Tower and Slab

Tower and Slab looks at the contradictory history of the modernist mass housing block—home to millions of city dwellers around the world. Few urban forms have roused as much controversy. While in the United States decades-long criticism brought about the demolition of most mass housing projects for the poor, in the booming metropolises of Shanghai and Mumbai remarkably similar developments are being built for the wealthy middle class. While on the surface the modernist apartment block appears universal, it is in fact as diverse in its significance and connotations as its many different cultural contexts.

Florian Urban studies the history of mass housing in seven narratives: Chicago, Paris, Berlin, Brasília, Mumbai, Moscow, and Shanghai. Investigating the complex interactions between city planning and social history, *Tower and Slab* shows how the modernist vision to house the masses in serial blocks succeeded in certain contexts and failed in others. Success and failure, in this respect, refers not only to the original goals—to solve housing crises and provide modern standards for whole societies—but equally to the changing significance of housing blocks within the respective societies and their perception by architects, politicians, and inhabitants.

These differences show that design is not to blame for mass housing's mixed record of success. The comparison of apparently similar projects suggests that triumph or disaster does not depend on a single variable but rather on a complex formula that includes not only form, but also social composition, location within a city, effective maintenance, and a variety of cultural, social, and political factors.

Florian Urban is Head of Architectural History and Urban Studies at the Mackintosh School of Architecture, Glasgow School of Art. From 2006 to 2008 he taught at the Center for Metropolitan Studies, Technische Universität Berlin. He holds a Master of Fine Arts from the Hochschule der Künste Berlin, an MA in Urban Planning from UCLA, and a PhD in History and Theory of Architecture from MIT. He is the author of *Neo-historical East Berlin – Architecture and Urban Design in the German Democratic Republic 1970–1990* (Ashgate, 2009).

Tower and Slab

Histories of global mass housing

Florian Urban

Routledge
Taylor & Francis Group

LONDON AND NEW YORK

First published 2012
by Routledge
2 Park Square, Milton Park, Abingdon, Oxon OX14 4RN

Simultaneously published in the USA and Canada
by Routledge
711 Third Avenue, New York, NY 10017

Routledge is an imprint of the Taylor & Francis Group, an informa business

British Library Cataloguing in Publication Data
A catalogue record for this book is available from the British Library

Library of Congress Cataloging in Publication Data
Urban, Florian.
  Tower and slab : histories of global mass housing / Florian Urban.
      p. cm.
    Includes bibliographical references and index.
  1. High-rise apartment buildings–Social aspects. 2. Housing. 3. Architecture
and society. I. Title. II. Title: Histories of global mass housing.
  HD7287.6.A3U73 2011
  363.5–dc22   2011010078

ISBN: 978–0–415–67628–1 (hbk)
ISBN: 978–0–415–67629–8 (pbk)
ISBN: 978–0–203–80413–1 (ebk)

Typeset in Aldine and Univers
by Swales & Willis, Exeter, Devon

Printed and bound in Great Britain by
TJ International Ltd, Padstow, Cornwall

Contents

Acknowledgments

My first words of gratitude go to the inhabitants, architects, planners, and scholars from seven different metropolises who took their time to share with me their experiences and opinions, and thus allowed me a glimpse into the diverse built environments that mass housing constitutes in these places. Their help was invaluable.

This book started in 2003 as a sideline project during my doctoral studies at MIT's History, Theory, and Criticism of Architecture program. Although the passages had long been discarded, the ideas connected with them lingered on. I would therefore like to thank my doctoral advisors Mark Jarzombek and Larry Vale for their guidance and support.

At the Center for Metropolitan Studies, Berlin Technical University, where I taught from 2005 to 2008 and where this project eventually came to fruition, I was surrounded by a collegial and supportive atmosphere that significantly contributed to the advancement of my work. Thanks to my colleagues Heinz Reif, Katja Sussner, Dagmar Thorau, Dorothee Brantz, Susanne Stemmler, and Oliver Schmidt. A generous grant from the Fritz-Thyssen Foundation funded the travels and research necessary for this book.

At the Mackintosh School of Architecture, Glasgow School of Art, I was able to work in an office with a direct view onto the built results of one of Europe's most ambitious mass housing programs, and encountered an inspiring environment to finalize some of my ideas. My warmest thanks to my students and colleagues.

I would also like to acknowledge the input and advice of various individuals who work on similar topics and helped me to clarify my thoughts. Thanks in particular to Richard Williams, Hervé Vieillard-Baron, Sofia Shwayri, Frank Wassenberg, Miles Glendinning, Richard Dennis, Rosemary Wakeman, Nikhil Rao, and Jean-Louis Cohen.

In particular I am grateful for the indispensable help of my graduate students who provided me with information, translations, photos, and insightful comments. My warmest thanks to Angelika Świderska, Ang Ye, Carsten Schmidt, Laurent Jachetta, and Di Wang.

Many friends and colleagues contributed to the growth of this work with astute comments, helpful feedback, and moral support; they helped to shape my thoughts, improve my style of writing, and clarify many doubts about the places they often knew so much better than I. Thanks to Michael Osman, Lize Mogel, Caroline Labusch, Silke Morgenroth, Kirsten Kofahl, Aleksandra Roth-Belkova, Gerald Roth, Kirsten Weiss, Cai Lin, Ying Zhou, Guzel Sabirova, Alla Vronskaya, Natalya Belkova, Priyanka Basu, Martin Schwegmann, Steve Rowell, Khadija Carroll, Alex Schweder, and Augusto Areal. Last but not least, I cannot thank my father and Marcela enough for their love and endless support.

Preface

by Mark Jarzombek

This book touches on a core problematic lurking within the concept of the modern city: housing. It is a rather innocuous word that emerged in the late nineteenth century in England, especially following the so-called "Housing of the Working Classes Act" of 1890. The word appeared subsequently in dozens of titles typically entitled "The Housing Problem in London" (1899), "The Housing of the Poor (1891), or "Housing of the Working Classes in Rural Districts" (1891). By the middle of the twentieth century, housing was not just a "problem," but in some places an investment opportunity, in other places an instrument of state-sponsored social control, and elsewhere even the core element of the lifestyles of the wealthy and middle classes. This leads to a question about the framing urban history. How does a city register its image unto itself when it comes to one of its obvious functional requirements, namely "housing"? In that sense, "housing" is still a problem, but of a different type than a hundred years ago.

In this book, Florian Urban—using the dual-faced concept, "tower and slab"—addresses a fundamental philosophical question about the efficacy of modernity in order to bring out of hiding the strangeness of the modern city. The story in some sense begins in the late nineteenth century in Haussmann's Paris, where the urban apartment was for the wealthy and "housing" for the poor. The apartment contributed to urbanity whereas housing was a problem to be solved. The slab and tower, as they became institutionalized in urban planning after the Second World War, inherited this fundamental antagonism to urbanity as both a promise and an accusation and, for a brief moment, as with Le Corbusier's Ville Contemporaine (1922), it was hoped that the tower could create a modern urbanity all its own. But "housing" could not quite escape its shadow and what seemed to be an aspect of forward thinking produced instead a vast set of problems, ranging from the social to the aesthetic, which eroded most of the utopian sheen that had been associated with the tower and slab prior to the Second World War. This, of course, did not stop the proliferation of these forms. But if we hone in on the debates, as is the project of this book, we realize that not all slabs and towers are alike and that the utopian dreams, social realities, and political justifications associated with them were often more complex and nuanced than one might think. Nor were slabs just for the poor, the urban disenfranchised, or socially progressive. Capitalism figured out how to make them compatible with the rich and the elite. In some cases, towers replaced the slum, but in other places, as in Mumbai, towers are effective in the reproduction of slums. In some places the slab was and still is an instrument of nationalist discourse; in other cases it epitomizes all that is wrong with state-sponsored capitalism. This book gives us a marvelously comparative—global—perspective on this phenomenon and in so doing lays the ground work for us to return to the philosophical question: What does it mean to live in our modern world, and also, what is our status as residents of a modern city?

Introduction

Mass housing – between glory and shame

Modernist mass housing is the most widespread architectural scheme of the twentieth century. From the central districts of Brasília to the housing projects of Chicago and from the Paris *banlieue* to the outskirts of Moscow, millions of city dwellers call a standardized apartment block their home. Its ubiquity notwithstanding, no urban form in history has roused such controversy. Since the completion of the first modular housing developments in the 1930s, towers and slabs have been alternately glorified as the salvation of mankind and scorned as generators of misery and distress. In the fall of 2005, the civil unrest in the French *banlieues* sparked an intense debate over the architect's role in creating crime and violence. In the United States, similar discussions had much earlier led to the extensive demolition of large-scale housing projects, which nevertheless continue to be sought after by the country's poorest today. In East Germany they are also being taken down, but mostly because they stand empty as a result of a shrinking population. In other contexts, however, mass-produced residences remain untouched by criticism. In the booming metropolises of Shanghai and Mumbai, tower blocks are continuously built for a wealthy middle class, and in Moscow the serial apartment buildings of the Khrushchev and Brezhnev eras generated a hybrid form of post-Soviet urbanity for those who are left out by the city's economic boom.

This book traces the changing course of mass housing in Chicago, Paris, Berlin, Brasília, Mumbai, Moscow, and Shanghai. Investigating the complex interactions between city planning and social history, it shows how the modernist vision to house the masses in serial blocks succeeded in certain contexts and failed in others. Success and failure, in this respect, refer not only to the original goals—to solve the housing crisis provoked by demographic growth and country-to-city migration and provide modern standards for the whole of society—but equally to the shifting significance of housing blocks within the respective societies and their perception by architects, politicians, and inhabitants.

The differences show on a global level that design is not to blame for mass housing's mixed achievements. The buildings did not produce the social situations they came to stand for, but acted as vessels, conditioning rather than creating social relations and channeling rather than generating existing polarities. The comparison of apparently similar projects in seven different cities suggests that triumph or fiasco did not depend on a single variable but rather on a complex formula that included not only form and programming, but also social composition, location within the city, effective maintenance, and a variety of cultural, social, and political indicators. If just one of these factors was slanted, the entire enterprise would be threatened, and a symbol of comfort and livability would easily become the epitome of misery and deprivation.

The mass-produced offspring of the so-called international style was therefore never truly international. The differences between the now demolished Robert Taylor Homes in Chicago, the Brasília *superquadras*, the Cité des Quatre Mille near Paris, and the Yanlord Gardens in Shanghai exemplify the scope of variation since the housing block was first theorized as a decontextualized one-size-fits-all solution to the modern age's demographic challenge. In this respect, the standardized housing block has always been a flexible category that includes both high-rise and low-rise dwellings, both prefab units and site-built homes. The evident local specificities point to the nature of what has been more aptly described as modernities than modernity, and what all over the world evolved from the continuous tension between an international discourse and local traditions. A history of mass housing architecture is thus also a history of globalization. Like any other innovation, towers and slabs did not spread across national borders without profound modification. Chinese fenced-in compounds and French satellite settlements are just two local examples of the seemingly universal tower block, whose form, program, and meaning were conditioned by the most diverse social and political situations. Thus the histories of mass housing in seven different contexts shed light on the factors that enabled the mundane magic of architectural metamorphosis: they show how boxes became palaces or cabins, battlefields or safe havens, and first and foremost, screens onto which a society's deepest fears and desires were readily projected.

Continuous principles: paternalism and standardization

What constituted the continuity of mass housing across cultural and political boundaries? The serial apartment blocks relied on two conceptual foundations, which originated in the late nineteenth century and soon came to be inseparably connected with the rhetoric of modernist architects and planners: first, the development of standardized design and industrial building techniques that profoundly changed the nature of residential con-struction, and second, a belief in egalitarian living conditions as a social goal and the paternalistic state as its most effective promoter. Mass housing rested on a conviction that state authorities were to take responsibility for the welfare of their citizens and counteract social polarization. This idea gave rise to diverse forms of state paternalism, whose most comprehensive forms were realized in the decades after the Second World War, on the one hand in Scandinavia and on the other in the socialist countries, with the significant difference that under socialism there was a wider gap between theory and practice due to more limited resources. Similar approaches were taken by the wealthy nations of Western Europe and East Asia, where welfare-state policies went along with a high degree of market regulation, and the development of an equalized middle-class society. In all these contexts, state-subsidized mass housing was part of a social program to guarantee material security for the whole of society, including the disadvantaged. But in the US, Brazil, India, Iran, or South Korea, where the welfare state never fully developed, the construction of mass housing was also based on increasing state regulation. Here, state influence was not mainly exercised through state-operated housing companies but rather through the different forms of cooperative and public utility housing, the legal framework for tenancy and home-ownership, the tax system, or the regulation of land use.

In a particular way, mass housing thus evidenced the contradictory nature of state paternalism, which next to its many beneficial aspects also carries the potential for oppression—assistance for the disadvantaged necessarily leads to the curtailment of individual agency. This contradiction played out very differently across the globe and had a significant influence on why otherwise similar projects succeeded in some contexts and failed in others.

This is illustrated in the US, France, Germany, and Russia on the one hand and in Brazil, India, or the People's Republic of China on the other. Spawned by an international discourse that was most effective in the post-war decades, public authorities in these countries erected similar tower-and-slab ensembles that soon came to develop in very different ways. In Chicago, Paris, and Berlin, mass housing developments acquired a bad reputation to the extent that local policy from the 1980s increasingly aimed at their demolition or redesign. In Moscow, Brasília, Mumbai, and Shanghai, in contrast, they are still pragmatically accepted as satisfactory dwellings—in the center of the Brazilian capital they are even designated as historic monuments. In all seven cities, public housing programs were discontinued between approximately 1975 and 1995 and restructured in favor of more market-oriented approaches. But while the public authorities in Chicago, Paris, Berlin, or Moscow chose to intervene less and less in the housing market, in Shanghai or Mumbai they maintained a comparably high degree of control.

In all these cities, the mass-produced apartment building was a strategy for modern-ization. Not only did the modular blocks come to stand rhetorically for progress and prosperity, they also literally promoted what are commonly seen as the conditions of modern urban life in contrast to those of a pre-modern society. These include not only certain sanitary and hygienic standards but also cultural conventions such as the cohabitation of a nuclear family with one or two children, a high degree of anonymity between neighbors, and the separation between home and work place. When the tower blocks were first conceived, this lifestyle stood in contrast to the habits of a large majority, and the ensuing tensions gave rise to numerous controversies. In all these contexts, the pre-modern ways of life disappeared or changed significantly, but contrary to what their promoters had hoped for, tower blocks did not transform into a global and superior modern culture. Rather, the modern dwellings came to be adopted by limited social groups whose significance in the respective societies differed considerably and, again, influenced the perception of the mass-produced abodes among the entire population.

Seven historical narratives

The diversity of mass housing is also a methodological challenge. Beyond the two common denominators of standardization and state involvement there is no category that encompasses the diverse typological, technological, economic, and social aspects of mass housing. Categories applied in different countries are highly idiosyncratic, thus giving rise to quite different social and political arguments. In France, it is the planning term *grand ensemble* (large compound) that frames both academic research and political debate. In the formerly socialist countries of Eastern Europe, the building technique is taken as the most prominent aspect, and the term "concrete slab" is applied to the whole building—*panel'niy dom* (panel house—Russian), *panelák* (panel building—Czech), *wielka płyta* (big slab—Polish), or *Platte* (slab—German) are the respective terms used by both scholars and the general public. In West Germany the concept of *Neubauten* (new buildings) came to be used for modern blocks as opposed to prewar buildings, but included different forms of financing and ownership. And in the United States the most significant debate evolved around public housing as opposed to privately financed construction, leaving other forms of standardized architecture aside. In India, China, and Brazil too, there has been no prominent category distinguishing the state-sponsored mass housing estates of the 1960s and 1970s from what was built before and after; rather, there are numerous distinctions applied to multi-family buildings with regard to design, comfort, size, and construction period. Given the impossibility of developing a comparative analysis from a common vantage point, an account of mass housing around the world can therefore only be a juxtaposition of historical narratives. One has to look at the respective buildings as contextual architectural expressions in their own right and at the same time as phenomena deriving from a global modern discourse. The simplifications and elisions resulting from an international perspective thus mirror the tensions between the global evolution of modernity and the local context in which it was framed.

A history of the apartment blocks in the sample cities would be incomplete without taking a look at the form of mass housing that has often been deemed the tower blocks' uncanny shadow: the slum. The different forms of overcrowded tenements, dilapidated huts, or self-built shacks originally gave rise to the discourse on mass architecture, and their continuous proliferation is often seen as an indicator of the failure of modernist housing. In India and Brazil, slum dwellers constituted the majority of the workforce on the construction sites, but rarely could afford to inhabit the very structures they built. In Mumbai or Brasília, mass housing blocks and informal settlements are located in close proximity to each other. The same contiguity could be found in the outskirts of Paris in the 1950s, where the aim to rid the city of self-built *bidonvilles* (shantytowns) became a major driving force in the tower block construction program. The slums thus not only constitute the lens through which the towers and slabs have been looked at in the respective contexts, but at the same time blatantly point to one of modernism's most limiting conditions.

The controversies spawned by tower-and-slab blocks were as multifaceted as their production was simple. To trace this maze of buildings, images, and ideas, this book draws from newspaper articles and scientific studies alongside interviews with residents, architects, and city officials. The diverse viewpoints pay due to the fact that the opinions of those who planned, designed, and inhabited these buildings changed over time and varied with regard to different projects. But the explanatory power of the sources is also contextual. In authoritarian countries such as China or the Soviet Union, written statements tend to reflect a government-sanctioned narrative rather than an independent perspective, but often still provide valuable information on state policy and the moments in which the official goals shifted. In countries where freedom of opinion is respected, on the other hand, newspaper reports and commentaries often reflect minority opinions and sometimes stand in blatant contrast to the views of professionals or inhabitants. The following chapters will thus draw from a variety of visual, oral, and textual snapshots to reveal seven parallel narratives that trace the conceptualization, construction, and perception of mass housing in six local contexts. These narratives exemplify the ambiguous role of state paternalism—embodying the conflict between empowerment and control—in the same way as the reciprocal relation between buildings and local conditions, thus illuminating the tortuous course of an architectural theme that in many countries continues to be debated and reinterpreted today.

1 Social Reform, State Control, and the Origins of Mass Housing

Housing and the social question

The social question, formulated with increasing pressure in all industrializing countries since the mid-nineteenth century, was fundamental for mass housing programs. Among the diverse groups of social reformers were radical aristocrats, bourgeois philanthropists, and labor activists, who shared an awareness of the miserable living conditions in which the industrial cities' lower two-thirds had to live, and the moral obligation to change them. The expressed commitment of the upper and middle classes to the poor went along with a protection of their own interests, including social stability and the prevention of workers' uprisings. From the very beginning, social reform oscillated between charity and domination. Measures to house and feed the needy went along with more or less coercive methods to categorize, regulate, and discipline the masses, to enforce moral rule and social hygiene. Like any type of assistance, social welfare helped the underprivileged, but at the same time strengthened the rule of the dominant groups and restricted the receivers' agency.

European countries started to introduce both state- and company-sponsored assistance around the turn of the twentieth century, and by the end of the Second World War had established comprehensive systems of social welfare of which mass housing would become a part. In Germany, the Verein für Socialpolitik (Social Policy Association, founded in 1873) united the most eminent proponents of state intervention in social and economic matters, who at the same time rejected socialist ideas. In France, the Musée Social (founded in 1894) came to be an important forum for similar approaches. General medical insurance for German workers was introduced in 1883, in the same year in which the Social Democratic Party was officially forbidden. In France, certain medical assistance was provided free of charge from 1893 and in Britain from 1911. The Societé française des urbanistes was founded in 1911 and the British Royal Town Planning Institute in 1914; the improvement of dwelling conditions subsequently became the backbone of municipal politics. In the United States, the "Progressive Era" of the 1890s and early 1900s spawned legislation on zoning, construction, and labor, and established the primacy of the state to regulate a variety of urban matters. Along with the rise of the social sciences, the smallest common denominator across national borders came to be the increasing reliance on comprehensive planning and state intervention. Policy relied mostly on quantitative analysis and scientific calculation to determine human needs and guarantee efficient remedy. The objective was to achieve what has never been achieved since the first cities were built: to provide adequate living conditions for all social classes.

These goals entered the architectural debate at the turn of the twentieth century. In the rhetoric of the modern movement in France, Germany, Britain, Russia, and the United States, housing assistance for the needy soon became inseparably connected with modernist architecture and urban planning. In France, Tony Garnier developed his proposal for a *cité industrielle,* in which the members of an industrialized socialist society would live in modular concrete homes. His ideas, which he worked out around 1900, anticipated the modular developments that were later built in many countries.[1] In the years after the Russian Revolution, visionary Soviet theorists such as Leonid Sabsovich, Mikhail Okhitovich, and Nikolai Milyutin thought of a thoroughly restructured urban landscape as the basis for a socialist egalitarian society. In Germany, architects such as Bruno Taut, Richard Riemerschmid, Hermann Muthesius, Hannes Meyer, and Peter Behrens thought of mass housing construction as the only way to mitigate the housing shortage and increase dwelling comfort for the disadvantaged. They took up the ideas of housing reformers such as Otto Schilling and Rudolf Eberstadt. Arguably the most consequential result of these efforts was the increasing foundation of public utility housing enterprises from the 1920s onward. All together believed in a strong and benevolent state that was to provide the regulatory framework for architects' activity, enforce minimum construction standards, and curb the most detrimental side effects of the free housing market.[2] These essentials could never-theless be provided by a diverse array of regimes from monarchy to socialism, and the political convictions of the housing reformers were accordingly diverse.

The origins of industrialized construction

Industrialized construction as was developed in the early twentieth century eventually became the fundamental technology for mass housing in most countries and simultaneously a stylistic principle for modern city design. Even in those contexts where industrialization did not become dominant—such as in Brazil or India—the underlying principles of these technologies inspired repetitive chains of production and determined the aesthetics of new design. There are two main characteristics of industrialized buildings as opposed to traditional site-built homes. First, they are assembled from prefabricated parts, and second, they are not constructed individually, but rather in series according to a rationalized process. Industrialized construction, in this sense, is an automated scheme that increases productivity through seriality and standardization. This definition also includes, for example, mobile homes or trailers and is not necessarily limited to multistory buildings. In any case, such a form of building not only invites production at a large scale but rather requires it, since the cost of the development of rationalized processes is very high and can only be amortized through large output that maximizes the cost-benefit rate.[3] The definition of industrialized construction is imprecise to a certain degree, since the difference to traditional construction is gradual rather than categorical. Most traditional site-built homes employ an array of prefabricated parts. Windows and doors are produced in series, beams and posts are cut in standardized measures, and the brick can be deemed a form of prefabrication. Similarly, the traditional divisions of labor, for example that between bricklayers and roofers, already means a rationalization of workflow. However, industrialized construction as practiced by modernist architects in the early twentieth century refined both prefabrication and stream-lining of procedures to an unprecedented degree and wedded them to their vision of a new society built on social equity. Hence in popular use industrialized construction is often connected not with a particular technology but rather with particular design principles and thus modernist architecture as such.

Some forms of prefabrication have been known since antiquity. Findings from Roman shipwrecks suggest that the elements for entire buildings were prefabricated at certain quarries and then transported to the construction site.[4] Colonial expansion in the nineteenth century played an important role in the improvement of prefabrication, since it brought about the necessity to provide shelter quickly for large amounts of people in remote places.[5] Along the same lines, military technology provided the basis for the civil use of mass-produced materials.

The industrialization of the construction process as we know it today was developed much later than that of materials. In the late nineteenth century, the engineer Frederick Winslow Taylor (1856–1915) invented scientific management, rationalizing each separate step of production. Henry Ford (1863–1947) applied Taylor's principles in his industrial plants. From 1913, his Highland Park Factory in Detroit produced motorcars on assembly lines. In the following decades, Fordist production became the model for the industrial-ization of the construction industry.[6] Flows of work were refined according to scientific rules, and similar buildings were produced in great numbers. The French term *grands ensembles*, and its German equivalent, *Großsiedlungen*, for large housing projects reflects the imperative of scale that lay at the heart of these industrialized operations.

New materials and technologies developed in the late nineteenth century furthered the industrialization of construction. Two innovations were particularly consequential: steel frames and reinforced concrete. As a construction material, concrete was known by the ancient Romans, but fell into disuse in later centuries. The experiments of the French engineer François Hennebique were crucial for the construction of concrete homes. Hennebique relied on the experiments of the gardener Joseph Monier, who stiffened his cast planters with wires for additional stabilization.[7] His 1892 patent on reinforced concrete opened the use of that material for large, industrially produced buildings. Other pioneers of concrete construction were the architect Auguste Perret, who in 1903 built his first all-concrete apartment house on Rue Franklin in Paris, and the Liverpool city engineer John Alexander Brodie, under whose auspices the apartment buildings on Eldon Street were built from prefab concrete slabs in 1905.[8] Like the construction of prefab wooden houses, concrete prefabrication was also furthered by colonial expansion. The French company Lippmann, Schneckenburger & Cie in Bastignolles near Paris, which pioneered the construction of houses from hollow concrete slabs, first and foremost exported its products to the French colonies, starting in 1860 with the Caribbean island of St. Thomas.[9] Their patents were taken over in 1893 by the Amsterdam firm Wittenburg, which also produced for export to overseas territories.

At the turn of the twentieth century, concrete slab construction was improved in England, Germany, France, and the US. Thomas Edison, the inventor of the lightbulb, experimented with the use of cast concrete. A series of two-story single-family homes were built in Philipsburg, New York, in 1909 according to his technology. The New York engineer Grosvenor Atterbury was best known for the further development of prefab concrete slabs. In 1908, he developed a construction system consisting of one-floor-high panels that were hollowed out for better insulation. Most famous was his Tudor-style townhouse community, Forest Hill in Queens, New York, which he designed from prefabricated concrete panels,[10] and his 1918 design of two-story single-family homes in Long Island, New York.[11] Paul Schmitthenner's traditionalist Garden City in Berlin-Staaken (1914–17) was built according to the latest development of standardization based on only five types.[12]

By 1920, the competition between steel frame and reinforced concrete construction was decided. In the eyes of most builders the advantages of concrete—it was inexpensive, resistant to corrosion and fire, and extremely stable—outweighed the disadvantages of its heaviness and the difficulty of transporting it. Many scholars also stress the political aspects of this development: the military industry depended on steel, which in many countries had become a rare commodity during the First World War.[13] The path was therefore set toward concrete as the preferred material for multistory homes. The age of concrete was about to begin.

The modernist movement in the interwar period: the first mass housing developments in Germany, France, and England

In the decade before the First World War, when mass-produced lamps, pens, typewriters, and automobiles already proliferated in British, French, and American cities, buildings were still erected as they had been a thousand years earlier: one at a time, and each by an individual builder. The only concession to the industrial age was the use of repetitive plans and façade models that were similar but not identical—to date the main feature of the now cherished late-nineteenth-century neighborhoods in New York, Paris, Berlin, and other cities. This apparent anachronism did not go unnoticed. In Germany and France, architects such as Walter Gropius (1883–1969), Ludwig Mies van der Rohe (1886–1969), and Le Corbusier (1887–1965) realized that traditional construction was not able to generate the output required by massive country-to-city migration and raged against obsolete building methods.

Industrialization, for them, was the mandate of the time. Supported by seductive images, they propagated standardized construction as both superior technology and signifier for modern life.

In Germany, where the Werkbund debate on standardization had peaked before the First World War, industrialized construction was increasingly brought to practice from the end of the war. Traditionalists such as the Staaken Garden City designer Paul Schmitthenner (1884–1972) played a similarly important role as the modernists associated with the Bauhaus. Walter Gropius and many of his colleagues espoused the aesthetics of the machine-produced good. They not only promoted standardization as the precondition for efficient factory-based production, but also cultivated a particular formal language that for its teachers embodied the spirit of industrialization: raw materials, geometrical shapes, and lack of ornamentation. The Swiss architect Hannes Meyer (1889–1954), Gropius's successor as director of the Bauhaus and one of the school's most radical architects, assigned such design a normative value, pointing out that typization and standardization were "the alphabet of socialist architecture" and most appropriate for a society without class differences.[14] Meyer held that the demands of the proletariat were absolutely equal and therefore required normalized buildings that were exclusively determined by their function. For him, a building was "neither beautiful nor ugly, just right or wrong."[15]

The new architecture was to be mass-produced in factories. In his 1926 article *Der große Baukasten* (The Great Construction Kit), Walter Gropius famously called for the industrialization of the entire construction industry.[16] Together with his colleague Konrad Wachsmann (1901–80) he developed numerous prefab construction systems.[17] For Ludwig Mies van der Rohe industrialization was "not so much a question of rationalizing existing working methods as of fundamentally remolding the whole building trade."[18] Mies van der Rohe thus called for a "total destruction of the building trade in the form in which it has existed up to now" and an adaptation to industrially produced materials.[19] Other Bauhaus teachers formulated similar ideas. Ludwig Hilberseimer (1885–1967), who taught at the Bauhaus from 1929, thought of modular new towns,[20] and Marcel Breuer (1901–81) developed various design schemes for modular housing. For them, building high blocks was a mandate of the time and supported by scientific calculations.[21]

The new technologies were carried out on an urban scale. In 1924 Martin Wagner (1885–1957) carried out the Splanemannstraße development in Berlin, the first *Siedlung* (residential development) from large precast concrete slabs. It inspired other ensembles of standardized residential buildings in Germany, such as Gropius's model ensemble in Dessau-Törten (1926–28) or the Horseshoe Development (1925–31) in Berlin by Wagner and Bruno Taut. These projects were heavily influenced by the British garden city movement, which since the late nineteenth century had promoted the idea of a lifestyle that remained connected with nature within modern industrial cities. Arguably the most successful serial developments of the 1920s were Ernst May's *Siedlungen*, which he planned during his tenure as municipal official for residential construction in Frankfurt between 1925 and 1930, and which included the serial developments in the Frankfurt suburbs of Praunheim, Westhausen, Bornheim, Römerstadt, and Niederrad. These *Vorstadttrabanten* (suburban satellites) were the first housing developments that constituted entire neighborhoods on the urban periphery; at the same time they pioneered the use of prefab concrete elements.[22]

Like their German colleagues, the architects in the newly founded Soviet Union also theorized principles of rationalization and standardization as a solution to an exacerbated housing shortage—and as the fulfillment of the socialist promise of equal housing standards for everyone. They celebrated industrialization with great enthusiasm, and an industrial aesthetic ranked high in their proposals. In the late 1920s, Moisei Ginsburg directed the Department of Typed Buildings at the State Committee for Construction in 1928, developing modular housing from industrial materials. His Gosstrakh Apartments (1926) and Narkomfin Apartments (1929) in Moscow embodied his ideas of transforming society through serial architecture.[23] At the same time, Andrei Burov and Boris Blokhin developed construction techniques from prefab blocks, and Nikolai Ladovski proposed buildings composed of entire prefab dwelling cells.[24] The rationalization of construction went along with a debate over the dwelling conditions not only for underprivileged groups but for the whole of society and led to investigations of floor plans, kitchen arrangements, and room sizes. During the 1930s, when Stalin suppressed the architectural avant-garde, experiments in the industrialization of construction nevertheless lingered on. At the Institute of Architecture in Moscow, Burov continued to investigate large-panel construction and eventually laid the technological groundwork for the architecture of the post-war era. After Stalin's death in 1953, Nikita Khrushchev forcefully promoted industrialized architecture and made it the most widely used form of construction in the Soviet Union.[25]

In France, Le Corbusier had experimented with modular house types since the end of the First World War. The most significant results were his two-story Maison Citrohan model (1920–22), and, most famously, his utopian Voisin Plan (1925), in which he proposed the rebuilding of Paris with modular high-rises in a park landscape.[26] In his 1925 book *Vers une architecture*, he called for a house that was mass produced like a car or ship and acted like a "machine for dwelling."[27] Le Corbusier advocated a completely restructured city and framed height, light, and geometrical order as the salvation from the dirt and chaos of existing urban agglomerations. His city of modular towers in a park became the emblematic model for a whole generation of architects—for later critics such as urban historian Peter Hall, this squeaky-clean vision evidenced an anal character, inherited from his family of Swiss watchmakers.[28] In 1933, Le Corbusier authored the Athens Charter, which combined many positions shared by architects united in the Congrès internationaux d'architecture moderne (CIAM) and propagated centrally planned mass construction according to rational principles. In the early 1930s, this thinking inspired the first large housing developments in the Paris outskirts: Le Plessis-Robinson (1924–39) by Maurice Payret-Dortail, Jean Demay, and Jean Festoc and the Cité de la Muette (1931–34) by Marcel Lods and Eugène Beaudouin.

The first mass housing developments in Britain were also completed in the 1930s. Among the earliest were the eight-story Highpoint One Apartments in London by Berthold Lubetkin (1933–35), who was a Russian émigré and in the 1920s had studied at the famous Moscow school Vkhutemas, which was founded by Moisei Ginsburg.[29] Other significant developments included Wells Coates's nearby Lawn Road Flats in London's Hampstead

(1934–35), the six-block development Pullman Court in London by Frederick Gibberd (1936), and the social housing complex Quarry Hill in Leeds by R. A. H. Livett (1938, demolished in 1978).[30] These ensembles were rather small: Pullman Court had approximately two hundred units, and even Quarry Hill comprised less than a thousand. They were also not very high by later standards; only Highpoint One Apartments had eight stories, and both Lawn Road Flats and Pullman Court were only five stories high.

In the US, mass housing construction began in the 1930s, when Roosevelt's New Deal strengthened the role of state in the provision of housing. The first state-sponsored projects went up in New York: The dumbbell tenement-style First Houses on the Lower East Side (1934) and the Harlem River Houses (1936) were built as compounds separated from the street. Here, serially produced apartment blocks were also built by private companies and designed for the middle class, such as Stuyvesant Town/Peter Cooper Village on the Lower East Side (1943–47), which closely resembled Le Corbusier's model of a cruciform tower in the park.

While the few German *Siedlungen* of the interwar period, the first *grands ensembles* in France, the industrialized buildings of the Soviet avant-garde, and the early British and American standardized blocks of flats only made a small contribution to the relief of the housing crisis, they evidenced a changing attitude. The works of the great social reformers had caught on: in most European countries and in the US the majority supported the regulation of the housing market. In light of a shortage that was enhanced by the destruction of the Second World War, state-subsidized mass housing came to be universally accepted as the most efficient answer to the challenges posed by social plight: it became synonymous with modernization.

The post-war era: mass housing goes global

In the post-war decades, mass housing construction reached its peak. The material qualities of reinforced concrete improved considerably in terms of insulation, stability, and endurance, and industrially produced buildings grew to an unprecedented size.[31] Serial apartment blocks were undoubtedly the most popular method of construction. If in the 1960s one had asked a random Swedish, French, or Russian schoolchild to draw a new house, he or she would be likely to have produced a rectangle with repetitive windows and not a pitched-roof home with scribbled tiles and a chimney. In countries such as South Korea, China, or Singapore, standardized towers and slabs became home to large parts of the urban population. Triggered by ambitious state-sponsored programs, these developments were designed to ameliorate the living conditions of common people who in most places continued to suffer from misery and overcrowding, and at the same time conspicuously stress that government's commitment to modernization and progress.

Mass-produced apartment blocks spread across cultures and climate zones; the right to a dignified dwelling was promoted more effectively around the world than democratic elections, freedom of speech, or racial equality. A strong state and egalitarian goals, the fundamentals of mass housing, were endorsed across the political spectrum by communists, nationalists, or catholic reformers. The social democratic government in Sweden cherished them in the same way as the nationalist-conservative regime in France. While in most countries the promise to provide modern kitchens, central heating, and running water was only fulfilled for a part of the population, all around the world the respective programs considerably changed the structure of large cities and the characteristics of urban life.

Towers and slabs were built on all five continents. In Europe, the prewar tradition of social housing was only briefly interrupted during the Second World War and resumed immediately after. Prefab construction proved to be the most efficient way to repair a continent in shards, and many a destroyed city was rebuilt from repetitive concrete parts. In England, state-owned council housing for poor residents was built denser and higher, with the ten-story mark reached around 1948.[32] Among the most famous were the Churchill Gardens in London by Philip Powell and Hidalgo Moya (1946), and the first point block in Britain, The Lawn in Harlow New Town by Frederick Gibberd (1950).[33] Hamburg, one of the most heavily damaged cities in Germany, sponsored the construction of the 16-story Grindelberg houses by Bernhard Hermkes and others (1946), the country's first residential high-rises.[34] Other projects appeared in the 1950s on the urban peripheries, like the Sennestadt in Bielefeld by Hans Bernhard Reichow (1956), or the Neue Vahr in Bremen by Ernst May (1957)—all were subsidized directly or indirectly by public agencies. France started its state-supported construction projects in 1951 with the formation of *zones d'urbanisation prioritaire* (ZUP, zones of prioritized urbanization), on which modular residential high-rises were erected. The Cité des Quatre Mille in La Courneuve outside Paris (1956) and the Les Minguettes development outside Lyon (1967) were among the most famous. In some European countries, housing culture changed radically in a staggeringly short amount of time. Vällingby new town on the Stockholm periphery was inaugurated in 1954. Between 1965 and 1974, Sweden carried out the ambitious *Miljonprogrammet* (Million Program), which was initiated by the ruling Social Democratic Party as the backbone of the Swedish welfare state, and which spawned more than a million dwelling units in a country with less than nine million inhabitants.[35] The Netherlands also built numerous state-subsidized housing developments, most famously the Bijlmermeer (begun 1966), which was to house one in every eight Amsterdam residents in one single development.[36] Industrialized construction became particularly widespread in the Soviet Union and its Eastern European satellite states. Soon after Khrushchev launched the program for the industrialization of the Soviet construction industry in 1953, tower and slab developments showed a higher degree of homogeneity than those in capitalist countries. The socialist planned economy provided the ideal conditions for standardization and high output. This applied for the Soviet Union in the same way as for Hungary, Poland, or East Germany. In all those countries, buildings were assembled from factory-produced concrete slabs that had been designed to be as simple as possible and combined structure, infill, and finishing. During the 1960s and 1970s, the few elements of any given series, such as the famous K-7 in the Soviet Union or the WBS 70 in East Germany, were employed nationwide without variation.

The political division did not stop the connections between the Eastern and Western blocs. In 1954, a group of French architects visited the German Democratic Republic, and ten East German architects in return went on a research trip to France, where they visited the communist governed *banlieues rouges* ("red suburbs") of Paris, Le Corbusier's Unité d'Habitation in Marseille, and the reconstruction of Le Havre.[37] The industrialization of the Soviet construction industry was favored by the purchase of two Camus factories in France in the late 1950s.[38] There was also growing exchange between Europe and other continents. As early as 1952, Soviet engineers were invited to China and oversaw the first experiments with prefabrication.[39] The architect Kisho Kurokawa, a pioneer of modular construction in Japan, traveled extensively to the Soviet Union in the early 1950s.[40] British professionals worked in Singapore and Hong Kong, and Asian, African, and Latin American architects studied in England or France. Their projects, however, can barely be deemed an offspring of European urban planning traditions, but rather constitute a complex adaptation of a discourse that by 1960 was debated all around the world.

A rapid production of housing for a growing population lay at the bottom of prefab programs in most countries, as did a relatively strong role of the state. In the United States, the most distinctive examples of mass housing were the state-sponsored projects that soon became the homes of the poorest. Many of them were built as repetitive high-rises, including the Pruitt-Igoe Homes in St. Louis (1951–56) and the Robert Taylor Homes in Chicago (1959–62).

But not everywhere were the modular blocks designed for the working class. Under the regime of Mohamad Reza Shah in Iran, legislation was passed in 1964 to encourage private investment in the housing sector. Great housing firms could profit from tax breaks if they built mass housing in towers of ten stories or higher.[41] The ensembles of tower blocks that were subsequently built in Tehran, such as Behjat-Abad (1965–68) or Shahrak-e Ekbatan (1970s) became luxurious residences for the privileged. These buildings had a comparably high material quality and for the Iranian bourgeois classes embodied the lure of modernity and a Western lifestyle. At the same time, a development such as Shahrak-e Ekbatan responded to cultural and climatic specificities: a careful design of the slabs prevented jealous looks from opposite windows, and those parts of an apartment designed for the reception of guests were clearly separated from the private ones.[42] Windows were predominantly oriented toward the south to reduce sunshine (the sun stands too high to shine into the apartments), and open spaces were laid out as places of encounter for the neighbors. After the Iranian Revolution in 1979, the Islamist regime also encouraged the construction of high-rise projects for lower classes, but since production fell far short of the need apartment blocks remained a luxury item.[43]

In India, the left-leaning government of prime minister Jawaharlal Nehru promoted state-subsidized mass housing as a means to fight a housing shortage that had afflicted the country's industrial working class since colonial times. In contrast to similar developments in other countries, India's apartment blocks continued to be built in situ using traditional technology—prefabrication offered no cost saving in an environment where labor was cheap and the means of transportation poorly developed. The wave of state-sponsored housing construction in urban agglomerations such as Delhi, Mumbai, and Kolkata was continued under Nehru's successors in the 1960s and 1970s.

The socialist regime in the People's Republic of China mandated standardized building designs from the 1950s. The industrialization of the construction industry according to Soviet models was started at the same time, but did not advance until the early 1970s, after the Cultural Revolution had come to an end. In the following decades, the government increasingly supported industrialized buildings, which in the 1990s became the country's most conspicuous urban design scheme.

Other Asian countries were much faster in absorbing the new housing types. In Singapore, the Housing and Development Board (HDB) started the large-scale construction of publicly owned housing projects in 1960, only one year after the former British colony's independence. The new policy was combined with an extensive slum clearance project. Between 1960 and 1965, about 118,000 units were built, mostly in standardized high-rise apartments. Forty years later, about 85 percent of the approximately 4.5 million Singaporeans lived in high-rise apartments that were built by the HDB.[44]

Hong Kong followed a similar pattern, initiating the "largest public housing programme in the non-Communist world."[45] The Hong Kong Housing Authority (HA) started the construction of public housing estates for low-income citizens in 1953. One of the first developments was the Shek Kip Mei Estate (1954), built on the site of informal homes that were destroyed in a fire. In the following decades, HA constructed hundreds of thousands of high-rise units, converting the British colony into one of the most densely built up areas on earth.

South Korea in the 1970s invested so heavily in prefab high-rises—called *tanji*—that these buildings became close to the norm of an urban dwelling. Comprising less than 4 percent of the housing stock in 1970, their number rose to 50 percent in 2000, while in the same period the percentage of individual houses decreased from 90 percent to approximately 25 percent.[46] The largest *tanji* house over 200,000 people. Despite many similarities to Western countries—a state-run program to fight a housing shortage exacerbated by demographic growth and country-to-city migration, large estates of identical buildings, and an ideology of modernization—South Korea's tower blocks developed in a quite different way. They were built in all parts of the major cities rather than on the periphery. They did not cater to society's most disadvantaged, but mostly to the middle classes. And they were built for owners rather than tenants. Their construction coincided with the period of rapid urbanization. Most *tanji* were thus not built on the site of razed pre-modernist buildings, but on newly developed land, such as on the marshy banks of the Han River in Seoul. Despite the fact that they were originally introduced by the much-hated Japanese colonizers, the *tanji* became a broadly accepted form of housing.[47] The government authorities forcefully propagated housing blocks as a symbol of modernization and progress and thus established a pattern of perception that is shared by many Koreans to date, despite the fact that the state has been reducing its role in providing housing since the 1980s and the housing situation is worse than, for example, in Singapore.[48]

Many South American countries also experimented with modernist mass housing. In Brazil, mass housing blocks were first built under the conservative-authoritarian regime of Getúlio Vargas in the late 1930s. The largest construction project to involve mass housing was the new capital city Brasília, which was begun in 1956 under president Juscelino Kubitschek and officially inaugurated in 1960.

Venezuela, which in the mid-twentieth century was one of Latin America's richest countries due to its oil exports, promoted large modernization programs. In Caracas, numerous high-rise developments were built during the 1940s and 1950s, such as the eight-story El Silencio development, extending over seven blocks (1941–45), and the Urbanización Veintitres de Enero (1954–57), both of which were designed by Carlos Raúl Villanueva.[49]

A quite different version of mass housing's egalitarian goals evolved in South Africa during the apartheid era (1948–94), when the government built large estates of cheap one-story pavilions for black workers.[50] South Africa's state-sponsored townships embody modernism's most rigid potential of ordering the city at the expense of disadvantaged groups. They provided certain minimum standards and at the same time confined their inhabitants to remote locations where they would be strictly separated from the white population. Comprehensive planning and ideas about sanitation were thus instrumentalized by a racist regime that violently oppressed the lower classes—in this context the country's black majority.

By 1970 modular housing blocks proliferated around the world. They were built anywhere where sand and cement were available, in the Sahara desert and in the Siberian taiga, in Chicago's inner city and on the shores of the Yellow Sea, outside the Bois de Boulogne and in the Brazilian bush. The modular apartment block was universally accepted as a visible sign of progress and the promise of a better world in a not too distant future. As a unifying force, it defied the dichotomy of the Cold War and an increasing polarization between the rich north and the "underdeveloped" south.

As great as the hopes connected with this type of construction was the disappointment in many countries, where the towers and slabs soon stood out as symbols for modernism's worst nightmare: the exclusion of the poor and their confinement to areas of high crime and violence. Some of the very projects that had come with an unprecedented rhetoric of hope subsequently became the incarnation of social dystopia. In the United States, the iconic image of mass housing's failure was the demolition of the Pruitt-Igoe Homes in St. Louis (built 1951–56, design: Minoru Yamasaki, 2,800 apartments). The blast in 1972 was transmitted as a media event of national significance and later canonized by the architectural historian Charles Jencks as "the day modern architecture died."[51] In the two decades that followed, state-sponsored mass housing programs came to an end all around the world. In France and the United States legislation was passed in the year of the oil crisis, 1973. Other capitalist countries followed in the late 1970s. And in Eastern Europe state support waned with the decline of the socialist regimes and was fully withdrawn with their demise. Concomitantly with the retreat of state intervention many countries started to operate the existing developments on the basis of apartment ownership rather than tenancy. Despite these changes, however, modular blocks continued to be built in many countries, seemingly unaffected by dystopian images or harsh debates. In contrast to what progressive architects and politicians had hoped, mass housing turned out to be highly uneven.[52] The architectural details of the buildings, the social status of the inhabitants, and the public perception differed extremely from country to country, and continued to take very different paths in the respective contexts.

2 Mass Housing in Chicago

Anti-high-rise America

"The US has always been anti-high-rise."[1] Thus Chicago scholar Roberta Feldman summarized the century-long history of modernist mass housing in a country which, ironically, is renowned the world over for its skyscrapers. Henry Cisneros, former secretary of the US Department of Housing and Urban Development and leader in the late-twentieth-century quest against high-rise mass housing, puts it equally bluntly: "High-rises just don't work, and we have to replace them."[2] Both statements exemplify an attitude that in the US in the early twenty-first century reflects the mindset of a broad majority. With the exception of Manhattan and some pockets on the Chicago Lakefront, modernist tower blocks are accepted only as hotels and office buildings in central business districts. In all other contexts, they rouse suspicion. Most Americans connect them not with the upscale towers of Louis Sullivan or Ludwig Mies van der Rohe that are much celebrated by architectural historians, but rather first and foremost with dismal housing projects such as Pruitt-Igoe in St. Louis or the Robert Taylor Homes in Chicago, which were both demolished only a few decades after their completion. Since the 1970s, these projects have been almost universally regarded as textbook examples of failed design. To the general public, they evoke gloomy images of broken windows, graffiti-ridden stairwells, and stony-faced children, most of them black, and embody everything that can go wrong with public assistance and government-sponsored construction. They appear as a state-subsidized nightmare locked in serial modern architecture, and a sharp contrast to the average suburban neighborhood, characterized by single-family homes and owner-occupancy. The distinct aspects of most American public housing—the box-shaped or cruciform brick-clad blocks with 4 to 20 stories are easily recognizable—have made them an apt projection screen for society's worst fears of crime and violence. High-rise public housing has a particularly bad reputation, and the overwhelming power of this image eclipses other forms of mass dwelling. The upscale condominium, the public housing block's unequal twin, is far less widespread in US metropolises than in other large cities around the world, and its popularity is limited to small circles of educated and well-to-do lovers of architecture. The perception of modernist apartment blocks to the present date is dominated by the potent controversies over public housing, and not by classy condominiums, such as the art deco Century Building on Central Park in New York (1931) or Mies van der Rohe's Lake Shore Drive Apartments in Chicago (1948). In contrast to the ubiquity of the former, the latter appear as exceptions, despite the fact that the residential skyscrapers, however unusual they might be in the American context, are well known throughout the world, and despite the fact that buildings such as the Lake Shore Drive Apartments are rightfully celebrated for their outstanding design.

This chapter will look at the history of mass housing in Chicago, where ideas about state involvement and equal housing standards have clashed with cultural dispositions, such as a deeply rooted individualism and a traditionally strong reliance on market forces.[3] It will show how modernist mass housing in the US—exemplified in the public housing block— came to be discredited more thoroughly than in all other sample cities in this book, and it

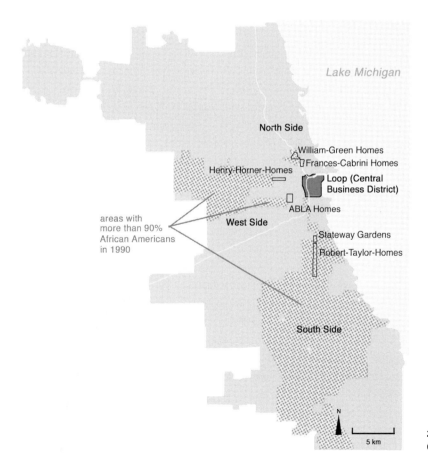

2.1
Chicago (Florian Urban)

Mass Housing in Chicago

will then briefly examine the one American exception to this general attitude: New York City. The invention of state-sponsored mass housing in the mid-twentieth century, its widespread application in the post-war period, and its disappearance in the 1990s have to be seen as a continuous development tied to a set of ideas, which were only slightly modified over the course of the century.

One of the distinct features of cheaply built mass housing in the United States is its inseparable connection with the painful history of race relations in America. Racial segregation, as enforced through both legal measures and racist practices, was at the root of construction, management, and perception of serial apartment buildings through most of the twentieth century. To an extent unknown in other countries, towers and slabs stood for the exclusion and oppression of blacks and other ethnic minorities. When they were built in the 1950s, they conformed with the numerous laws that denied non-whites free choice

2.2
Upscale apartment block on Lake Shore Drive (Florian Urban, 2007)

of their residence and equal opportunities, and even when segregationist legislation was abolished in the 1960s, the connection between mass housing and black marginalization proved to be surprisingly resilient. This crude association was reinforced by the numerous news reports on African Americans and urban decay that have been pervasive in the media since the 1960s. Perhaps the most significant goal of the demolitions at the turn of the twenty-first century was therefore to exorcise the spirits of segregation and open up this architectural type to reinterpretation.

Tower blocks in the Black Belt

Nowhere is this specific history better illustrated than in Chicago, which like few other Northern cities was built along the color line. The Windy City was also both birthplace and closing stage of American high-rise housing. Here the skyscraper was invented, and America's first office towers were erected during the 1880s and 1890s. Half a century later, the country's largest high-rise housing projects were built in Chicago's so-called "Black Belt"—the neighborhoods that form a half circle south, west, and north of the Loop (the central business district) and lie like a barrier between the commercial center and the wealthy suburbs. Since the early 1900s, they have been the center of Chicago's African American community. The public housing projects of the 1950s and 1960s, such as the Cabrini-Green, Robert Taylor, and Henry Horner Homes, were all built in this area.

Like few other American cities, Chicago witnessed both the enthusiasm for public housing and the subsequent disenchantment. Several particularities marked the local situation. Like other Northern cities, Chicago had been the destination for African Americans fleeing Jim Crow laws in the South. Between 1940 and 1960, the black population almost tripled—from 278,000 to 813,000.[4] Most of these new residents settled in the poor inner-city area, where housing soon became scarce. In the same period, the city as a whole grew only marginally, as white middle-class families increasingly moved to the suburbs.[5] Chicago's demography at that time showed two contradictory tendencies: on the one hand, a dispersal of the population, with a decrease in the city and an increase in the wider metropolitan area, and, on the other hand, a strong population growth in the Black Belt.

The city administration reacted with a mixture of patronizing care and racism. While the white city officials were eager to "develop" the black areas and thus improve the situation for poor migrants, they also carefully sought to maintain segregation and prevent blacks from moving into white neighborhoods. The selection of sites for public housing reinforced the color line. African Americans were not admitted to most white projects, and in mixed projects, their number was limited. In other contexts, the connection between urban renewal and segregation was less direct but equally effective. The transformation of the Hyde Park Kenwood neighborhood (situated at the fringe of the Black Belt in south Chicago) in the 1950s is just one of many examples. Supported by the University of Chicago, one of the largest institutions in the area, Hyde Park Kenwood was one of the largest urban renewal projects at the time. The plan succeeded in revitalizing the area in economic terms and, at the same time, large portions of the African American community were driven out.[6] Chicago authorities were particularly keen to convert "slums" into showcase examples of modern housing. City officials took it for granted that large parts of the city were beyond salvation and had to be razed and rebuilt. A 1949 estimate classified as "conservative" called for the construction of 105,000 apartments to replace the slums—about 20,000 were actually built in the following 20 years, about 15,000 on demolished "slum sites."[7]

The Chicago Housing Authority (CHA) was a major player in the slum clearance policy, embodying the ambiguity of modernizing policies with their blend of charitable assistance and deeply rooted racism. Elizabeth Wood, the executive director from 1948, was the city's leading housing progressive. Promoting racial integration, Wood clashed with both reactionary city officials and conservatives in the CHA and had to resign in 1954.[8] Many of the CHA's most infamous large-scale public housing projects were planned and built in the years that followed her resignation, including the Robert Taylor Homes and the William Green Homes. And most were built on the site of two-story wooden houses classified as "slums."

Chicago's first housing projects were low-rise. The shift toward high-rises took place shortly after the Second World War, and was initiated after Elizabeth Wood and her staff visited New York City and saw the high-rise development East River Houses (built 1938).[9] In the following years, 90 percent of the low-income units mentioned earlier were built in high-rises.[10] The first was the Dearborn Homes, an 800-unit development on the South Side that consisted of 16 cruciform buildings and was begun in 1947.[11] Originally planned with six stories, it was eventually built with nine stories, first and foremost because of the better proportion between the number of units and the acreage of the open park space.[12] Five additional high-rise projects followed between this time and 1950: Loomis Courts, Ogden Courts, Harrison Courts, Maplewood Courts, and Archer Courts. These buildings conformed with what would become the stereotypical image of American public housing: repetitive rectangular or cruciform plans, compounds set off from the streets, and brick façades with no adornment and no balconies.

In contrast to mass housing in France or in the Soviet Union, America's serial tower blocks were mostly steel-frame structures with brick infill rather than prefab buildings. There was, however, a debate about the introduction of industrialized construction in the US. In 1970, for example, the Berkeley engineers T. Y. Lin and S. D. Stotesbury issued a vigorous call for industrialized housing, which they saw as the only possible response to the expected population increase, and pointed to the exemplary policy in many European countries, including the Soviet Union.[13] Other voices were also favorable toward industrialized mass housing, including the 1968 Kaiser Report by the US Government.[14] One can only speculate as to why prefab construction remained the exception in the US; among the reasons might be the ready availability of steel and cheap labor, and the fact that in the absence of large-scale, state-sponsored institutions, projects were carried out by local builders who shunned the investment in prefab technology.

Given the widespread resentment against high-rise housing from the very beginning, what circumstances led to their construction? First, one can assume that in the 1950s the worldwide lure of the Corbusian tower-in-the-park also had its impact in the United States and thus seemed to be the proper embodiment of progressive policy. And second, high-rises were the cheapest solution in a country where private landownership was inviolable. In contrast to many other countries, where mass housing was built on state-owned real estate or where land-use regulations were modified to decrease cost for public clients, US authorities had to buy land at market prices. For politicians this was a significant incentive to reduce cost by building their projects in undesirable and thus cheap neighborhoods and at increased density.[15] Already in master plans from the early 1940s, slum clearance was not expected to reduce overall density and the new buildings on the sites were to house the same number of people as the overcrowded shacks.[16] Multiple stories and repetitive design, therefore, appeared as the most economical solution. In addition, there is little evidence that the earliest residents of these towers had any prejudices against high-rises. And if they had, their worries were certainly eclipsed by their relief at living conditions that in most cases were far better than the ones they had left behind. Enjoying running hot water and central heating for the first time, they wasted little time worrying about potential elevator blackouts.[17]

In any case, the opinions of the inhabitants counted little at the time, and the developments of the 1950s and early 1960s became the textbook examples of high-rise housing. Most prominent were the Robert Taylor Homes in Chicago's Near South Side neighborhood (1959–62), named for Robert Rochon Taylor (1903–59), the Chicago Housing Authority's first African American chairman.[18] Housing approximately 27,000 people in more than 4,300 apartments, it was one of the largest housing projects in the US at the time. The bleakness of the project soon became proverbial. The Robert Taylor Homes were composed of 28 identical 16-story buildings, arranged in clusters of 3, and set at a great distance to any of the city's cultural or commercial centers. The isolation of the Homes from the surrounding working-class neighborhoods was deliberate; according to CHA head Elizabeth Wood, they were supposed to constitute "islands in a wilderness of slums."[19] Other projects followed, all situated in the Black Belt, such as the Cabrini-Green Homes (1942–62, 3,600 units) in the north, the Stateway Gardens (1955–58, 1,600 units) and Ickes Homes (1955, 800 units) in the south, and the Rockwell Gardens (1961, 600 units), Henry Horner Homes (1957–61, 900 units), and the ABLA development (1937–62) in the west.

Equal dwelling conditions in a market economy

Most historians are skeptical about American mass housing's humanitarian pretensions.[20] In the eyes of many recent scholars, the projects were stillborn from the beginning. They conclude that the state-sponsored residences were in fact never directed toward egalitarianism and sharing society's wealth with the disadvantaged, but rather aimed at their exclusion from the start. They thus continued a long tradition of anti-poor laws and deeply rooted racism. Federal housing programs did not relieve the plight of the poor, but rather destroyed more affordable living spaces than they created and subsidized those who needed it least.[21] At the same time, they excluded blacks from economic opportunities and societal participation. The confinement of the poor in inner-city ghettos was therefore not an

undesired outcome of good programs gone awry, but, on the contrary, their intended consequence.

The Chicago housing projects, according to the critics, thus demonstrate that despite the genuine idealism of many housing reformers, two major principles underlay the construction of mass housing throughout most of the twentieth century: racial segregation and the belief in private enterprise as a social benefactor.[22] As a consequence of the first, the color line was never effectively blurred and Chicago in 2001 remained the second most segregated city in the US after Gary, Indiana.[23] As a result of the second, in the US, unlike in Europe, government efforts to relieve the misery of the lower classes had to follow a commercial logic, and housing reform was carried out only if it was profitable. Ideas about state-sponsored equal housing standards were particularly difficult to establish, because they collided with one of the country's dearest founding myths: the promise of unlimited advancement through entrepreneurialism and individual effort. Rejecting the class constraints of the Old Continent, many Americans believed in the power of the individual to shape his or her life and conceived of poverty as self-inflicted and potentially well deserved. In most Western countries, the tension between the two conflicting Christian traditions of charity and forbearing acceptance of social circumstances remained unresolved, but nowhere did they more openly favor the rich and successful. The American promise of opportunity, individual strength, and the power of role models was thus particularly difficult to reconcile with progressive ideas about the state eradicating social inequality.

When the discourse on social reform gained international significance, Americans were more receptive to proposals aiming at physical rather than social improvement. A

prominent example is the approach of journalist Jacob Riis (1849–1914), who in the 1890s indicted the miserable housing conditions of America's poor.[24] To his contemporaries, his reports appeared particularly convincing because Riis knew what he was writing about. A Danish immigrant from a working-class family, he had for many years suffered hunger, unemployment, and homelessness in America's great cities. His traumatic experience, however, did not prevent him from proposing shortsighted solutions. He vigorously endorsed slum clearance projects such as the 1895 demolition of Lower Manhattan's infamous Mulberry Bend neighborhood and, at the same time, failed to present a convincing plan for what to do with the displaced inhabitants. Riis's activities were seminal for the widespread adoption of a demolition policy among progressive politicians.[25] Like most reformers at the time, he believed that social behavior was conditioned by accommodation— removing the most dilapidated buildings was therefore enough to build a better society.

The legacy of physical determinism weighed heavily upon later proponents of equal housing standards and was noticeable even in the proposals of those housing reformers who, influenced by early British and German social housing projects, called for government-sponsored housing to accommodate the poor. Prominent representatives of this group included housing lobbyist and government consultant Edith Elmer Wood (1871–1945) and the secretary of the New York Tenement House Commission Lawrence Veiller (1872–1959).[26] Under Veiller's auspices the city's 1901 tenement legislation, which included reforms such as the outlawing of rooms without windows, was passed. Other famous advocates of state intervention included Catherine Bauer (1905–64), Mary Kingsbury Simkhovitch (1867–1951), Clarence Stein (1882–1975), and Lewis Mumford (1895–1990).

The physical aspects of the proletariat's disastrous living conditions were particularly emphasized by American housing reformers, since gloomy back alleys and overcrowded tenements fitted in with a traditional American view of great cities as the incarnation of bodily and moral sickness. In the late nineteenth century, this anti-urban sentiment was disseminated by bestselling novels such as Josiah Strong's *Our Country* (1885), Joaquin Miller's *Destruction of Gotham* (1886), and Edward Bellamy's *Looking Backward* (1886). In the twentieth century, it protracted an approach to reform that centered on physical improvements and set the parameters for mass housing long before the first tower blocks were built.

Given the scope of the misery of the urban underclass and the vigorous finger pointing of housing activists beginning in the late nineteenth century, there was surprisingly little action. It took a major catastrophe like the Great Depression and the impoverishment of thousands of middle-class families for social reformist thinking to play a prominent role in national policy. It seems that only the temporary plight of the former middle class, rather than the ongoing suffering of the proletariat, was effective in instigating wealthier citizens' solidarity with the poor, to whom they now felt closer than any time before and whose "undeserved" distress they now saw as the consequence of force majeure rather than of individual deficiency. With Franklin D. Roosevelt's New Deal, the American government for the first time reached what historian Peter Hall has called an "unlikely coalition between conservative and progressive interests" and formulated the goal of assuming responsibility for the material well-being of the disadvantaged.[27] Such policy was nevertheless far more controversial in the US than it was in Europe, and eventually resulted in what housing reformer Charles Abrams called "socialism for the rich and free enterprise for the poor"— a concentration of state subsidies on the middle rather than the lower classes.[28]

Following the traditions of the Progressive Era, the federal housing programs begun in the 1930s and expanded until the 1950s put a stress on physical improvements. Slum clearance played a major role. The National Housing Act of 1934 established the Federal Housing Administration (FHA) as the major institution dealing with public housing; subsequent institutional modifications converted it into the Department of Housing and Urban Development (HUD), which was established in 1965 and still exists today. The construction of mass housing in the inner city for the poor and the promotion of a suburban lifestyle for the middle class went hand in hand. The 1934 legislation that established the Federal Housing Administration, which was repeatedly amended over the following years, also established the federally insured system of long-term mortgages. It thus, for the first time, made homeownership available to a large segment of the population and laid the foundations for the triumph of the suburban single-family home as the all-American middle-class dwelling.[29]

Another major legal piece of housing legislation was the 1937 Housing Act, also known as the Wagner-Steagall Act, which declared it to be the government's responsibility to provide decent housing for its citizens. It provided a significant incentive for cities to start slum clearance programs, since the federal government paid 90 percent of the total cost, which included the demolition of the old buildings and design and construction of the new ones. The remaining 10 percent could be earned by the cities through tax exemptions.[30] Federal money only paid, however, for land and construction costs but not for the running costs. This legislation thus excluded the poorest, who could not afford the expense of maintaining their homes. The designated clientele of the original projects was thus clear: not blacks, not recent immigrants, but rather the white middle class affected by the Great Depression. Public housing was merely thought of as a form of temporary aid for these "deserving poor." It was only when the original target group had recovered that the housing programs were extended to social and racial minorities.

To a greater degree than in Europe, state-sponsored housing programs followed a business agenda and did not significantly restrict the free housing market. Private actors retained strong influence in the process, and policies were tailored to their needs. In 1935, for example, Federal Justice Dawson declared eminent domain for public housing unconstitutional. Subsequently, the government had to pay for housing sites, which necessarily limited the output of state-sponsored apartments. The specific ways in which public housing was established revealed the influence of a powerful real estate lobby. Housing projects were geared toward a maximum profit for private developers rather than maximum benefit for future inhabitants.[31] The bias in favor of business increased when laws were gradually geared to support a comprehensive redesign of the city. Two additional Housing Acts were passed in 1949 and 1954.[32] The first one famously stated the goal of providing "a decent home and a suitable living environment for every American family," while the second established what would become the catchphrase of the time: policy was no longer aimed at "slum clearance and redevelopment" but rather at "urban renewal." The widespread demolition and new construction in the inner city was not so much targeted at aiding poor inner-city dwellers but mostly benefited the interests of business owners who had suffered from the relocation of their clients to the suburbs. On several occasions, commercial developers advocated the demolition of "slums" in the inner cities but failed to build the promised accommodation for the poor.[33] Among the most famous inner-city areas gentrified through slum clearance projects were the Golden Triangle in downtown Pittsburgh (1946), Bunker Hill in Los Angeles (1955), Washington Square Village in New York City (1957), and the West End in Boston (1959). The working-class population in these areas—which by far was not the most impoverished in the respective cities—was forcibly displaced and replaced by wealthier groups. In Chicago, the urban renewal projects in the Black Belt also served business needs on another level: they kept the mostly black urban underclass out of the white suburbs and out of the white central business district.

"Brutal buildings"

Chicago's public housing units shared a conceptual deficiency with many other state-sponsored mass housing units in this book: from the beginning, the costs of maintenance were underestimated. As in the cheaply built tower blocks in Paris, Moscow, or Mumbai, the state institutions were too poorly funded to guarantee the upkeep of the buildings. Hence almost from the date of their completion, the blocks deteriorated at an increasing pace. Roofs leaked, windows broke, steam pipes and cables burst. The textbook image of how many resources were wasted by lack of maintenance appeared in a widely read report on the Henry Horner Homes: in the apartment of a single mother with eight children the broken bathroom faucet was not fixed for years, and the whole family suffered from sleepless nights due to the noise of boiling hot water constantly rushing into the bathtub.[34]

At the same time, the composition of the inhabitants changed rapidly. While in the early stages there was still a certain mix of working-class and middle-class tenants, those who could afford it soon left. In addition, federal legislation from 1969 onward based the

rent level in subsidized housing on the tenants' income, making housing projects more and more unattractive for those who had a job. From the 1970s on, almost all residents of the Robert Taylor Homes were black, unemployed, and extremely poor. By the late 1990s, the population had dropped almost two-thirds to 11,000. The Robert Taylor Homes became an "unrelenting wasteland of brutal buildings and broken lives," embodying the worst aspects of public housing.[35]

Among America's white middle class, mass housing became the archetypal image of America's urban nightmare. The first account of the terrible conditions in the Robert Taylor Homes shook the nation in 1965, only three years after the project had opened. The Chicago *Daily News* painted a nightmarish picture of poor maintenance, excessive vandalism, and ongoing violence.[36] Over the following years, interest in first-hand accounts of the housing projects was widespread. Most were nevertheless written by observers rather than inhabitants of these buildings. The story of two African American brothers growing up, as the author put it, "in the other America," soon became a bestseller.[37] The author, the white journalist Alex Kotlowitz, portrayed two boys who were raised by a single mother amid drug abusers and gunfire from rivaling gangs in the Henry Horner Homes Extension, a cluster of seven high-rises. Kotlowitz described all facets of his young protagonists' everyday life. In his account, the unwelcoming architecture of the high-rises acted as a negative force in the lives of the two boys and their family. He focused on dramatic events, particularly on their experience of the deaths of several of their fellow residents from gang-related shootouts. Kotlowitz's reportage is a sensitive account of the public housing tenants' daily joys and hardships. The abundance of such reports nevertheless contributed to the fact that, in the eyes of the white majority, inner-city tower blocks and black tenants on welfare were soon meshed into an undifferentiated scary "other."

In public opinion, poor maintenance was increasingly depicted as the key feature of the projects' failure. Broken windows and littered hallways became signifiers of the fact that public authorities were obviously incapable of taking care of their tenants. The inference was convenient, since it fit Americans' deep-rooted mistrust of state intervention: their belief that if one depends on the government, one always ends up losing. The focus on physical features was nevertheless not limited to a general audience. Many scholars followed a similar argumentation. City planner Oscar Newman, in his well-known analysis of buildings and crime prevention, blamed bad design for the high crime rate in the housing projects.[38] Along the same lines, the "Broken Windows" theory maintained that the key to crime prevention was the creation of a safe atmosphere, in which certain physical aspects such as the absence of visible decay played a fundamental role.[39] Critics such as Peter Blake and Tom Wolfe ridiculed the tower blocks as dysfunctional and ugly.[40]

At the same time, too, a criticism of the social and political context increased. Residents associations, supported by intellectuals such as Jane Jacobs and Richard Sennet, waged a great war against urban renewal and opposed the demolition of historic neighborhoods.[41] In this context, many housing activists criticized the mass housing developments for not taking into account the needs of the projected inhabitants. For them, the one-size-fits-all architecture of the housing block promoted a white middle-class lifestyle incompatible with that of other classes and ethnicities, for example in not allowing for extended families and in not catering to the needs of families with many children—the great majority of households in Chicago's projects. Critics thus accused public housing of being biased against its very inhabitants.[42] Such views were embedded in a widely held view that rejected the toolkit of modernist urban planning, including top-down decision-making, a belief in impartial experts, and the conception of a universally acknowledged public weal.[43]

By the early 1970s, a negative vision of modern architecture dominated the public debate and for decades to come left the connection of serial apartment blocks and social misery unchallenged. When the St. Louis city authorities decided to blow up the infamous Pruitt-Igoe Homes in 1972, the step was widely applauded.[44] In 1973, the Nixon administration confronted the consequences of the ongoing criticism and, at the same time, reacted to the internationally fading reputation of direct-housing subsidies. Instead of providing funding for individual projects, the federal government now supported state entities for the construction of housing. The era of large-scale developments thus came to an end, and large-scale mass housing projects were no longer built. And finally, when a decade later America experienced the "renaissance of the inner cities," the real-estate industry pushed for the privatization of state property, which now carried the potential for increasing profit margins.

The scare stories in the media, the objective plight in the housing projects, and public opinion that increasingly opposed apartment blocks were nevertheless unable to affect the perception of mass housing among its inhabitants: most did not feel uncomfortable living in serial high-rises as such but rather suffered from their wholesale depiction as ciminals.[45] Among those on low incomes, public housing is far from being considered obsolete. In 2005, the Chicago Housing Authority had more than 148,000 persons on its waiting list—roughly two-thirds of them were black.[46] To date, for the few remaining housing projects, both high-rises and low-rises, vacancy rates are next to zero. Despite all attacks and despite its apparent failure in many respects, public housing still seems far more attractive than all alternatives to it.

New York exceptionalism

America's main argument against physical determinism is New York City, where serial residences have been surprisingly successful. While the residents often suffer from comparable race and class prejudices to those in Chicago or other American cities, high-rise housing as such has not been stigmatized in the same way.[47] The city that boasts some of the most famous high-rises in the world is thus an exception in the US context. The reasons are both historical and geographical. In New York, verticality has been part and parcel of residential culture since the early twentieth century and has traditionally been associated with the wealthy. A decade before the first public projects went up in New York's disadvantaged neighborhoods, the well-to-do in the Big Apple delighted in dwelling in similarly tall, albeit very different, buildings. New York's luxury high-rise condominiums were a product of the Roaring Twenties, a time when the city was already one of the most populated in the world but long car commutes were not yet an attractive option for the rich. The residential skyscrapers were mostly erected in midtown locations close to Central Park. One of the earliest and to date most prestigious is 740 Park Avenue. Built in 1930 by Rosario Candela, the 17-story art deco tower was once home to John D. Rockefeller Jr. In 2000, his 24-room, 12-bathroom apartment sold for approximately 30 million dollars.[48] Equally famous is the San Remo, built in 1929 on Central Park West, and former or present home to Bruce Willis, Dustin Hoffman, Demi Moore, and Steven Spielberg. In the San Remo Building, the average unit has 3,200 square feet; on several floors, there are spacious terraces with spectacular views of Central Park.

In the late 1930s, New York City's mayor Fiorello LaGuardia pioneered the implementation of the federal public housing laws passed a few years before. The first federally funded projects were low-rises of five stories or less. The first project, First Houses (1935–36, 120 units) on the Lower East Side, was a small-scale dispersed version of block perimeter four-story tenements, of which every third one was taken out to reduce density and create open space. The second, Harlem River Houses (1936–37, 600 units, design: John Louis Wilson), had only five stories but already contained many of the elements that would compose the archetypal image of public housing:[49] a large compound set off from the street, with bleak, unadorned brick façades, standardized crossbar windows, and no balconies. Compared to later projects, there were many amenities: the compound included a nursery school, a health clinic, stores, and sports facilities. Harlem River Houses stood out among the early housing projects as one of the few that was built for African Americans. Media reports stressed the pride and contentment of the residents of these first projects, which lingers to date. Long-term tenants still point out the considerable improvements that these apartments presented to their personal living conditions at the time they moved in, including providing electricity and warm running water.[50]

2.6
Polo Grounds Towers in Harlem, New York City. This public housing project on 155th Street was completed in 1968 and comprises approximately 1,600 apartments, which are situated in four 30-story buildings (Florian Urban)

What accounted for New York's exceptionalism? There are three major reasons. First, mass housing typologies were not restricted to the poorest of the poor, but inhabited by all social classes. From the 1940s onward, tower blocks were built in great numbers for the middle classes. Perhaps the most perfect image of Le Corbusier's tower-in-a-park vision published in his Voisin Plan was carried out in New York: the Stuyvesant Town/Cooper Village on the Lower East Side, a series of cruciform high-rises. Built in 1947 on a cleared "slum site," it has remained a sought-after location for middle-class residents who enjoy living in a central location.

Second, New York's public housing projects were much better funded than those in other American cities. Only in New York did city and state authorities contribute extra funds to the paltry federal ones. Hence the New York City Housing Authority (NYCHA) was better able to maintain its public housing projects and better integrate them into the city. Established in 1934, NYCHA was the only large US housing authority that made serious efforts with regard to social and economic integration.[51] Unlike in other cities, public housing did not begin to decay physically and socially immediately upon completion. As a result, no project was ever singled out as a textbook image of inner-city decline comparable to Chicago's Robert Taylor Homes. On the contrary, many areas that in the 1960s acquired a notoriously bad reputation—such as Harlem or the South Bronx—were neither high-rises nor public housing, but rather poor neighborhoods of three-story brownstone houses from the late nineteenth century.

A third reason for the relative success of New York public housing was geographical. The island situation of Manhattan disfavored suburbanization and accounted for the fact that since the late nineteenth century land prices were high enough that only a tiny minority of those living in the "city proper" could afford single family homes—the rest had to live in multistory buildings. Few public housing dwellers could therefore afford to leave their homes, even if their economic situation put them significantly above the welfare line.[52] Public housing dwellers were thus not as stigmatized as in other cities, since many middle-class families also lived in such projects. The broad acceptance of the high-rise type in connection with the better funding of the housing projects and the unaffordability of single-family homes led to the different valuation of high-rise housing in New York in comparison with the rest of the country. A long history of racism notwithstanding, the equation between poverty, people of color, and high-rise housing thus never became as poignant as in other American cities.[53]

Replacing towers with pitched-roof houses

Public support for housing had never been a major force in American cities, and the few existing subsidies were gradually removed in the 1990s. In 1992, the federal authorities started the redevelopment program HOPE VI (Housing Opportunities for People Everywhere), which provided funds to cities to knock down crumbling public housing and replace it with so-called mixed-income developments. A small portion of the new units was to be assigned to low-income tenants; the others were to be sold at market rate. At the same time, HOPE VI promoted the demolition of modernist towers and the construction of "traditional" low-rises with wooden structures, porches, bay windows, and pitched roofs, which, ironically, often resembled the buildings that in the 1950s had been demolished as "slums" to make way for the tower blocks.[54] Presented as a means to prevent ghettoization and concentration of poor households along with aesthetic improvement, the measure in fact sharply reduced the amount of affordable housing.

Chicago became a principal location for the new policy. In 1995 federal officials took over the Chicago Housing Authority's holdings and property, after enhanced allegations of corruption. The institution, which since its incorporation in 1937 had been an independent state agency, was run by the federal government until 1999. The first tower block demolitions were carried out in the Cabrini-Green project in 2000. In the following years, almost all projects exceeding five stories were razed in favor of mixed-income developments. For example, the Cabrini-Green project, which had once provided 3,200 public housing units in repetitive high-rises, was torn down and replaced by neo-traditional two-story townhouses. The developers hoped that the new development would "prove attractive to both renters and prospective homebuyers," and poor neighbors were likely to disturb this image. Only 700 public housing units were developed, complemented by 340 market-rate and 140 "affordable" housing units (rented at slightly less than market rate). Of the public housing units, less than 200 were on the site of the demolished buildings and the rest were scattered throughout the city. The amount of state-subsidized housing was thus effectively reduced by almost 80 percent.[55]

For other Chicago projects such as the Stateway Gardens or the Robert Taylor Homes the rates of affordable housing units are similarly disillusioning.[56] On the site of the latter, the low-rise redevelopment Legends South is currently under construction. The first new building, Mahalia Place, opened in 2004. As if to mock the displaced residents, it was named

2.7
The Stateway Gardens (built 1955–58) immediately before their demolition in 2007. On the right side the neo-historical "mixed-income developments" are being built on the site (Florian Urban)

for gospel singer and former South Side resident Mahalia Jackson, whose impoverished family of 13 would hardly be tolerated there. In all the redevelopments, the former tenants had no right to stay. The total number of apartments in the new pitched-roof buildings was significantly smaller than that in the demolished high-rises, and only a portion of them was rent-subsidized. Thus only a tiny minority of the old tenants could secure a space in the few new subsidized apartments; the rest were given "housing vouchers," called "Section 8 certificates," that would subsidize their rents in other buildings.[57] Their situation was thus much worse than under the old conditions, since there was no guarantee that they could find affordable private housing in a city plagued by soaring rents. Most were scattered throughout low-income neighborhoods on the periphery, such as Englewood, South Shore, Gresham, West Garfield Park, East Garfield Park, and South Austin.[58]

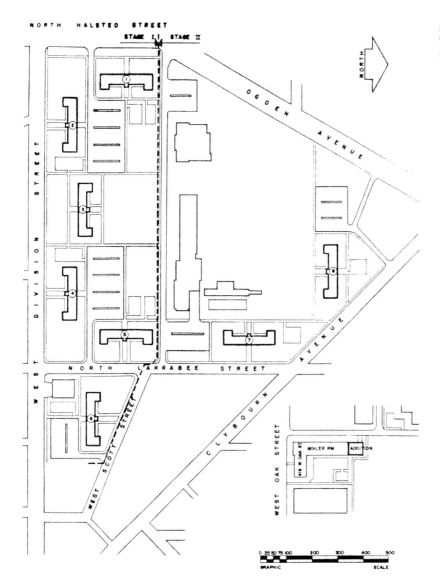

2.8
William Green Homes, plan
(drawing: Steffen Seidel)

2.9
William Green Homes, seen from Elm Street (background) and "mixed-income projects" (foreground) built under the HOPE VI program in the 2000s on the site of the demolished Frances Cabrini Homes (Florian Urban, 2007)

The rigid design guidelines for the HOPE VI projects combined different threads of anti-modernist criticism and corresponded to what by now had become the mainstream image of a beautiful city: compact block perimeter buildings with no more than five stories and façades that reflected pre-modernist European design and local traditions. The widely acknowledged positive connotations of these forms suggested a solution to the social problems that in fact were merely shifted to other areas. Federal policy thus resumed the centuries-old strategy that had already inspired the slum clearances of the mid-twentieth century or Oscar Newman's studies of the 1970s, but which had hardly ever yielded the desired effect: social ills were to be cured through aesthetic means.

Exorcising the spirits of the past

The contradictory history of mass housing in the US illustrates how the enthusiasm for city-based progress and technology was always accompanied by an anti-urbanist undercurrent.[59]

At the same time, it demonstrates that certain principles of the late nineteenth century have remained surprisingly stable: social advancement is to be reached through entrepreneurialism and private business, physical improvements are to guide social betterment, and there is little collective responsibility for the poor. As a result, visions of a city that integrates rich and poor have always remained weak. Scholars and activists therefore rightfully indicted the futile replacement of high-rise projects with low-rise mixed income projects, which in most cases lowered the living conditions of the most disadvantaged rather than improving them, and merely masked the displacement of the poor with colorful façades.[60] Investigating different housing projects, these critics pointed to local specificities and assigned general questions of design less significance. Katherine Bristol, for example, pointed out that it was not its design that made Pruitt-Igoe a failure, but rather urban politics in St. Louis and social factors.[61] Lawrence Vale, in his research on the evolution of three apparently similar Boston housing projects, argued that housing projects succeeded or failed due to specific neighborhood struggles, and not because of certain aesthetic features.[62] And sociologist Sudhir Venkatesh, in his highly acclaimed account of life in the Robert Taylor Homes, saw the development of housing projects in Chicago as determined by social factors rather than the condition of high-rise mass housing.[63] In political scientist Eugene Meehan's words, public housing fell victim to a "condemnation without a trial."[64] Despite these findings, the few liberal activists who argue for continuing housing subsidies face an uphill battle. In contemporary Chicago, no political faction shares their opinions, and support for the poor has completely vanished from political agendas.

Compared to other countries, mass housing in the United States thus took a distinct path. It did not become a city-building institution as in Europe, but rather enhanced the polarity between poor inner cities and wealthy suburbs—the latter being equally subsidized through federally supported mortgages and a state-built highway system.[65] Public housing was also never public in the sense that the majority shared its underlying values of state-sponsored redistribution of wealth. From the very beginning, the incongruence of vision and reality was largely determined by long-standing cultural dispositions and the specific economic situation of the post-war period. The seeds of international ideas about state intervention and equal living standards fell on the local soil of a polarized society that was largely unwilling to alter the status quo of racial segregation and an unshakable faith in private business.

The demolition and redesign of various housing blocks evidence the power of an architectural image that had remained unchanged in the previous five decades. In Chicago's one-dimensional symbolic economy, the high-rises represented the oppression and exclusion of blacks in the same way that neo-traditional forms came to stand for an integrated society and the promise of community and social cohesion. For politicians and a large share of the population, the only solution to this perceptual deadlock was to dynamite the towers and thus exorcise the spirits of the past. In this respect, pulling down the mass housing blocks met an actual need beyond the profits of the real estate industry. Removing one of the most painful symbols of exclusion and oppression, the redesign demonstrated, at least on a surface level, an outspoken rejection of the principles that high-rise mass housing had come to symbolize. Creating the opportunity for a reinterpretation of this architectural type is likely to become the demolitions' most beneficial effect.

3 The Concrete Cordon Around Paris

Victims of modernism?

In few European countries have tower block developments developed such a negative public image as in France at the turn of the twenty-first century. In October of 2005, they were prominently featured as backdrops for burning cars and enraged teenagers. Countless television reports and newspaper articles showed that in the *grands ensembles*, as the vast modernist developments in the outskirts of French cities are called, the promise of *liberté, égalité,* and *fraternité* stood in blatant opposition to a sad reality of oppression, exclusion, and xenophobia. Modernist apartment blocks became signifiers for poverty, marginalization, and a racist society in which the French-born children of Middle Eastern and North African immigrants are still denied equal treatment despite their legal status as French citizens. The potency of the message was enhanced by the fact that the bleak serial tower blocks looked decidedly different from the images that the world had so far connected with French cities, and with Paris in particular. The high-rises in the Paris suburbs of Créteil, Clichy-sous-Bois, or Sarcelles did not fit with the idea of tree-lined boulevards, lushly decorated squares, and art deco metro entrances. To an international public, they appeared as an eerie flipside that the City of Love for a long time has managed to bar from both its municipal boundaries and public image.

What role did mass housing play in the exclusion and violence of the French suburbs? Were the revolting youth, as a Swiss journalist put it, "victims of modernism," rebels against a totalitarian order imposed by functionalist design?[1] And how does the French situation differ from other contexts in which, as in the United States or West Germany, tower blocks reinforced social exclusion? While there is little evidence of a direct relation between serially built high-rises and violent behavior, the towers do, however, offer a key to the understanding of a social situation that resulted from a particular evolution of modernist mass housing in

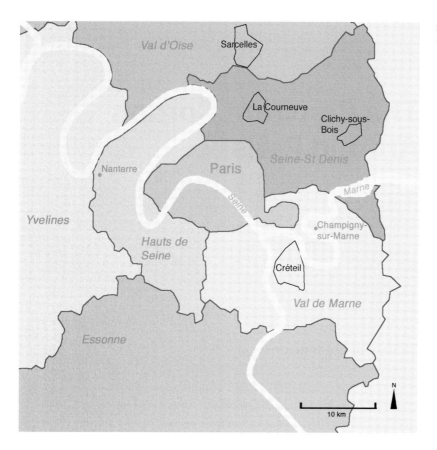

France. Approximately 10 million of France's 60 million inhabitants currently live in tower-and-slab developments—a greater percentage than in Germany or the United States, but smaller than in Russia. To an extent unknown in other countries, the *grands ensembles* came to form a world of their own, clearly separated from other architectural environments—as a contemporary French urbanist put it, a world of "irreducible strangeness and insularity."[2]

The *grands ensembles*, also known as *cités*, or simply *les quartiers*, became a conceptual entity in its own right, researched intensely like few other living environments to the extent that in France urban studies became almost a synonym for the investigation of mass housing developments. A list of scientific publications during the first two decades fills more than 200 pages.[3] The studies were carried out by sociologists, urban planners, geographers, and historians, and covered every possible aspect, from building technology to leisure activities. The tower blocks mostly appeared as symbols for broader social matters, be it a global crisis in the relation between the French and their urban habitat,[4] an unjust society that failed to provide social equity,[5] or even, ironically, a successful strategy that eventually fell victim to its own accomplishments after having witnessed the social advancement and subsequent moving out of the first generation of inhabitants.[6]

Criticism of these environments has been widespread since the 1960s, but has followed a different line of thought than, for example, in the US. The deficiencies in the architectural design and planning guidelines were discussed in great detail in both countries, but in France this was connected to a broader debate on the value of high architecture—in contrast to the US, the first tower blocks were designed by the country's most famous architects. In France, tower block developments also did not perpetuate an existing spatial exclusion like the racially segregated neighborhoods in the US—the obvious connection between colonialism and the evolution of modern urban planning notwithstanding.[7] Most *grands ensembles* were built before the country came to be divided into natives and immigrants. Unlike in the US, business interests were not very significant for the course of housing programs; in France, the state traditionally held a strong position in organizing city matters and throughout the twentieth century retained much of its authority.

Grand ensemble refers to a type of neighborhood which, despite its fixed image in French public debates, shows considerable variations. However, the developments have several things in common. They were all centrally planned, financed by some kind of state subsidy, and built on the peripheries of existing cities. All were built for tenancy rather than ownership and most remained tenant-occupied to date. Each development houses between 1,000 and 20,000 inhabitants in mass-produced towers and slabs of 5 to 20 stories. Almost all were built between 1953 and 1973. They are thus a product of the *Trente Glorieuses* ("glorious thirty"), the approximately thirty years between 1945 and 1973, when France experienced unprecedented economic growth, which accounted for rising wages and full employment. Hence they are connected with a period in which French society, along with the built environment, changed radically as rarely before. The country recovered from the Second World War and at the same time lost its colonial empire. A growing awareness of the housing crisis went along with a yearning for social unity and a commonly shared belief in the qualities of an orderly city. This vision, ironically, eventually resulted in a particularly obtrusive geography of exclusion. This chapter will trace the evolution of this new spatial order, stressing some key moments and focusing on the Paris region, where the great majority of French tower block developments were built.

The concept of a *grand ensemble* precedes the post-war era. The first modernist housing developments of the Paris region were erected in the 1920s, such as the *cité jardin* in the town of Le Plessis-Robinson (1924–39, 24 units, design: Maurice Payret-Dortail, Jean Demay, and Jean Festoc) or the Square Dufourmantelle development in Maisons Alfort (1930s, 600 units, design: Roger Hummel and André Dubreuil). The term *grand ensemble* first appeared in the title of a 1935 article by Maurice Rotival, one of France's most eminent urban designers at the time. Rotival vigorously called for the provision of public housing for the working classes (*HBM—Habitations à bon marché,* cheap apartments; after 1949 called *HLM—Habitations à loyers modérés*, moderate rent apartments). Anticipating much of the construction that was carried out in the following decades, he proposed independent clusters of homogenous 10–20-story towers on the cities' peripheries. The *ensembles* were to contain offices, healthcare centers, stores, and other services surrounded by large park spaces, and they were to be connected with the city via high-speed highways and suburban railroads. Rotival was hopeful "that one day, leaving Paris . . . one will find the length of large highways harmonically arranged between large woods, parks, stadiums, and large, clear and well-oriented settlements on which the sun shines brightly." Laying open the ambiguity between paternalistic help and control, he concluded that "we will arrive at redressing the morale of the laboring population of our great cities, and thus prevent them from gradually transforming into true insurgents."[8]

Rotival was a pioneer and passionate advocate of a comprehensive modernist approach to the city that the French call *urbanisme*, and his ideas about fundamental renewal extended far beyond the outlay of streets and buildings. His article appeared 24 years after the Societé française des urbanistes had been founded in 1911 and 16 years after the Cornudet Law had established planning as a mandatory element of municipal policy in 1919. At the bottom of his vision lay a conception of the city as a harmonious community of citizens, free in their thoughts and actions, and at the same time tightly controlled by a commonly accepted political system. Rotival's city of the future exposed the basic principles of French urban planning since the nineteenth century: social responsibility and tight rule.

In the discourse advanced by Rotival and his supporters, orderliness ranked high. The tower developments were conceived as improvements of the existing cities, albeit in a different way than in Germany or the United States. In contrast to the German quest against the gloomy backyards of late-nineteenth-century tenements, French housing reformers showed less contempt for the existing urban fabric. They typically raged against a form of dwelling that played a minor role in the housing debates elsewhere and even showed a certain similarity to the well-reputed American suburbs: the masses of cheap individual buildings on the urban periphery. These *pavillons*—mostly one-story structures—were erected on small plots of subdivided estates (*lotissements*) during the interwar years. Most were unplanned, and they often lacked proper infrastructure. In the eyes of the critics at the time, they were "ridiculously crammed together," generating "soulless suburbs."[9] In 1950, Eugène Claudius-Petit, the socialist Minister of Reconstruction and Urbanism, denounced the *pavillons*, warning against the "anarchy of the agglomerations" and "monotonous anonymity."[10] His successor, the moderately right-wing Minister of Construction Pierre Sudreau, in 1959 warned against repeating "the errors of the preceding generations" who produced "sleep cities, alignments of dead houses, and buildings without character."[11]

In these proposals, chaotic planning was seen as the source of all evil, and rationality and order as the keys to a good society. It was this comprehensive vision, both emancipatory and exclusionary, which came to embody the spirit of France's tower-and-slab developments. The connection of these ideas with forced relocation, racial segregation, and the oppression of native peoples in the colonies have been repeatedly acknowledged, and the roots of French mass housing in the "laboratories of modernity" in North Africa, Indochina, and elsewhere are well known.[12] While the liberating promise of rational planning had always clashed with rationalism's oppressive potential, the *grands ensembles* came to embody the contradiction inherent in two of the French Enlightenment's most cherished ideals: the tension between equity on the one hand and tolerance on the other.

Charity and control

The French mass housing developments evolved against the background of a period in which economic upturn went along with a strong belief in state paternalism that was shared across the political spectrum. In the winter of 1954, shelter became a question of life or death for many French. In January and February of that year, the country experienced one of the harshest cold waves in decades. In the Paris region, where snow is unknown in normal years and many houses lack a heating system, temperatures dropped to minus 15 degrees Celsius. The inclement weather was particularly threatening for those who lived in shantytowns or on the street. Their precarious situation is mostly remembered for the activities of the Catholic priest and social activist Henri Grouès, who became known under his Résistance pseudonym Abbé Pierre. At the peak of the cold wave, he successfully roused the French bourgeoisie's awareness of the suffering of the country's *sans abris* (homeless). In one of his most popular actions, he convinced the Gaullist Minister of Reconstruction Maurice Lemaire to assist at the funeral of a baby who had fallen victim to the frost. Lemaire subsequently supported the opening of emergency shelters. Upon Abbé Pierre's intervention, so-called *restaurants* for the homeless were installed and metro stations were opened at night. Following his emergency call on the radio on February 1, 1954, his charity organization Emmaüs received 120 million francs and 120 tons of clothes.[13]

Abbé Pierre's activities were significant for the future development of *grands ensembles*. He helped to forge a public consensus that state funds be funneled into the accommodation of the disadvantaged. The collective experience of the life-threatening cold and the ensuing solidarity across classes evidenced the social climate of the early 1950s. Exclusion and marginalization—exemplified by the many who had to live in appalling conditions—stood next to a broadly shared belief that a polarized society is morally wrong and will be overcome in the near future. Abbé Pierre also directly targeted the housing situation. As a consequence of his emergency call, the government passed a program to build 13,000 *logements économiques de première nécessité* ("economical housing units for first necessity")—the first batch was inaugurated in the spring of 1954 in the Paris suburb of Le Plessis-Trévise. These dwellings were soon dilapidated and, ironically, criticized as examples of *taudification* ("slumification").[14] The fact that these cheap, low-rise buildings were associated with the "chaotic" *pavillons* and increasingly censured as new slums became a significant factor in the promotion of the high-rise *grand ensemble* type.

The housing situation in France was indeed precarious. Wartime destruction, country-to-city migration, a high birth rate, and a general depression of the war-ravaged national economy accounted for the shortage. The lack of adequate dwellings, in part, was the result of a policy that in the early post-war years invested public funds predominantly in the reconstruction of productive capital rather than in housing. The statistics show a desolate situation. In the early 1950s, 29 percent of the French lived in substandard conditions. Ninety percent of dwellings were not equipped with indoor showers or bathtubs, and only 58 percent had running water.[15] *Bidonvilles* (literary "canister towns"), informal settlements of self-built shacks, were a common sight on the peripheries of large cities. They were inhabited by French citizens, but, as will be shown in the following, also by an increasing number of immigrants. The squatter settlement in Nanterre on the western fringe of Paris, built from makeshift cabins and wooden shelters, grew over the late 1950s through the influx of Algerians. Its immediate surroundings later became the location not only of an ambitious mass housing project but also of the newly founded Université de Paris-10 campus, which a few years later would become a hotspot of the 1968 protests. The *bidonville* in the eastern Paris suburb of Champigny-sur-Marne in the 1960s was home to 15,000 inhabitants, most of whom were North Africans and Portuguese. Makeshift settlements also spread in other inner suburbs of Paris, including Noisy-le-Grand, Colombes, Bondy, and Aubervilliers. Contemporary reports described lives of utter misery and appalling sanitary conditions.[16] While squatter settlements could also be found in other European countries at the time, in France they experienced extraordinary growth throughout the 1960s. Their disappearance during the 1970s is often seen as the one positive effect of the massive high-rise construction.[17]

At this time the political situation was also unstable. The PCF (Parti communiste français) had gained from its role as a major force of resistance against the German occupation and acted almost as an autonomous power within the state. Its strongholds in the Paris region lay precisely in the peripheral communities where many of the *grands ensembles* were later erected, the so-called *banlieue rouge* (red suburbs). The PCF consistently received around 30 percent of the vote and controlled some of the country's major intellectual publications, including *Les Lettres françaises*, the evening daily *Ce Soir*, and the official communist organ *L'Humanité*. Given its strong ties to the Soviet Union, its rejection in principle of parliamentary democracy, and its support of Algerian independence, the Communist Party was a significant factor in the instability of the French political system.

But on the right margin there were also strong anti-democratic powers, and many supported a violent response to what they considered a communist threat. Right-wing forces gained support with the outbreak of the Algerian War in 1956, attempting a coup d'état two years later and dealing the deathblow to the Fourth Republic. Between 1944 and 1958 France was ruled by 24 different governments, most of which lasted less than a year. Despite their political opposition, both communists and nationalists favored state intervention and agreed on the necessity of public housing. Hence, despite the frequent changes in political leadership and the lack of personal continuity in the Ministry of Construction, housing policy was fairly consistent during that time. There was an overwhelming solidarity between both French politicians and the general public with the homeless and badly housed.

This moral spirit, which inspired the strong response to Abbé Pierre's calls for charity, and which is often related to the collectice memory of the Résistance, was nevertheless ambiguous from the very beginning. It seems to have been perfectly compatible with the widespread resentment against immigrants who made up an increasing share of the slum dwellers. No call for social cohesion demanded equal opportunities for them, and no radio messages pleaded for their integration. The increasing presence of immigrants in France contrasted with their almost complete absence from the public debate throughout the 1950s and 1960s. Coverage was limited to pitiful reportages of the hardships foreign workers had to suffer in France, and occasional denouncements of the racism they encountered on the job and in the housing market.[18] Immigration as such only became a political topic with the economic crisis in the 1970s, and only from the late 1970s were immigrants connected with the *grands ensembles*. The reason is obvious: throughout the 1960s the tower block developments, albeit already the target of harsh criticism, were still privileged and comparably expensive residences. Immigrants frequently worked on their construction, but could rarely afford to inhabit them.

In the post-war period, immigrants from different countries went to look for work in French cities. In the early years they came predominantly from Italy and Spain. They were favored by a pro-immigration policy that catered to the needs of the booming economy. The influx continued over the following decades. In 1982, 3.7 million of 54 million French were immigrants—the share has slightly dropped since that time. Currently 20–25 percent of the population are estimated to have an immigrant background.[19] When the political situation in Algeria heated up in the late 1950s, Algerians flocked to France in increasing numbers. While the exact numbers are unknown, the 1954 census mentioned approximately 30,000 for the city of Paris and 46,000 for the suburbs—still a small number in comparison with the Paris region's approximately 5.5 million inhabitants at the time.[20] Most immigrants lived in dire conditions. They frequently suffered from racism and xenophobia. The government built so-called *foyers*, simple dormitories resembling military camps, but could not keep up with the need. In 1962 one out of four, and in 1965 one out of two, immigrants ended up in a *bidonville*. At that time, an estimated 80 percent of the slum residents in the Paris region were foreigners.[21]

While similar tensions between long-term residents and newly arriving migrants could be found in many northern European countries in the 1960s, the situation was particularly bad in France. On the one hand, the housing situation was extremely poor, and slums widespread. On the other hand, much of the immigration was related to the Algerian War (1954–62), which in 1958 led to the end of the young Fourth Republic after only 14 years of its existence and brought France to the brink of a military dictatorship. When the war broke out, French society was polarized not only over the questions of whether or not to grant Algeria independence but also of how to deal with an extremely violent conflict. On the one side, Algerian terrorist groups organized attacks not only against French policemen but also against Algerians who belonged to rival parties. On the other side, police violence and the disappearance of Algerian detainees was the order of the day. Terror and systematic torture was used on both sides. French troops regularly bombed Algerian villages and executed or forcibly relocated Algerian civilians. Both French settlers (*pieds noirs*) and loyalist Algerian fighters (*harkis*) were frequently killed in deterrence or retaliation. And eventually 1.4 million—close to 3 percent of the French population at the time—had to flee Algeria to settle in a state they accused of failing to protect their lives and property.

The social and economic effects of the war were also disastrous. The death toll among the combatants alone is estimated to be more than 140,000. The self-esteem and political culture of the *grande nation* was in tatters. In Algeria, France faced its defeat after having pulled out all the stops to avert it. The motherland of civic liberties in Europe, which for two decades had been taking pride in its resistance against Nazi Germany, now had its own record of war crimes. And it did everything possible to repress the unpleasant memories. Whether or not their arrival was directly related to the Algerian War, immigrants in France suffered from the deeply felt insecurity about the foundations of French society.

The insecurity was also reflected in the newcomers' legal situation. At the height of the Algerian War, France insisted on Algeria's status as a part of the motherland and not a colony such as, for example, West Africa. At the same time, the French state continued classifying Algerian immigrants as French subjects rather than French citizens, thus denying them civic participation. As holders of French identity cards, Algerians were theoretically entitled to many of the civil rights French Enlightenment thinkers had once fought for, and yet in reality they were socially ostracized and subject to arbitrary arrests and police brutality.

The consequences of this situation can still be traced in the Paris region, where the exclusion of immigrants from the "city proper" took place long before the high-rises were built. The administrative and architectural disparity between the city of Paris and the adjacent communities mirrors the conflict between democratic liberties and authoritarian control, and in addition carries the memories of the 1961 riots, which led to the biggest massacre among unarmed civilians since the Second World War. In that year, the de facto confinement of Algerians to poor neighborhoods outside the Paris borders was granted legal status when, after a series of bomb attacks against French policemen, Police Chief Maurice Papon issued a nightly curfew for "French Muslims of Algeria." Subsequently, nightlife on the French capital's grand boulevards was officially restricted to ethnic French. Protests against these measures culminated on the evening of October 5, 1961, when tens of thousands of the approximately 150,000 Algerians that lived in the Paris region at the time followed a call of the FLN (National Liberation Front) and peacefully marched the streets of the inner city. After blocking streets and metro entrances to prevent the Algerians from entering the city, the police opened fire on the crowd. For decades official sources tried to downplay the incident, and current estimates on the number of death range between 40 and 200.[22] The 1961 massacre was not only the eerie peak of a long, violent struggle between French and Algerians. It also once again demonstrated the ambiguity of an urban planning tradition that since Haussmann's times has produced both arenas for democratic debate and operative tools for state repression, and that subsequently came to set the stage for the construction of the cordon of mass housing around Paris.

Building a concrete cordon

Combining support and segregation, the idea of housing the disadvantaged turned into a collective enterprise. The years 1953 and 1954 saw the beginning of the French building boom. Housing construction increased steadily over the 1950s and 1960s and by 1973 constituted more than 25 percent of all national investment.[23] When in 1953 Pierre Courant succeeded Eugène Claudius-Petit as Minister of Reconstruction and Urbanism, the construction of *grands ensembles* ranked high on his political agenda. Famously, he worked out the "Courant Plan" to increase output of housing, funneling additional state funds into construction and facilitating eminent domain. The Courant Plan included a series of legislative improvements that would facilitate the construction of *grands ensembles*. The total number of dwelling units produced in France during the two decades following is estimated to be 6 million.[24]

In the early 1950s, the government started to support industrialized construction methods. Construction was rationalized through cranes operated on rails that were set up in front of the buildings. Prefabrication played a particularly important role in the early phase of large-scale housing construction between 1954 and 1963, when factory-produced parts were used on construction sites across the country. This technology was later modified to allow for on-site production of prefab parts.[25]

Construction on the periphery of Paris was imposed in a quasi-colonial way. The Paris HLM (public housing) office provided organization and funding, while the municipalities in the outskirts were forced to provide the land. A 1958 decree, which remained valid until 1967, enabled the formation of *zones d'urbanisation prioritaire* (ZUP, zones of prioritized urbanization), designated areas for the construction of *grands ensembles*. The sites lay almost exclusively on the fringes of big cities. The great majority was concentrated in the Paris region, eventually laying a concrete cordon of about 800,000 apartment units around the French capital.[26] Most were erected in the northern and northeastern *départements* Seine–Saint-Denis and Val-de-Marne, but some were also built in the south and west. Although the Paris *banlieue* continued to comprise other building types, including many upscale single-familiy homes on the western fringe, they came to be more and more identified with the *grands ensembles*. The new built environment came to embody the double meaning that Le Corbusier had already foreseen in his Athens Charter, in which he stated that "the banlieue is the symbol of both waste and experiment."[27] Separated from Paris's famous nineteenth-century fabric, the peripheral tower settlements were not only architecturally distinct but also gave rise to a local identity born of exclusion. Rather than Parisians, proud inhabitants of the French capital, the tower dwellers were "only" *banlieusards*, citizens of the urban periphery.

Sarcelles, situated 6 miles north of the Paris border in the Oise Valley, was one of the first *grands ensembles*. Between 1955 and 1970 apartments for approximately 40,000 people were built, mostly in tower blocks (design: Roger Boileau and Jacques-Henri Labourdette). They eventually housed 65 percent of the municipality's inhabitants. The development was composed of enormous slabs assembled in an orthogonal system of interior roads, and crammed between a railroad line and a high-speed road. The plan aimed at an entire self-sufficient city that included commercial centers, offices, a youth club, a movie theater, a dance venue, and a police station. Critics at the time celebrated the vast parking spaces and stressed the sophisticated traffic pattern that separated roads from pedestrian walkways.[28]

Another famous *grand ensemble* was the Cité des Quatre-Mille (City of Four Thousand) in La Courneuve in the northern suburbs (1956–67, design: Clément Tambuté and Henri Delacroix). It was literally an outsourced community, founded and administered by the city of Paris and only in 1984 handed over to the HLM office in the municipality of La Courneuve, on whose grounds it was built. The development derived its uninspired name from the original 4,000 highly standardized apartments. They were situated in repetitive buildings—15 stories high and up to 500 feet in length—which were distributed on the site, as a critic put it, "like regiments on the plans of a military school."[29] Around 1970, the development had 17,000 inhabitants. Famously and very critically portrayed in Jean-Luc Godard's 1967 film *Deux ou trois choses que je sais d'elle* (Two or Three Things I Know

3.2
Sarcelles, apartment
building at Avenue Frédéric
Joliot-Curie, designed by
Roger Boileau and
Jacques-Henri Labourdette,
1955–70 (Di Wang, 2008)

about Her), the Cité des Quatre-Mille soon turned into an epitome of bleakness as embodied by visible dilapidation, constantly broken elevators, and smelly corridors. In 1986, the 300-apartment "Debussy slab," which had been one of the worst, was demolished.

In Clichy-sous-Bois, situated northeast of Paris, plans were prepared in the late 1950s to house approximately 10,000 people in a new development (plan: Jean Sebag, building design: Bernard Zehrfuss and others), thus tripling the number of Clichy residents. The plan followed the principles of "space, light, and nature," and the first apartments were built in 1965. Slabs of 5 or 11 stories were assembled around the intersections of three major traffic routes. Clichy-sous-Bois made it to the headlines all over the world for triggering the October 2005 riots, when two teenagers died from electric shocks while hiding from the police in a transformer building. Currently, plans are being discussed to demolish a substantial number of the buildings.

French politicians and critics hailed the construction of the first tower block developments with great drama. They presented cities in general as a national achievement

3.3
Sarcelles, apartment building at Rue Peter Rubens designed by Roger Boileau and Jacques-Henri Labourdette, 1955–70 (Di Wang, 2008)

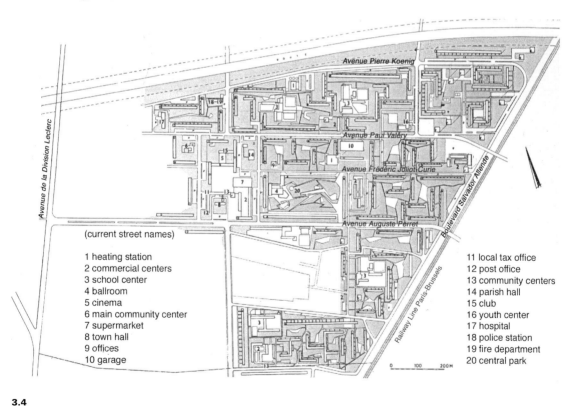

(current street names)

1 heating station
2 commercial centers
3 school center
4 ballroom
5 cinema
6 main community center
7 supermarket
8 town hall
9 offices
10 garage

11 local tax office
12 post office
13 community centers
14 parish hall
15 club
16 youth center
17 hospital
18 police station
19 fire department
20 central park

3.4
Plan of the Sarcelles development, designed by Roger Boileau and Jacques-Henri Labourdette, 1955–70 (Courtesy *L'architecture d'aujourd'hui*, published in v. 29 n. 80, October–November 1958, 15)

that evidenced the high level of French civilization, and their extension through towers and slabs as an endeavor of epochal significance. Such statements could be found across party lines. The socialist Minister of Construction Eugène Claudius-Petit, for example, pulled out all the stops and called for "Architecture" (with a capital A) to "protect our civilization," which, in his words, was to be defended "not only occasionally on the battlefield but also on an everyday level in our cities."[30] His liberal successor Pierre Sudreau reminded architects that French cities "bear witness to the genius and vitality of generations,"[31] and Sudreau's technical advisor Gérard Dupont greeted the new cities as a "factor in human progress."[32] The debate was loaded with bold predictions. The architectural critic Alexandre Persitz, who was the chief editor of the journal *L'Architecture d'aujourd'hui*, announced the end of the traditional city declaring that "the street as such has expired,"[33] and the daily newspaper *La Croix* celebrated the "birth of a civilization."[34] The pathos of the enterprise was underlined by the frequent calls for high architecture as opposed to mere construction.[35]

The calls were taken seriously at least with regard to the choice of the designers. They included France's most famous architects at the time. Many of them had won the prestigious Rome Prize that the Ecole de Beaux-Arts awarded every year to only one or two architects in the entire country, including Eugène Beaudouin (1928), Charles-Gustave Stoskopf (1939), Robert Camelot (1933), Bernard Zehrfuss (1939), and Xavier Arsène-Henry (1950). Some, like Beaudouin or Zehrfuss, were later appointed life-time members of the Académie de Beaux-Arts, the most prominent distinction to be attained by a French designer. As a consequence of the caché connected with the tower blocks, it was considered a privilege to be assigned an apartment in one of the *grands ensembles*. Tenants were not the poorest of the poor, but rather comparably privileged members of the working class. In line with the enthusiasm of the general public, the response of the architectural world was generally positive. In 1953, France's largest architectural journal *L'Architecture d'aujourd'hui* published an unreservedly congratulatory article on the *grands ensembles*, celebrating the large-scale construction of mass housing in the Paris

3.5
Slab blocks at the Chemin des Postes, Clichy-sous-Bois, designed by Bernard Zehrfuss, plan by Jean Sebag, 1950s (Wikipedia Commons)

3.6
Cité des Quatre-Mille in La Courneuve north of Paris, designed by Clément Tambuté and Henri Delacroix, 1956–67 (Di Wang, 2008)

region, Le Havre, St-Etienne, and other cities that had started in that year.[36] The towers and slabs were not only seen as a bold effort to tackle the housing shortage, but also commonly trusted to offer both an environment that fostered community values and a dignified life.

Sarcellitis: the mass housing disease

Only a few years later, the picture was very different. In 1962, a neologism was coined and immediately caught on: "sarcellitis," the mass housing disease. Derived from the Sarcelles development, the new pathology stood for all psychological evils mass housing inhabitants were supposedly suffering from, from claustrophobia to dying social relations.[37] Sarcelles was now seen as an architectural deadly sin. The liberal newspaper *L'Aurore* called the development a "factory of hooligans and school of violence" and "one of the worst plagues our society ever invented,"[38] and the writer Christiane Rochefort shocked the nation with her best-selling *Les petits enfants du siècle* (translated as *Children of Heaven*), the story of a fictional working-class girl who after moving to Sarcelles leads a state-subsidized lifestyle of monotony, ennui, and an absence of norms.[39] The standardized apartments in Sarcelles and elsewhere were now tarnished as "depressing landscapes of cement boxes against the background of empty lots,"[40] and increasingly referred to as *clapiers* (rabbit stables), *casernes civiles* (civil barracks), *cages à poules* (chicken cages), *cités termitières* (termite cities), and *cités ghettos* (ghetto towns).[41] Another peculiar metaphor also became widespread at the time: Sarcelles was declared an *univers concentrationnaire*—a universe resembling a concentration camp.[42] Two decades earlier, the loaded term had been reserved for a completely different urban environment: the overcrowded early-twentieth-century tenements in the inner ring of Paris's suburbs.[43] Other critics denounced the "slumification" of precisely those *ensembles* that had been built only a few years earlier to house former shantytown dwellers.[44] The deteriorating image of Sarcelles and other tower block developments evidenced the widespread disenchantment with the modernist promise. A new urban civilization, as became clear in the early 1960s, was not going to happen. The hope for a utopia of light, air, and green had to be buried along with that of comprehensive social integration—be it in a classless society, as desired by the socialists, or in a proud French nation, as fancied by the center and right.

How did the sudden swing in opinion come about? The first critical views were published in the spring of 1959, at the peak of the Algerian War, when several well-known psychiatrists and sociologists pointed at "a new social ill, infinitely more frightening than that of the slums."[45] Their statements triggered a big debate in the press and instigated a wave of architects' self-criticism.[46] State construction officials now censured the very projects that their offices had authorized only a few years earlier. The tone was harsh. Minister of Construction Pierre Sudreau, for example, spoke of developments that "disfigure unchangeably the site on which they were built" and warned that such "errors" weigh even graver since they "will persist for several generations."[47] He asked whether the authorities had not merely "changed the scale of the error by replacing 'the small shack' with 'the big barracks'."[48] Other critics lamented technical malfunctioning, traffic congestion,

and soil erosion. They decried missing recreational facilities, and a general lack of social cohesion—precisely what had been the very goal of the towers in the first place. All in all, less than five years after the full-bodied announcement of a new civilization, observers spoke instead of ready-built slums.

3.7
Cité des Quatre-Mille in La Courneuve north of Paris, designed by Clément Tambuté and Henri Delacroix, 1956–67 (Di Wang, 2008)

Even some of the designers joined the public slashing. Eugène Beaudouin, who was the architect of several *grands ensembles* and the president of the influential Societé française des urbanistes, pointed out in 1959 that simply providing people with sun, air, and green was not enough to make them happy. He censured the endless repetition in many projects leading to "mental fatigue."[49] In 1960, *L'Architecture d'aujourd'hui* also turned to burning its idols. The magazine, which had so far served as a mouthpiece of the architectural establishment and steadfast supporter of the tower blocks, published an entire issue denigrating the *grands ensembles* as "dispersion" and "mediocrity."[50] Two years later, the same journal published a rogue gallery called "the museum of errors," assembling what it considered buildings that "disfigure irreparably the site on which they are built."[51] The "architectural disasters" included, ironically, the Cité Joliot-Curie in Argenteuil by Marcel Lods, Jean de Mailly, and Bernard Zehrfuss, who were all on the journal's editorial committee.

The early criticism focused, on the one hand, on formal deficiencies such as monotonous, over-dimensioned blocks and small and noisy apartments, and on the other on faulty planning resulting in insufficient communal facilities, geographical isolation, and lack of public transportation. Alexandre Persitz of *L'Architecture d'aujourd'hui* interpreted the bad social relations between tower block neighbors as a result of too many apartments per landing and the lack of recreational activities. Ironically, he also censured the absence of contact with nature—precisely this had been a key promise of modernist tower-in-the-park architecture.[52] Sociologist Paul-Henry Chombart de Lauwe further specified a desire to appropriate, arrange, and furnish one's space and a desire to establish social relations with the exterior—the inflexibility of the planned environment and its segregation from the rest of the city were already seen as fundamental ills.[53] Along the same lines, Henri Lefebvre, at the time one of France's most eminent sociologists and theorist of urban space as being socially produced, joined the discussion, decrying the lack of a "ludic element" in *grands ensembles* and calling for ample resistance: "The fight against the ennui just started."[54]

In France, as in neighboring Germany, the public opinion on the tower block developments switched from positive to negative in a surprisingly short period of time. There was nevertheless a particular local twist. While in Germany the swing took place between 1968 and 1970 along with the student protests, the public outcry in France was heard almost a decade earlier—that is, between 1958 and 1962. The early timing of the criticism shaped the thrust of the argument. French critics to a much smaller extent targeted top-down planning and the synchronized inhabitant, and focused rather on formal, aesthetic, and technical shortcomings. The medical terminology—critics explicitly spoke of "neurosis of the banlieue"[55]—figured prominently in France, where the tower blocks were seen as pathogenic. A similar rhetoric of "cancer" and a "sick urban body" was used in Germany to promote tower block architecture as an alternative to nineteenth-century tenements.[56] This interpretation somewhat echoed the origins of urban planning in the mid-nineteenth century, when the living conditions of the working class were construed first and foremost as a problem of hygiene. It also showed to what extent the French commentators were indebted to the very approach of radical renewal whose built results they criticized.

Improving the *grands ensembles*?

The following years were characterized by a contradictory approach. The tower blocks were torn to shreds by the critics, and at the same time built at an unprecedented scale. State intervention in matters of housing was as strong as never before, and centralized planning remained unquestioned. Public institutions put together numerous commissions on the *grands ensembles* to pin down the problem. Unlike German critics a decade later, many French reviewers around 1960 firmly believed that the shortcomings of the first tower-and-slab ensembles in principle could be fixed and "better" developments could be designed.[57] Their confidence was supported by the fact that not all French *grands ensembles* were viewed as badly as those in Sarcelles or La Courneuve—among the better reputed were, for example, Le Mirail in Toulouse by Georges Candilis, Alex Josic, and Shadrach Woods, and the HLM housing on the riverfront in the city of Tours.[58] Politicians, journalists, and designers thus expressed their optimism with regard to correcting the mistakes of the early years and censured the results rather than the methods.[59] Their trust in scientific methodology was not shattered, and neither was their confidence in the benefit of large-scale construction, as long as "extraordinary precautions" were taken.[60] For a long time, the principles of urban design thus remained largely unchanged.

Next to technological shortcomings, aesthetics was a key point of criticism. In 1963, the government started to systematically photograph and file thousands of apparently unspectacular buildings, streets, and squares.[61] The underlying idea was to arrive at comprehensive rules for a good life in French cities. A similar attitude spawned the *grille Dupont* (Dupont Table) in 1958, which was named for the Construction Minister's technical advisor and promoter of "human progress," Gérard Dupont. The Dupont Table was designed to perfect the meticulously calculated tower blocks through even more meticulous calculations. One reads about "Monsieur Urbain," the imaginary standard city dweller, who together with his family needs exactly 16 square meters of ground floor space for dwelling, 5 square meters for shopping, 3 square meters for social and cultural facilities, 2 square meters for administration and worship, 28 square meters for traffic and parking, 46 square meters for sports and recreation, and 72 square meters of green spaces.[62]

"Monsieur Urbain" and the Dupont Table were particularly preposterous attempts to improve a technocratic living environment through technocratic means. Such proposals generally claimed to address "the human dimension." For example Xavier Arsène-Henry, the Rome-Prize-winning architect of the *grand ensemble* in Monterau-Fault-Yonne, in 1960 conjured the ideal of a "human urbanism" and pointed out that this could be found in the principles of the Athens Charter.[63] For Minister of Construction Pierre Sudreau, the challenge was to "subordinate technology to the human"[64] and build "at a human scale"[65]— he eventually started a policy of adjustment that aimed at small modifications in mass housing design. And even number-crunching housing official Gérard Dupont pointed out that the fulfillment of technical needs such as apartments, schools, and parks did not suffice and that the most important task, rather, was to "create a human community."[66] "Human scale" was the catchword at the time, repeated throughout the media.[67] Due to a blurry definition, the term comprised any real and imagined shortcoming of the traditional city. It could refer to a six-lane road that permitted the traffic to flow and thus allowed for individual mobility or to a 20-story tower amidst asphalt and shrub that catered to the human need for sun and air.

Most noteworthy were the plans to "improve" the over-dimensioned tower block developments with even bigger and more daring dwelling compounds. Critics repeatedly complained that the *grands ensembles* did not yet fully satisfy the principles of modern city planning. In a 1962 reportage, the founder of *L'Architecture d'aujourd'hui*, André Bloc, who at the time was in his late sixties, repeated an argument that modernist architects had waged against the pre-modernist city two decades earlier, censuring the "urbanistic disorder" of the high-rise developments around Paris.[68] Bloc based his analysis on one of the modern movement's most cherished methods: the aerial photograph. His calls for audacity and big gestures also eerily recalled the battle cries that Le Corbusier and his disciples in the 1920s had directed against the pre-modernist city. In a similar move, a group of well-established architects suggested building not new satellite cities but rather a "Parallel Paris"—a new town for 400,000 inhabitants, 25 miles west of the French capital.[69] The new city was to consist of dense, industrially built high-rises financed by the state. The group, ironically, had designed many of the *grands ensembles* that by now had come under criticism. Marcel Lods, one of the architects of the prewar development Cité de la Muette, also acknowledged the "sometimes unfavorable reaction" of the public, which he saw as stemming from noise and unresolved parking issues. According to his new ideas, both could be efficiently resolved by covering the entire surroundings of the high-rises with a second deck for pedestrians. Cars, then, would circulate and park on covered tunnels at ground level, while people would walk on the artificial floor above.[70]

Despite the criticism, tower-and-slab developments were built at an increasing rate over the course of the 1960s, despite the fact that municipalities were increasingly resistant to new projects on their territories. Around 1965, the impressive number of 400,000 apartments per year was achieved.[71] Only the means of finance changed. In the early phase of large-scale high-rise developments, direct or indirect state involvement had accounted for the bulk of investment. From 1963 on, private housing investment—of course supported by state legislation and subsidies—exceeded public funds, which were now mostly concentrated on housing for the neediest. The "zones of prioritized urbanization" legislation was modified in 1967, now allowing for some flexibility.[72] The goal was to involve multiple actors in the planning process, including private and community organizations.

The era of French *grands ensembles* officially ended in 1973, the very year in which the French economy started to suffer from the oil crisis, and the same year in which the federal authorities in the US also withdrew their support for large-scale public housing. The decisive document was the "Guichard circular," which was authored by the Minister of Spatial Planning, Olivier Guichard, and which removed subsidies for large developments. It also limited the number of units to be built in any new development to 2,000 in cities with more than 50,000 inhabitants and to 1,000 units in cities with less. Guichard, who quoted Henri Lefebvre's "Right to the City" in the Chamber of Deputies in support of his new approach, openly directed his circular against "social segregation by residence" and thus initiated a policy that supported small-scale construction of individual buildings.[73] After decades of broadly shared enthusiasm and years of rising criticism, the economic crisis eventually dealt the deathblow to the concept of state-sponsored large-scale housing. By that time, the structure of French cities had been irrevocably changed.

Cité de la Muette: mass housing and mass murder

The tension between emancipation and oppression had its precedent in what is considered the first *grand ensemble* in France. The social housing project Cité de la Muette in the eastern Paris suburb of Drancy (1931–34; demolished 1976, design: Marcel Lods and Eugène Beaudouin) came to be connected with both the modern dream of mass housing and the modern nightmare of mass killing. Between 1942 and 1944, the German invaders converted some of the empty buildings into an internment camp. Up to 76,000 mostly Jewish prisoners were held captive here before being deported to the death camps.[74] The uncanny connection between industrialized housing and industrialized murder also recalls the parallels between modernity and the Holocaust that were famously analyzed by the Polish-born British sociologist Zygmunt Bauman.[75]

The use of the Cité de la Muette as a Nazi prison camp was accidental, but nevertheless related to its modernist design, as the scale and shape of the huge U-shaped *grande cour* (big courtyard) building was the prerequisite for the incarceration of large

3.8
Cité de la Muette in Drancy,
east of Paris, designed by
Marcel Lods and Eugène
Beaudouin, 1931–34,
demolished 1976 (postcard
edited by Godneff)

amounts of people. This building lay on the west end of the complex. Next to the low-rise *grande cour*, there were two other building types that formed five similar compounds called *peignes* (combs): 16-story point-access towers and 5-story slabs that were connected with each other in U-shapes, forming long, narrow courtyards like the teeth of a comb, forming five similar compounds. In the towers, studio and one-bedroom apartments were built, while the low-rise slabs contained one- and two-bedroom apartments. The *grande cour* had apartments, stores, and community spaces. Schools and sports fields complemented the ensemble.[76] The entire development comprised 1,200 units. Commissioned by the HBM Office, it was designed to offer a garden city environment for low-income tenants.

The Cité de la Muette anticipated the key principles of the *grands ensembles*. The project was supposedly based on rational principles and carried out through strict top-down planning. Neither the municipality of Drancy on which the towers where built nor the future inhabitants were allowed to participate.[77] The architecture made consequent use of prefabrication. Factory-produced reinforced concrete parts were erected on a steel frame. The steel frames could be assembled without cranes, and were covered with precast concrete panels that included different shapes for doors, walls, and balconies.[78]

The compound soon became a showcase project.[79] Most contemporary reviewers were overwhelmingly positive, lauding the high degree of technological efficiency and innovation, the use of factory-produced parts and rationalized work flows, the inclusion of electric and gas hot water heaters, and details "dear to the French housekeeper" such as balconies, laundry-drying rooms, ventilated food safes, and louver blinds.[80] A particularly positive aspect, according to observers in the 1930s, was the scientifically calculated plans— the shadows of the buildings were designed never to fall upon each other.[81] A reviewer in 1936 concluded that "one senses that life does not have the pettiness that is all too often evoked by the poor small barracks ... in the banlieues" and thus elevated the Cité de la Muette to the pantheon of true art: "This is not merely construction, this is Architecture."[82]

After the Second World War, the buildings stood empty for a long time, then were bought by the French army in 1973 and used as barracks. In sharp contrast to the 1930s, Cité de la Muette was now remembered as a site of murder and oppression rather than one of architectural vision. In 1976, the towers and most slabs were demolished. Only the U-shaped courtyard block was spared. The former prison now stands like an eerie presage for similar blocks of the post-war era, which their marginalized and impoverished inhabitants often perceive as instruments for life-long imprisonment.

Mass housing and the geography of exclusion

By 1970s, the *grand ensemble* had acquired textbook status as an undesirable living environment. At the same time, the country went into a massive economic crisis, and it was felt hardest in the tower block developments. In the 1960s, the majority of the tenants had been employed, but with the downturn the conditions rapidly deteriorated. Those who could afford it left for other forms of housing, and the prefab developments turned into the residence of the poor and unemployed. While up to the 1960s, the overwhelming majority of residents were ethnic French, many residents now belonged to the groups who traditionally had been in the weakest position on the housing market: first- and second-generation immigrants, many of them from North or West Africa.

From the 1970s onward, immigration became a major issue in French politics. Along with the economic downturn, right-wing parties with a racist and xenophobic agenda gained voters. The extremist Front National, in particular, grew from the early 1980s; during the 2002 presidential campaign its leader Jean-Marie Le Pen received more than 5.5 million votes. At the same time, the first- and second-generation immigrants formed organizations and their cause received increasing attention in the media. In October 1983, the *Marche des beurs* (March of North African French) from Marseille to Paris started—French of Tunisian, Algerian, or Moroccan descent marched against racism and exclusion. Upon their arrival in Paris two months later they were greeted by 100,000 demonstrators.[83] In the following years, films such as *Le thé au harem d'Archimède* by Mehdi Charef (Tea in the Harem, 1985), *L'Oeuil au beurre noir* by Serge Meynard (The Bedouins of Paris, 1987), and *La haine* by Matthieu Kassovitz (Hatred, 1995) depicted a life characterized by racism, violence, and poverty. The original footage from a 1995 riot shown in *La haine*, presented in black and white, turned into the archetypal shock pictures of a dehumanized world within French society. At the same time, the prejudices based on class and ethnic origin came to be extended to the place of residence. Scientific research suggests that the chances of a *banlieue* dweller getting invited to a job interview are significantly lower than those of a Paris resident, even if his first name is Olivier or Gérard rather than Mohammed or Saïd.[84] It is thus safe to say that an apartment in a French mass housing development is a serious obstacle to social advancement.

The first riots broke out rather late—almost 15 years after similar incidents in American housing projects that were built at the same time. In 1979, a *grand ensemble* in Vaulx-en-Velin, a Lyon working-class suburb, became the site of France's outburst of urban violence. The pictures of burning cars and enraged teenagers would show up time and again over the following decades, turning into an icon for the nation's most pressing ills. Vaulx-en-Velin was burning again in 1990, and subsequently Les Minguettes near Lyon (1983), Le Val Fourré near Paris (1991), Dammarie-lès-Lys near Paris (1993), and so on.

From the 1980s, politicians repeatedly declared their willingness to improve life in the *grands ensembles*. The overall conditions, however, did not change fundamentally. Infrastructure and education remained substandard, crime and juvenile delinquency rates high. Citizens with an immigrant background still enjoyed far fewer opportunities than their fellows with French ancestry. In light of this gloomy situation, the French Minister for Employment and Social Cohesion Jean-Louis Borloo followed the way that his American colleagues had already embarked on. In 2004, he launched a program to demolish an initial 240 of France's most troubled neighborhoods.[85] A spectacular demolition had already occurred in 2000: one of the largest residential buildings in Europe was taken down, the 270-meter-long, 20-story-high Muraille de Chine ("Great Wall of China") in the industrial city of St. Etienne. The event was interpreted as a symbolic expiation comparable to the 1972 demolition of the Pruitt-Igoe Homes in St. Louis.[86]

Current policies toward the *grands ensembles* are ambiguous. While the term "urban renewal" in other countries was discredited for its association with bulldozed city centers, forced relocation, and technocratic top-down planning, the French had no qualms about calling their 2000 city improvement legislation *Loi solidarité et renouvellement urbains* (Law on solidarity and urban renewal). The law arose from the debates of the 1990s, but remained silent about some of the questions that had already been left unanswered forty years earlier. On the one hand, it proposed an increase of market forces, resident mobility, and mix of uses. On the other hand it promoted state-sponsored demolitions—this time addressing the high-rise blocks rather than the tenements and *pavillons*. Overall, the new law retained a fundamental shortcoming of the *grands ensembles* from when they were first conceived: their position outside the social dynamics of the rest of the city.

One aspect of the social segregation in the Paris region is administrative. Exclusion is inherent in the municipal boundaries that define the residents' identity. Paris is the only capital in Europe that has not extended its borders in more than one and a half centuries. At the turn of the twenty-first century, three quarters of the metropolitan region's 8 million inhabitants lived outside the city line that was established in 1860. They are therefore defined as *banlieusards*, natives of the outskirts, rather than Parisians and heirs of the symbolic capital. The focus of Paris's centrality, which for centuries has been fundamental in French spatial thinking, eclipses the visibility of the *banlieue* residents and their dwellings in the public discourse. And all too often, their categorization as not belonging to the French capital is paralleled by a characterization as non-French. The municipal boundaries thus eerily reflect the daily experience of many *banlieusards* who are not only excluded from equal opportunities but also from the mind-map of French self definition: "The problem," said a young Frenchman of Senegalese descent during the 2005 riots, "is that the French don't think I'm French."[87]

The particularity of this situation is best illustrated by the one big French city that displays a different structure. Marseille stuck out as being the only major urban agglomeration that did not experience violent protests in the fall of 2005.[88] This was even more surprising since Marseille has one of the country's largest proportions of citizens of North

African and Middle Eastern descent and a consistently high unemployment rate. The level of racism and marginalization is certainly not lower than in other parts of France, as the high scores of the right-wing party Front National in several elections show. Why, then, did the Marseillais of Arab descent not take to the streets in the same way as the second-generation immigrants in Paris, Lyon, or Toulouse? One explanation has to do with urban design. Unlike most other cities, Marseille has very few tower block developments. Gentrification is not as palpable as in Paris. The lower and middle classes still live in the city center, while the rich build their homes in the outskirts or even in neighboring cities such as Aix-en-Provence. This spatial configuration has helped the city to conserve a vibrant mixture in its central eighteenth- and nineteenth-century district. The status of outsiders and intruders from the periphery, from which the inhabitants of the Paris outskirts frequently suffer, does not apply for the Marseille, where the urban design supports a common local identity and to a certain extent transcends the boundaries of class and ethnicity. If not classified as French, the immigrants are at least accepted as Marseillais. While this does not prevent them from becoming the target of racism, at least in the fall of 2005 it seemed to have been key in conserving social peace.

However, the absence of modernist mass housing can hardly be deemed a key to peaceful cohabitation—at least not if mass housing *ensembles* are understood in purely architectural terms. The French example shows the double edge of paternalist care. For many decades, the impulse to create a homogenous civic community was particularly strong in France, and at the same time the exclusion of those who were left out was particularly rigid. The confinement of Portuguese and Algerian immigrants to peripheral *bidonvilles* in the 1950s and 1960s was only one sad chapter in this history of exclusionary urban design. Physical improvement based on segregation was already palpable in Haussmann's mid-nineteenth-century transformations, which created sanitary facilities and integrative public spaces while simultaneously confining the working classes to backyards and peripheral neighborhoods. The *grands ensembles* merely continued this ambiguous urbanistic aproach. While being successful in mitigating the housing shortage and improving the living conditions of the *bidonville* dwellers, including many immigrants, they did not change the social gap epitomized in the substandard dwellings that they came to replace. The *bidonvilles* dwindled concomitantly with the erection of the tower blocks, but the geography of exclusion remained. The *grands ensembles* were also situated "outside Paris," thus reinforcing an already existing exclusionary identity and continuing the marginalization of disfavored groups—not by virtue of their form but of their location.

The historical continuity of spatial exclusion in Paris notwithstanding, there is nevertheless a certain semantic flexibility in any urban form. This is evidenced in Paris's mid-nineteenth-century squares and boulevards, which were to become the stage for the most diverse events, and, simultaneously, subject to numerous reinterpretations. They were the backdrop for the 1871 Commune, the demonstrations of the interwar period, and the student protests of 1968. They came to be associated with democratic negotiation, social mixture, and civic debate as well as with repression and violent class struggle. Along these lines, there is hope that one day the *grands ensembles* too will be subject to reframing and reappropriation.

4 Slabs versus Tenements in East and West Berlin

Battles over buildings

The new housing development Märkisches Viertel in West Berlin was apparently a straightforward success. According to a journalist in 1966, the architects paid homage to the urban design tradition of Berlin's grand boulevard Unter den Linden and the city's most symbolic monument, the Brandenburg Gate. They created an "expressive composition" that embodies a "will to art" and a "sensible and not only mechanistic spatial order."[1] Another writer called it "a symbol of hope for designers in many European countries."[2] The triumph, however, was short-lived. Only a few years later, the very same buildings were scorned as a "depressing mass of monotonous slabs" and the "realization of a dismal science-fiction movie."[3] The paper *Die Welt*, which in 1966 had still praised "the colorful residence of the future"[4] and the "plasticity of the forms" that resonated the rhythm of the surrounding landscape[5] only two years later reviled the new homes as "factories for dwelling" bearing strong resemblance to "the Stalinallee in East Berlin . . . and to the products of urban renewal in the black neighborhoods of Manhattan."[6]

Hardly any city has experienced harsher debates over tower-and-slab developments than the birthplace of Walter Gropius. The Märkisches Viertel (1963–74, designers: Werner Düttmann, Hans Müller, Georg Heinrichs, and others) was a textbook example. It comprised more than 17,000 apartments in tower blocks with 10 to 14 stories, and in 2006 it had about 36,000 inhabitants. It was typical of what was considered the most advanced urban design of the time. *Großsiedlungen* (great settlements) were built on the peripheries of big cities in both East and West Germany from the 1960s. They were rooted in the Weimar Republic tradition of public utility housing, and at first widely applauded. In both German countries their reputation rapidly deteriorated in the late 1960s.

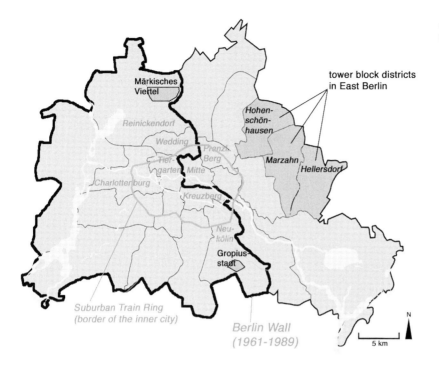

tower block districts
in East Berlin

Märkisches
Viertel

Hohen-
schön-
hausen

Reinickendorf

Wedding

Prenzl.
Berg

Marzahn

Tier-
garten Mitte

Hellersdorf

Charlottenburg

Kreuzberg

Neu-
kölln

Gropius-
stadt

Suburban Train Ring
(border of the inner city)

Berlin Wall
(1961-1989)

N

5 km

In the socialist East, one can detect a growing dissatisfaction with a policy that officially was not to be questioned; eventually this led to a modification and downsizing of the slab developments. In the West, prefab housing triggered a massive bout of mudslinging in the media, which continued for several years. The controversy over the Märkisches Viertel was the most salient example; it stood, however, for an architectural debate over form, function, and physical determinism that went far beyond academic and architectural circles and shook large parts of the population. What was at stake in Germany at the time was nothing less than the modernist promise of development and progress. This was not limited to the rebellious students of 1968. In the late 1960s, Germans of different generations and political colors formed a strange coalition to settle a score with the apostles of the new modernist city who were increasingly perceived as pretentious and oppressive. The *Großsiedlungen* came to be the symbolic battleground for a struggle in which radical college students sided with bourgeois traditionalists against an establishment of liberal developers and Social Democratic politicians.

Organic concrete blocks

Mass housing developments had been planned in East and West Germany with similar enthusiasm. They were seen as an efficient alternative to the loosely scattered low-rise settlements of the immediate post-war period, and, in the East, also to the costly neoclassical residences of the Stalin era. They were also interpreted as an expression of "organic urban

4.2
Märkisches Viertel, plan by
Werner Düttmann, Hans
Müller, Georg Heinrichs,
design by various architects,
1963–74 (Florian Urban, 2008)

design." This concept was formulated in works such as Hans Bernhard Reichow's influential manifesto *Organische Stadtbaukunst* (Organic Urban Design) of 1948.[7] Reichow was called to design one of West Germany's first large high-rise projects, the Sennestadt new town on the periphery of Bielefeld (1956–65, approximately 20,000 inhabitants), which was subsequently incorporated as a city of its own. The development was to constitute a functionally separated "urban landscape" based on individual motor traffic. In the Sennestadt and other developments, Reichow evoked a picture of a city that is derived from the aesthetics of the bird's eye view, with a plan ordered like a plant. Industrial areas were the roots of a tree, expressways the trunks, branches, and twigs, and residential neighborhoods the leaves and flowers. He saw the "organic" curved thoroughfares as a counterproposal to the angular geometry of nineteenth-century squares and boulevards.

In the 1960s, large-scale tower block developments were first completed in West Germany. Between 1957–62, Bremen developed the Neue Vahr (design: Ernst May, 25,000 inhabitants). In Cologne planning for the "new city" of Chorweiler began in 1957 and building began in the 1960s and 1970s (design: Gottfried Böhm and others, 20,000 inhabitants).[8] Hamburg started planning the Steilshoop development in 1960 (various architects, 19,000 inhabitants); Frankfurt the Nordweststadt (1963–68, design: Walter Schwagenscheidt and Tassilo Sittmann, 25,000 inhabitants) and Limesstadt (1962–73, design: Hans Bernhard Reichow, 10,000 inhabitants); Hamburg the Mümmelmannsberg development (1970–80, 19,000 inhabitants); and Munich the tower block city Neuperlach (1963–78, design: Bernt Lauter and others, 50,000 inhabitants). Although peripheral, German high-rise developments were relatively well connected to the city centers. Frankfurt-Nordweststadt and Köln-Chorweiler had their own subway lines planned simultaneously with the residential buildings, and even Bielefeld-Sennestadt, which had originally been designed for a high degree of car ownership, was part of the city's rapid

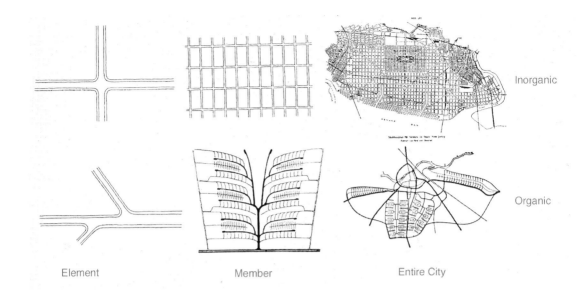

Inorganic

Organic

Element   Member   Entire City

transit system. In 1957 West Berlin had celebrated the *Interbau* building exhibition in the newly built Hansaviertel, where individually designed, loosely scattered tower blocks in a park landscape were presented as showcase examples for West Berlin's new "democratic architecture" and as counterproposals to the gigantic neoclassical Stalinallee in the East.

In the 1960s, two projects epitomized the city's search for the organic city. The first was the Gropiusstadt on the southern fringe of the city (1962–75, 50,000 inhabitants), which was originally planned by Walter Gropius and eventually executed according to a modified plan by Wils Ebert. The second was the Märkisches Viertel. Both were presented as showcase projects for Berlin's new housing policy. At the fourth *Berliner Bauwochen* building fair in 1966, approximately 40,000 visitors flocked to the information pavilion that the city-owned developing firm GESOBAU had erected near the construction site. The press was full of praise, commending a model city of the future that was to remove all shortcomings of the past.[9] In Berlin, as in other German big cities, most "old" neighborhoods were composed primarily of the despised *Mietskasernen* (rental barracks)—late-nineteenth-century tenements with five-stories, an ornamental stucco façade, and courtyards with barns and workshops in the inner parts of the block. Comprising more than two-thirds of Berlin's urban fabric despite wartime destruction,[10] they epitomized the downside of the city's early industrial past. Planners, designers, and large parts of the population considered them the city's slums, and an architectural cause of social and psychological misery.[11] In their eyes, stucco ornaments were symbols of social misery and political oppression, which embodied the built-in inequality of the tenements: contrary to the "egalitarian" modernist blocks, they were seen as classist architecture that distinguished between spacious apartments in the front for the wealthy and narrow one-room apartments in the backyards for the workers. The rejection of the tenements also implicitly announced liberation from the shadows of the past, which included both the German Empire under which the tenements were built and the Third Reich, whose rise and fall they had witnessed.[12] Hence in the late 1950s and 1960s,

4.3
Comparison between "anorganic" and "organic" city planning, adapted from Hans Bernhard Reichow, *Organische Stadtbaukunst* (Organic Urban Design) (Braunschweig: Westermann, 1948), 122

4.4
Neue Vahr development in Bremen, designed by Ernst May, 1957–62. In the upper left corner is the high-rise by Alvar Aalto (Wikipedia Commons)

4.5
Gropiusstadt, planned by Walter Gropius and Wils Ebert, buildings by various architects, 1962–75 (Wikipedia Commons)

both East and West Berlin governments propagated ample demolition of this building type—and the relocation of the inhabitants into the newly built high-rise developments on the periphery became part of the program.

Fall from public grace

In the case of the Märkisches Viertel, the fifth *Bauwochen* (Building Fair) in 1968 marked a sudden swing in public opinion. The official program of the fair was complemented by the *Anti-Bauwochen* (Anti-Building Fair), an exhibition where young architects were supposed to present their visions of a better city. The Berlin government subsidized the show with the considerable amount of 18,000 German marks (equaling approximately 15 years of rent payments for a two-bedroom apartment at the time)—and in return received merciless criticism of its own construction policy.[13] Instead of showing design proposals, the young architects aired their discontent with the state-sponsored slab buildings. The Märkisches Viertel was criticized as a textbook example of modernist hubris that entailed both ugly architecture and bad planning. The lack of daycare, transportation, and shopping opportunities—many of them were planned but not yet finished—was denounced as a fundamental defect of tower-and-slab developments. The Märkisches Viertel was also criticized on an aesthetic basis: the buildings were too big, as were the "dead" spaces between them, and the standardized forms were too monotonous.

The students' criticism was eagerly published in Germany's most eminent news magazine, *Der Spiegel*, which censured the Märkisches Viertel as "the bleakest product of concrete architecture." The diagnosis: "This is a gray hell!"[14] The periodical followed up with a cover story five months later, quoting frustrated inhabitants of large prefab settlements all over Germany: "I feel like I am in a prison camp," "I will die in this monotony," and "Every night when I come home I curse the day we moved into these barracks." The projects were indicted as "monotonous orthogonal high-rise towers," "inhospitable square mountains," "shabby dwelling cubes," and "bleak groups of barracks."[15] The report triggered a sudden change in media coverage. Suddenly, apocalyptic descriptions of the Märkisches Viertel abounded. Newspapers called the area a textbook example of "rigid uniformity and sterile monotony," "perhaps the most depressing outcome of both freelance and bureaucratic building technology . . . where housewives, apparently for no reason, become alcoholics," and "concrete blocks" where "four-year-olds are already condemned to spend their future lives as unskilled laborers."[16]

The criticism targeted different aspects. The works were often shabby, the apartments relatively small. The endless repetition of the same forms was perceived as monotonous, the scale as inflicting insecurity upon the inhabitants.[17] The vast green spaces rarely served as the meeting places that the architects had envisioned; indeed they were dangerous to cross at night. The dissolution of old neighborhood structures and the anonymity in the huge towers led to mistrust and neglect of public spaces. Another problem was the negative selection of inhabitants. Most were relatively poor—more than 20 percent were on social welfare—and the proportion of Märkisches Viertel youth involved in criminal activities was about 30 percent above the average in the adjacent areas.[18] Compared to Chicago housing projects of the same period, where close to 100 percent of the inhabitants were on social welfare, the West Berlin slabs of the 1970s were still relatively wealthy and well integrated.[19] But the gap between rich and poor in German cities was wider than a decade earlier, and the change was perceived as substantial.

The "murdered city"

For the many left-leaning architects of the Märkisches Viertel, who conceived of their work as the best possible solution to the shortage of working-class housing, the assault struck like a bolt out of the blue. The ground for this different perception, however, had been plowed in the decade before. One of the most vigorous attacks was launched by journalist Wolf Jobst Siedler (born 1926). The German Jane Jacobs published his pamphlet *Die gemordete Stadt* (The Murdered City) in 1964. Together with his co-author, the photographer Elisabeth Niggemeyer (born 1930), Siedler indicted modernist designers for having "murdered the old city."[20] The book became a best seller, convincing first and foremost because of its visual appeal. It was an effective retaliation in the war of images that modernist designers had long dominated without ever being able to decide it in their favor. Niggemeyer's evocative images of children playing in quaint backyards were persuasive counterproposals to her bleak depictions of the no-access signs and forbidding pathways of the tower blocks. The book spectacularly positioned stucco ornaments against concrete walls and chatting corner-store patrons against deserted parking lots. Referring to the negative connotations of the post-1870 period when the tenements were built, Siedler accused his contemporaries of launching a *"zweite Gründerzeit"* (second founding period) a hundred years later, which this time had not resulted in overcrowded working-class homes but—worse—in the demolition of the liveable city.

Contemporaneous with Siedler and Niggemeyer, psychologist Alexander Mitscherlich indicted modernist architects for producing "inhospitable" environments.[21] Mitscherlich abstained from illustrations, but his text was equally suggestive.

> "Cubic meters are being piled upon one another. The whole thing looks like a signalman's lodge that through selective breeding has grown to a monstrous size. In the late bourgeois era, which cared about slums, one would have spoken of a petrified nightmare; it is surreal that this has become reality sixty or seventy years later, in a society that calls itself progressive."[22]

Siedler/Niggemeyer's and Mitscherlich's presentation anticipated many elements that a few years later would enter the standard negative perception of the Märkisches Viertel in the media. The formal attributes of the new developments, such as large open spaces and greater functional separation, were interpreted as driving changes in Berlin's economic and social structure, such as the disappearance of mom-and-pop stores, the diminishing of close contact with neighbors, and the decreasing significance of the extended family. Their

critique also revealed what at the time was rarely debated but becomes evident in the planning documents of the time.[23] The long-term goal of construction policy was to rid the city of "obsolete" buildings and replace large amounts of the existing urban fabric.

Blurred party lines

Confronting the modernist mass housing developments, the critical media coverage of the late 1960s, ironically, reproduced the undercurrent of physical determinism inherent in the texts of modernism's most fervent defenders. Only the values were reversed. Once seen as the breeding ground for a just society, towers and slabs were now construed as generators of crime and deviancy. Now the Märkisches Viertel was called a "slum"—a term that before was restricted to old tenement neighborhoods. It was criticized as a "modernist backyard"— echoing the image of the gloomy backyard as the most inhuman trait of the old tenements. And it was reviled as *Zille-Milieu*—a reference to early-twentieth-century artist Heinrich Zille, who had portrayed the poverty of Berlin's tenement dwellers.[24] Modern developments were also seen as the result of "greedy speculators"[25]—freewheeling real estate speculation in the nineteenth century had been the standard explanation for the particularly

4.6
The "inhuman" modernist Hansaviertel (left, built 1957), set against the "charming" late-nineteenth-century neighborhoods (right) in Wolf Jobst Siedler's and Elisabeth Niggemeyer's 1964 bestseller *Die gemordete Stadt* (The Murdered City). The signs on the left say "private road, no trespassing" and "private playground," while the one on the right says "Wild Boar Square" (courtesy Wolf Jobst Siedler)

unhealthy structure of Berlin's old neighborhoods. The diagnosis of the modernization was thus blunt: the slums were merely "displaced"[26] and "removed from the blighted areas of our cities to inhuman modernist housing ghettos and satellite cities."[27] Journalists stressed their disappointment with the modernist architects' promises to engender a more human society. Or, as a daily paper put it: "Even the most credulous should have realized by now that this [concrete slab] construction method cannot possibly engender lively and functional housing and urban design."[28]

The rhetoric, however, remained the same. Like in the decades before, architecture was blamed for social conditions. The persistence of late-nineteenth-century images to describe the conditions of the 1960s was particularly evident in the diatribes against "speculators," which appear rather awkward in a city where state control over matters of construction was stronger than at any time before in modern history, and where profiteers tended to gain from state commissions rather than market speculation.

In the search for a scapegoat on which to blame Berlin's planning disaster, party lines soon blurred. Both Siedler's and Mitscherlich's books showed aspects of a bourgeois opposition. Mitscherlich mourned the loss of bourgeois values such as "urbane dignity" and "civic obligation,"[29] and Siedler defended the charming insignia of the Prussian aristocracy on Berlin's ornamented nineteenth-century façades.[30] At the same time, both claimed to speak for the underprivileged classes. Mitscherlich frequently referring to poor tenants in the towers, and Siedler's wholesome old town dwellers are almost exclusively factory workers, inn keepers, and allotment gardeners—decidedly not the upper classes of post-war Germany.

To understand this blurred partisanship within Germany's anti-high-rise movement, one has to bear in mind that the state-subsidized construction of large-scale housing developments had been a project of West Germany's Social Democratic Party (SPD) and its allies in unions and labor organizations. At the same time their policy received considerable support from socially conscious conservative circles. The case of the Märkisches Viertel was typical. It was built and operated by a state-owned corporation, headed by Berlin's social democratic Minister of Construction Rolf Schwedler. West Berlin, arguably the least capitalist city in the Western world with regard to the absence of big corporate players, a majority of left-wing voters, and a tenant-friendly legislation, thus became dominated by a policy that its critics called "social authoritarian."[31] In no other city in the Western bloc was the leftist dream of a state-supported solution of the housing question carried out with greater consequence, and nowhere was its failure so obvious.

The most fervent criticism came not from the conservatives, but rather from the far left. In West Berlin, like in the entire Federal Republic of Germany, this was the growing student movement, known as *Außerparlamentarische Opposition* (APO, opposition outside parliament). In an article sympathizing with the APO's position, the magazine *Der Spiegel* attacked the foundations of the capitalist economic system. "If any modern planning and renewal was to succeed," the authors noted, "private landownership has to be reformed."[32] The possibility of gaining profit from land speculation, in their eyes, was among the main reasons for the poor quality of the large-scale developments.[33] Similarly, journalist Ulrike Meinhof saw the main frontline in the Märkisches Viertel as being not between proletarians and the middle class, but rather between the working-class inhabitants and the state-operated landowner and developer GESOBAU.[34] Meinhof at the time was a social activist in the Märkisches Viertel and soon afterward famously became a protagonist of the terrorist group Red Army Faction. She and her leftist colleagues did not question state planning; rather, they attacked moderate state officials for their insufficient pursuit of the tenants' real needs. They blamed cooperative developers for reaping large profit margins, and the Federal government, which since 1966 had consisted of a coalition of the conservative and the social democratic parties, for backing the developers with tax breaks. Individual landowners and large corporations, who would be the protagonists of real estate development in other cities, were conspicuously absent from the debate.

The inhabitants of the Märkisches Viertel had mixed feelings. While they shared a general discontent with the infrastructural shortcomings and voiced their protest against the shortage of daycare centers, retail stores, and public transportation, they were equally shocked by newspaper reports that depicted them as criminal riff-raff, or, at best, as helpless victims of inhuman architects. Thus their criticism of the new residences was soon eclipsed by a defense mechanism against the muckraking in the media. Reporters who painted the area as a tower block ghetto encountered growing mistrust and aggression from the locals who felt deeply insulted—the objection that the press only defended their interests fell on deaf ears.[35] In addition, there were also increasing signs that many Märkisches Viertel inhabitants were more or less happy with their modern environment compared to the tenements in which they had lived before.[36] The biggest challenge for them, it seemed, was neither the inhuman architecture nor the bad planning but rather the high rent. Albeit subsidized and state-controlled, rents were twice the rate that many residents had paid for their old and substandard inner-city tenements—a problem that proved to be irresolvable even for Social Democratic politicians.[37]

The "slab" in East Berlin

Die Platte (the slab), as East Germans still call the numerous prefab housing developments built under the socialist regime, is the most conspicuous relic of the late German Democratic Republic (GDR). In 1990, 23 percent of East German citizens lived in standardized housing estates with more than 2,500 apartments, compared to only 1.7 percent of West Germans—the figures do not include the numerous inhabitants of smaller prefab developments.[38] Although referring to a constructive element—the prefabricated concrete slab—die Platte is more a cultural than a technical term. To date, it is more commonly associated with East German prefab developments than with similar architecture in the West. Given the strong ideological implications under which the slabs were planned and built, they are even referred to as a cipher for the East German state.[39] Slab developments in the GDR were more standardized and much larger; apart from that, however, they showed numerous similarities to their counterparts in the West. Like in West Germany, the slabs originated from a state-driven impulse to improve the housing shortage exacerbated by wartime destruction and at the same time liberate city dwellers from late-nineteenth-century neighborhoods. What in the West was seen as the mandate of progress and modernization, in the East was tied to the narrative of socialist advancement. In 1955, the Politburo under Head of State Walter Ulbricht decided on the "industrialization of the building industry" and subsequently restricted the use of other constructive methods. In this respect, the focus on towers and slabs was more one-dimensional than in the West and by the end of the German Democratic Republic prefab technology had virtually become the only method of construction.

Like in the West, the first slab developments were started in the late 1950s. In 1957, construction began in the small town of Hoyerswerda near Dresden, close to a newly incorporated coal plant. The large-scale settlement increased the population from approximately 7,000 in 1955 to more than 70,000 around 1980. In 1964, the government mandated the construction of East Germany's largest tower block development: Halle-Neustadt (Halle New Town), a development for 100,000 people across the Saale River from the old town of Halle, which was subsequently incorporated as a city of its own. Similar developments followed in many cities, including Lütten-Klein in Rostock (1965–69, 18,000 inhabitants) or Grünau in Leipzig (1976–80s, 100,000 inhabitants). From 1973, these developments constituted the backbone of the 1973 Housing Program, through which Erich Honecker, Head of State from 1971, promised to resolve the housing problem. Honecker planned to construct more than 3 million apartments in the German Democratic Republic between 1973 and 1990, approximately 2 million of which were actually built.[40] Next to the already mentioned new towns in Hoyerswerda and Halle, the three

4.7
East German Head of State Erich Honecker (left) visiting a workers' family in the East Berlin slab district of Marzahn on July 6, 1978, and inaugurating the allegedly one millionth apartment completed in the German Democratic Republic since the start of the Housing Program in 1973 (source: *Neue Wohnkomplexe in der DDR und der UdSSR*, ed. Ministerium für Bauwesen der DDR, East Berlin: Verlag für Bauwesen, 1987)

developments on the East Berlin periphery were known best. Marzahn (started in 1977), Hellersdorf (started in 1981), and Hohenschönhausen (started in 1984) in 1989 together housed approximately 350,000 of the East German capital city's 1.1 million inhabitants. The one-sided concentration of the state-operated construction industry on prefabrication led to a continuous "production" of prefab developments until the end of the German Democratic Republic. Like in the West, however, there was continuing criticism from the 1970s onward, which in some respect entailed a modification of the prefab buildings and a focus on construction in the inner city.

Since the 1960s, the modernist mass housing developments in East Germany were increasingly labeled "monotonous," "uniform," and "carelessly designed." Taking into account the extent of censorship in East Germany, the criticism was surprisingly blunt.[41] A 1975 report to a high-ranking party leader pointed out the gravity of the situation, suggesting that the low aesthetic quality of East German housing blocks seriously endangered the citizens' identification with the socialist state.[42] East German theorists, however, initially neglected such findings since, as they pointed out time and again, aesthetic appearance was not to be looked at as a problem of its own, but always in connection with the surrounding social conditions. They assumed that socialism, which aimed at an improvement of these conditions, would necessarily produce satisfactory buildings and that the aesthetic concerns voiced in the West were mere placeholders for the unjust conditions under capitalism.

4.8
Marzahn district, East Berlin
(Florian Urban, 2005)

Referencing Alexander Mitscherlich's criticism of "inhospitable" modernist urban design, the well-known East German theorist Bruno Flierl claimed in 1973 that there was "no exit from the inhospitable city within inhospitable capitalism."[43] That socialist cities could also be inhospitable was originally not provided for in the mindset of East German officials. Hence coming to terms with the monotony of the slab developments was a painful process, and it was only achieved through sleight of hand and selective forgetting.

Bruno Flierl was a pioneer of this process. In the 1970s, he pointed out that formal similarities between capitalist and socialist architecture were insignificant, since the difference lay in the societal structures, but at the same time insisted that the actual buildings were a factor of these conditions.[44] That could be understood as: although West German slabs are rightfully being criticized as monotonous we should continue to build them in the East, since our East German slabs are not inhabited by underprivileged and marginalized social groups but by a proud working class, and this is all that counts. It could also translate into: one should not take for granted that "socialist" slabs are good and "capitalist" ones bad, but rather investigate how the inhabitants relate to either buildings. Thus Flierl opened a backdoor for an analysis of aesthetic appearance. He agreed with orthodox Marxists that it was "bourgeois ideology" to look at aesthetics as an autonomous expression, but he allowed for an academic analysis of appearance.[45]

Such research reflected an international concern with city perception and contextual urbanism, which in Western discourse is connected with the works of Aldo Rossi, Colin Rowe, or Kevin Lynch. On this basis, modernist slab developments were criticized for their lack of a recognizable *Stadtbild* (city image or skyline). In the late 1970s, East German researchers Olaf Weber and Gerd Zimmermann compared the perception of Old Town Halle by its inhabitants with that of the slab development Halle-Neustadt.[46] Using mental maps and surveys, they found out that in Old Town Halle city image was anchored to streets and squares and in Halle-Neustadt to individual buildings. As a consequence of the lack of *Stadtbild*, orientation in Halle-Neustadt was only possible through habitual sequences, which explained why strangers regularly lost their way. Their study contained a clear criticism of modernist design on the basis of its insufficient communicative qualities.

While East German authors were increasingly critical of the tower developments, there were numerous attempts to modify prefab construction. In 1982, the Politburo mandated that future construction projects were to be executed in the inner city.[47] Although this did not affect the tower developments on East Berlin's periphery that were still under construction, such developments were no longer planned. A 1989 study carried out by the Building Academy eventually declared the necessity of a "densification" of these settle-ments.[48] Criticizing the old strategy, the study referred to the "struggle of the residents against the demolitions [that] is among other things grounded in experiences with . . . the poor and careless design of the 'products' [=apartment blocks], which does not take into account the specific character of the neighborhood."[49]

Such publications suggest that by the late 1980s, East German authorities in the majority acknowledged the necessity of reforming the construction of "the slab." Seeing the repetitive concrete boxes as the peak of technological and aesthetic progress had become hard even for steadfast believers in the accomplishments of the real existing socialism. Had the German Democratic Republic continued to exist, it is likely that such construction would have come to a complete halt. The efforts to modify the monotonous settlements, however, were tightly restricted by the constant shortage of labor and materials and by the production methods set up during the 1960s, that is, by an exclusive concentration on prefabricated parts and by the closing down of small firms offering alternative methods of construction. While both East German officials and the populace increasingly perceived industrialized construction as a straightjacket, the regime nevertheless proved to be too inflexible to admit substantial reforms.

Demonic tower blocks, homely late-nineteenth-century tenements

In West Germany, too, the image of modernist towers deteriorated further in the 1970s, and started to be associated with drugs and child prostitution. The connotation relied on a 1978 best seller that infamously featured a girl from West Berlin's Gropiusstadt development. The book *Wir Kinder vom Bahnhof Zoo* (We, the Kids from Zoo Station) is the autobiography of a heroin user who from the age of 14 has to steal and prostitute herself to finance her addiction.[50] Vera Christiane Felscherinow, who appeared under the pseudonym Christiane F., had managed to escape the grip of the substance at 16 and subsequently told her story to two journalists. The book presents an unequal struggle between a rebellious girl and a demonic big city, which, unlike the asphalt jungle in Alfred Döblin's famous 1929 novel *Berlin Alexanderplatz*, was now epitomized in the modernist slab development. The report opens with the description of an environment that is not only dysfunctional but also designed to smell. The reason: Small children who play outside the tower blocks hardly ever make it to their upper-floor apartments when they have to pee; since the panoptical surroundings of the block offer no place to hide, they urinate in the corridors. The lot of the "wooden-spoon-kids" was equally deplorable. These children frequently lost the spoons their mothers had given them to press the doorbells and operate the intercoms. Too small to reach the buttons by themselves, they sometimes remained locked out from their high-rise apartment homes for hours. Christiane F.'s drug use and delinquency is thus shown as an outcome of the inhuman surroundings she had experienced since her early childhood.

The report was one of the best-selling German books since the Second World War—in 2006 the forty-eighth edition was released. Immediately after its first publication it acquired textbook status in German secondary schools, where a social activist generation of post-1968 schoolteachers tried to keep their students clean of drugs. Its success among both schoolchildren and their pedagogues derived from its particular style, which on the one hand gave a realistic glimpse of the horrors of drug addiction, and on the other hand vividly transmitted the anxieties and insecurities of a teenager without a moralizing undertone. In addition, the story rearranged the centuries-old themes of love, death, and the salvation of a fallen girl and combined them with modernist architecture. The book thus powerfully canonized the negative image of the tower blocks.

With the modernist developments being more and more discredited, efforts to preserve the late-nineteenth-century tenements were gaining ground. This happened simultaneously in both parts of the divided Berlin. In the East, the first large-scale tenement remodeling started in the Arnimplatz neighborhood in 1973, with significant repercussions in both East and West Berlin. The demolition of old buildings was eventually outlawed in 1979, although the prohibition was never enforced efficiently and renovations remained the exception.[51] From the 1970s onward there was also a growing opposition to the relocation policy in East Berlin's tenement neighborhoods.[52] The Arnimplatz project had shown that it was in fact possible to have one's cake and eat it, too. The tenants could remain in their old social context and at the same time enjoy in-house toilets, showers, and warm water. It thus became possible to disassociate the opposition between old and new buildings from the question of unequal sanitary standards. The public opinion about the tenements thus became a merely social, functional, and aesthetic question, and their reputation grew steadily.

In West Berlin, one of the first tenant associations to successfully fight the forced relocation from their old apartments was founded on Klausener Platz in the Charlottenburg district in 1973. The neighborhood was eventually remodeled in 1976. Other remodeling projects started with the incorporation of the International Building Exhibition in 1979. In the following two years, a growing squatter movement vociferously denounced the deliberate neglect of late-nineteenth-century tenements, and in 1982 West Berlin eventually adopted comprehensive legislation that mandated the preservation of these buildings.[53] The 12 principles of what was called *Behutsame Stadterneuerung* (Careful Urban Renewal) were the direct opposite of the urban renewal policy of the 1960s. Extensive state funds were now funneled into the preservation of tenements and the fitting out with modern amenities such as central heating, showers, and toilets inside the apartments. The new respect for what was now considered a historic monument went along with a policy change toward participatory forms of planning that regarded the tenants as partners rather than subjects of the renewal process. A system of community workers was set up to provide the tenants with substitute apartments while their buildings were renovated—they all retained the right to return to their old apartments and enjoy rent control. Despite the numerous legal provisions aimed at *Milieuschutz* (protection of the milieu), some tenement areas were gradually gentrified—the rent level in desirable neighborhoods such as the Mitte and Prenzlauer Berg districts in former East Berlin in particular rose after the turn of the twenty-first century. At the same time, no designer, theorist, journalist, or politician in East or West Germany called for the knocking down of tenement neighborhoods any more. The value of the historic city had become a part of mainstream culture.

Reconfiguring old and new

One of the distinctive characteristics of Berlin mass housing is the strong-felt dichotomy between old and new, as embodied by the opposition of tower blocks and tenements. In most countries, the modernist promise was directed against a "traditional" lifestyle and the buildings that were connected with it, but in few places was the dichotomy of old and new as clear-cut and the struggle as passionate as in Berlin. Both the proponents of modernist architecture before 1970 and the defenders of the historical city after 1970 saw the two forms of dwelling as mutually exclusive. This is already reflected in the terminology *Neubau* (new building) versus *Altbau* (old building), which in popular use first and foremost did not refer to the age but to the typology of modernist apartment block versus late-nineteenth-century tenement. And it is evidenced by the fact that in Berlin, more than in other cities, the construction of mass housing followed what its critics dubbed *Kahlschlagsanierung* (chop down remodeling), the large-scale urban renewal program of the 1963 that foresaw the demolition and rebuilding of 56,000 apartments in the historic inner-city districts and in the long term aimed at ridding the city of the tenements. The construction of the Märkisches Viertel and other tower block estates was an integral part of this strategy.

From the very beginning, the tenets of modernist architecture, such as light, air, and the absence of ornamentation, were derived from the rejection of the tenement type, particularly the "gloomy backyard" and the "deceptive stucco ornaments" allegedly devised to mask overcrowding and poverty.[54] Before 1970, tenement neighborhoods were deemed "unhealthy" because of their overcrowded apartments and their insufficient sanitary facilities, "monotonous" because of their standardized height and repetitive stucco ornaments, and "chaotic" because of their backyards and the mixture of residential and commercial spaces. After 1970, the same terms were used against the modernist satellite settlements, which were called "unhealthy" because of their concrete façades and paved yards, "monotonous" because of their repetitive geometry and unadorned façades, and "chaotic" because of their lack of a recognizable block structure. While before 1970 the modernist apartment blocks promised social justice, an authentic lifestyle, and the protection of the pedestrian, the same potentials were later attributed to the tenements.

A number of historical conditions favored the peculiar reinterpretation of old and new dwellings. First, Berlin's demographic development was different from that of most other sample cities in this book, since its population had barely increased since the early 1900s and in the late twentieth century was significantly less than at its peak around 1940.[55] Hence, the number of old buildings was high compared to the population: despite wartime destruction, tenements for a long time outnumbered other building types, and only since the 1970s has the ratio changed in favor of modernist towers and other post-war typologies.[56] The relative stability of Berlin's population in connection with ongoing construction accounted for the fact that the housing shortage was significantly mitigated and over the years the tenements came to be less and less overcrowded. Second, in contrast to the wooden houses of old Moscow or Chicago, Berlin's late-nineteenth-century homes were made from durable materials and could therefore be adapted to a modern lifestyle more easily. And third, the population in both German states around 1970 had attained an unprecedented standard of living, and the differences between working-class and middle-class lifestyles were smaller than ever before. In a way, the tower blocks also fell victim to their own success: since they contributed to a partial solution of the housing crisis, they cleared the view on the qualities of traditional tenement dwellings that before was dulled by poverty and overcrowding.

Ghettos for immigrants?

The connection between Berlin's serial apartment buildings and the city's marginalized minorities of Turkish or Arab descent was never as fixed as in France. Unlike many Paris *banlieues*, which from the 1970s came to be home to a majority of non-ethnic French, mass housing developments in Berlin remained predominantly "German." While the overall degree of ethnic segregation in Berlin is low compared for example to Chicago, the percentage of immigrants in tower blocks roughly corresponds to the city's average or, particularly in the eastern half, is even lower.

Immigration played out very differently in both German states. West Germany experienced its largest wave of immigration in the 1960s, when the government actively encouraged immigration from southern Europe and Turkey to satisfy the booming economy's demand for labor. Until 1973, when official recruitment was stopped, approximately 2.9 million workers migrated to West Germany, mostly from southern Europe and Anatolia. During that time, West Berlin became home to approximately 120,000 Turkish expatriates; with more than 12 percent non-Germans in the 1980s, the walled city had one of the largest foreign populations in Germany.[57] The migrants were originally called *Gastarbeiter* (guest workers), reflecting the fact that both the West German government and most of the workers themselves regarded their presence as temporary. It was not until the late 1970s that the migrants were increasingly understood as permanent residents. Given their provisional status in the early years, their weak economic situation, and xenophobic resentment from the Germans, most settled in the least desirable neighborhoods. In West Berlin, those were the late-nineteenth-century areas of Wedding, Tiergarten, Neukölln, and Kreuzberg, whose low-standard five-story tenements were often scheduled for demolition in the long run.

The German Democratic Republic also recruited so-called *Vertragsarbeiter* (contract workers) from overseas, mostly from befriended communist states such as Vietnam or Angola, but their number was much smaller. When the socialist regime ceased to exist, there were 91,000 contract workers living in East Germany—less than 0.5 percent of the population. By the late 1990s, only 13,000 were still living in Germany, most of them Vietnamese. While they were poorly integrated into East German society—under the socialist regime they had to live in strictly controlled group homes—their number was too small to have a lasting influence on East Germany's urban life.[58]

As in France, immigrants were conspicuously absent from the planning debates of the 1960s and early 1970s.[59] West German journalists occasionally reported on the hardships of the newcomers facing xenophobia and an unfamiliar environment, but not until the late 1970s were they perceived as an integral part of Germany's urban culture. This changed in the 1980s, when West Berlin increasingly embraced its new identity as a "multicultural metropolis." The Eastern portion of the Kreuzberg district around Schlesisches Tor, which by then featured Germany's largest concentration of baklava bakeries and kebab stands, attained national reputation as "Little Istanbul," a term that for many Germans conjured both fears of a cultural infiltration and the lure of an exotic "other." It also showed the extent to which West Germans were puzzled by the new ethnic diversity—in few other large cities would an area whose population is only slightly more than 25 percent Turkish be deemed an ethnic neighborhood.

Some immigrants also moved to the tower block neighborhoods on the periphery, but their presence never became as strong as in the tenement neighborhoods. In 2006, the Märkisches Viertel had only 9.3 percent residents with a non-German passport (2.5 percent Turks)—quite low compared to the Berlin average of 13.8 percent (3.6 percent Turks), and to the 39.5 percent in Kreuzberg's "Little Istanbul" (26.5 percent Turks).[60] The low to average number of foreigners in the Märkisches Viertel is reflected in other West Berlin mass housing districts, such as Gropiusstadt (14.3 percent foreigners, including 5.5 percent Turks),[61] and is even more blatant in the East Berlin tower block development Marzahn-Hellersdorf, where the percentage of non-Germans has always been very low (only 3.4 percent foreigners).[62] In this respect, the early descriptions of the Märkisches Viertel as an "inhuman ghetto" resonate exclusion based on income rather than on ethnic origin.[63]

Berlin, though, seems to be a special case. In other German tower block developments, including Köln-Chorweiler, Hamburg-Mümmelmannsberg, or Munich-Neuperlach, the percentage of non-ethnic-Germans is much higher than the local average.[64] In those cities, many historic central city neighborhoods were gentrified in recent decades and many poor immigrants were pushed to the tower blocks on the periphery, which often offered the lowest rents. Some people claim that in Berlin—to date one of the poorest large cities in Germany—this development is just beginning and with the rents in certain inner-city neighborhoods on the rise, working-class non-ethnic Germans are now increasingly moving to the slab developments.[65] Whether or not this tendency will increase, immigrants are not likely to become the dominant group in the near future.

The calm after the storm

By the late 1980s, the storm against the mass housing developments slowly waned. The images of hope and despair that had been alternatingly attached to the standardized blocks blurred while at the same time the old neighborhoods became more important. Public perception, after changing from white to black, eventually faded into gray. At the same time, the tower-and-slab idea had run its course. Not only were modernist developments no longer built, there was even talk of listing them as protected monuments, since they were, according to West Berlin's head preservationist Helmut Engel in 1988, "a significant testimony of a past cultural epoch."[66] The public decided to care less and less. Since the demolition of these projects was beyond question, it seemed that one had to live with them, and negative reports on the alleged ghettos disappeared from the media. By the 1980s, there was also an increasing awareness that Germany's great settlements were far from being homogeneous. Some still had a disproportionately high rate of poverty, but at the Märkisches Viertel, for example, this was no longer the case. According to a 1985 survey, only 13 percent of the inhabitants received rent subsidy as a form of social welfare.[67] By 2004, the number had risen only marginally to 14.5 percent (Berlin average: 8.1 percent).[68]

The unemployment rate of 17 percent among the approximately 36,000 inhabitants was also only slightly higher than the Berlin average of 13 percent.[69] At the same time, statistics showed that the slab tenants' degree of contentment with their environment was comparably high. Sixty-nine percent were "pleased" or "very pleased" with their dwelling situation, and 85 percent were happy to remain.[70] The Märkisches Viertel received better and better press. Journalists commended the amount of street life, the many playgrounds, and the civic spirit among the inhabitants, which, ironically, was enhanced by the common fight for a better neighborhood.[71] The result: little fluctuation and increasing positive identification with the new neighborhood.[72] The numbers confirm that the Märkisches Viertel is a neighborhood with significant social challenges, but not a ghetto.

City slab developments in the eastern half of the city also became less controversial. Traditionally more socially mixed than their West German counterparts, the tower blocks on East Berlin's periphery for a long time had a far better reputation among the majority. Independent surveys were rarely permitted in the German Democratic Republic, but individual accounts suggest that the attractiveness of central heating and hot water tended to eclipse discontent with bleakness and standardization. An analysis of classified ads by a West German scholar further suggests that by the late 1980s the physical form of the building—1970s slab versus late-nineteenth-century tenement—had little influence on the average East Berlin citizen's dwelling preferences.[73] After the German reunification in 1990, the East German slab developments were thoroughly renovated and often repainted in flashy colors, thus further increasing their appeal.

Is all well that ends well? Not quite. While not being the condensers of crime and misery in the way the 1970s media had depicted them, Germany's slab developments continued to be the residences of society's lower strata. Even in the East, where once the medical doctor had lived wall to wall with the construction worker, a new social stratification became palpable: those who stayed tended to be those who could not afford to leave. This was especially visible in the many German areas that since 1990 had suffered from a population decrease. East Germany's former industrial cities, such as Hoyerswerda or Halle, all of a sudden had countless empty apartment blocks, and both residents and politicians started to call for their demolition. At the same time, slabs in central locations were rediscovered as fashionable locations for art shows and other cultural events—in the same way that artists had appropriated the tenements twenty years earlier.

While physical determinism has largely vanished from the popular discourse, the reputation of the slabs remains ambiguous. A possible path for the future can be detected in a pilot project subsidized by the Berlin government. In the peripheral East Berlin neighborhood of Ahrensfelde, architects Stephan Schüttauf and Michael Persike tried to remove the shortcomings of the slab developments while preserving their advantages. Their 2002 project *Ahrensfelder Terrassen* (Ahrensfelde Terraces) presented a peculiar restructuring of the slabs.[74] Former 11-story buildings were cut off above the fourth floor, and an irregular silhouette was carved out, allowing for inventive maisonette apartments with roof terraces. The inhabitants could thus enjoy the environment of a quiet and green district that at the same time was well connected to the city center by public transportation; the modular variations of the slab system were nevertheless still visible. The social mix that was once

characteristic for East Berlin's slabs was to be restored by attracting wealthier groups—Schüttauf's and Persike's Ahrensfelde Terraces were built for both owners and tenants. The project might remain unique. It nevertheless showed a development that bore surprising resemblance to the strategies applied to the tenements 20 years before: a once broadly despised architectural type gets restructured and at the same time reinterpreted as an acceptable form of housing.

4.9
Ahrensfelde Terraces (design: Stephan Schüttauf and Michael Persike, 2002). The 11-story prefab slab buildings were cut off above the fourth floor and converted into low-rise condominiums (Florian Urban, 2007)

5 Brasília, the Slab Block Capital

Order and progress: a new metropolis as a condenser for modernization

In Brazil, the principles of modernist mass housing are painted in golden letters on the country's flag. *Ordem e progresso*—"order and progress"—was the promise on which the Brazilian Republic was built in 1889, and for a long time the slogan also inspired national policy. The most famous outcome of this attitude, the city of Brasília, stands out as one of the largest number of residential slabs built in the twentieth century, and at the same time, modernism's most radical project.

Brasília is quite different from the Chicago housing projects or the Paris *grands ensembles*. First, the representative function was crucial. The city was founded as a capital, political center, and model for a modern Brazil; the symbolic dimension of both plan and architecture was therefore particularly strong. Second, Brasília was designed to house the country's political elite and not the working class. And third, modern design did not come along with modern technology such as prefabrication, but was carried out using traditional methods of construction. Despite these differences, the international discourse of state intervention and egalitarianism is palpable in Brasília's slabs in the same way as in the American or French tower blocks.

Most early reviews centered on the city's ambiguous symbolism. Brasília had been intensely debated since its foundation in 1956, but never became abruptly discredited like so many other formerly revered modernist projects. Admiration and reservation always coexisted, and the acknowledgment of Brasília's humanist potential and egalitarian goals always went hand in hand with caveats against the architects' hubris and the criticism of many unfulfilled promises. Under the military regime, which lasted from 1964 to 1985 and suppressed both freedom of the press and open academic debate, the media coverage

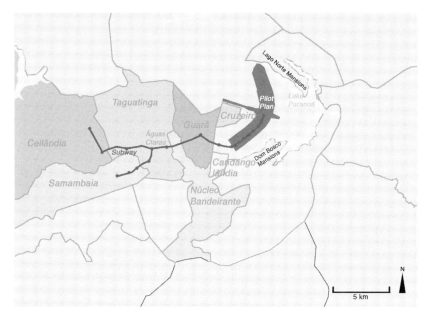

5.1
Brasília (Florian Urban)

decreased significantly—international reviews also dwindled. This chapter thus relies mainly on sources published in the early 1960s and since the 1980s.

Brasília was inaugurated in 1960 after only four years of construction. It was built on a largely uninhabited plateau, close to the country's geographical center. The original planned city—to date known as the Plano Piloto (Pilot Plan) and constituting the center of the urban agglomeration—occupies an area of approximately 40,000 square miles; the same as the city of Paris. However, while Paris has some 2 million inhabitants, the Pilot Plan has only 200,000—originally residences, offices, and public institutions had been planned for half a million.[1]

Brasília evolved as a joint project of two ambitious men: president Juscelino Kubitschek and architect Oscar Niemeyer, who had been friends since the 1940s. When Kubitschek campaigned for the presidency in 1955, he promised to fulfill a centuries-old Brazilian dream and build a capital city in the country's vast and underdeveloped interior. Elected a year later, he promoted modernization on many levels, opening new iron ore mines and developing the automotive industry. The new capital city was to crown his efforts. Since the Brazilian constitution forbade reelection, he knew that he had only four years to advance construction to a point where the plan could not be abandoned by his successor. Niemeyer was game. An open competition was held to determine the urban design, merely asking for a plan on a scale of 1:25,000 and a brief commentary. Under Niemeyer's influence the famous airplane-shaped plan by architect Lúcio Costa was chosen. Niemeyer knew him well, since he had worked in Costa's office in 1934. The city was erected following the British model of a development corporation by the state firm Novacap (Companhia Urbanizadora da Nova Capital = Company for the City Planning of the New Capital), which was commissioned to prepare the site for construction and erect the public buildings. Ground was broken in 1956, and in the same year the seat of the president was officially

5.2
Brasília's south wing in 1959
(postcard edited by Colombo)

transferred to Brasília—provisionally housed in a wooden structure called *catetinho*. Costa subsequently did not take an active role in the construction process, but Niemeyer designed the most prestigious buildings.

Among the first completed structures were the presidential residence (1959) and the Brasília Palace Hotel for state guests (1958). Costa's plan was based on the tenets of modernist urbanism: functional separation, traffic based on the automobile, and dispersed multistory buildings surrounded by large park spaces. The population was to be housed in four- to seven-story slab blocks, grouped around communal facilities. Brasília was largely a state enterprise. Like the large-scale developments in Germany and France, the city was built on state-owned land, although tradable construction rights, referring to the floors above the public ground floor between the pilotis, were later transferred to private developers. Amid clouds of dust and half-finished buildings, the city was officially inaugurated on April 21, 1960, the legendary date of Rome's foundation. Juscelino Kubitschek later called it the happiest day of his life and it was the first time that a Brazilian president had shed tears in public.[2]

The *superquadra*

To an extent unprecedented in Brazil, Brasília came to be a city of residential slab buildings. At first glance, this fact surprises. The area was sparsely inhabited, owned by the Brazilian state, and traffic was to be based on cars—it could have been designed as an agglomeration of dispersed low-rise structures like Los Angeles. While the significance of the housing block

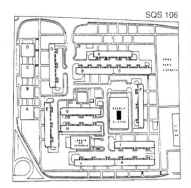
SQS 106

SQS 308

SQS 409

type as such was hardly mentioned in contemporaneous reviews, one can only assume that it was chosen for symbolic reasons, derived from the modernist ideas that at the time were discussed in Paris or London in the same way as in São Paulo or Rio de Janeiro: Le Corbusier's Unité d'Habitation and the CIAM debates on minimum dwelling and functional planning. Niemeyer and Costa, who had both studied at the Escola Nacional de Belas Artes in Rio, were indebted to this discourse and it is likely that for them, too, apartment bocks embodied the promise of modernity.

The city was designed to provide a comprehensive living environment for its inhabitants—offering modern standards, which at the time only a minority of Brazilians enjoyed, but which, it was optimistically assumed, would become the rule in the not-too-distant future. In this sense, Brasília became a mass housing project for the privileged few. Already the plan was to guarantee a high level of comfort. Brasília's slab buildings were erected on the famous *superquadras* (super-blocks), rectangular plots of 280 × 280 meters that typically contained 11 apartment blocks each, plus schools, kindergartens, and park spaces. Four *superquadras* constituted a neighborhood and shared communal facilities such as shopping spaces. The scaled layers of reference paralleled the hierarchical subdivision of Soviet or French modernist residential compounds.

The *superquadra* is a variation of the "neighborhood unit" theorized in the 1920s by Clarence Perry and others and famously realized in the garden city of Radburn (1928, design: Clarence Stein and Henry Wright).[3] In Brazil, the best-known equivalent is the Parque Guinle development in Rio de Janeiro, which is often quoted as the model for Brasília's *superquadras* (1948, design: Lúcio Costa and Roberto Burle Marx). Each *superquadra* is limited by large streets on all four sides and communicated by access streets and interior pedestrian walkways. The percentage of green spaces is high. Only 14 percent is occupied by buildings.[4] Thus the number of residents is also moderate—200–300 per slab and 2,000–3,000 per block. The *superquadras* comprise both wings of the airplane-shaped Pilot Plan. They are connected by the residential axis, the 9-mile-long main avenue that runs through both wings. Each is referred to by a number, such as Superquadra South (SQS) 102 on the South Wing or Superquadra North (SQN) 104 on the North Wing. The best-known *superquadras* are the three rows in the south with the numbers SQS 101 to 116, SQS 202 to 216, and SQS 302 to 316. By the time of the inauguration in 1960, only SQS 105–108

5.3

Three types of *superquadras* on the South Wing of the Pilot Plan (Sylvia Ficher on the basis of a plan by the Brasília District Government)

5.4
The first completed
superquadras in 1960
(postcard edited by Edicard)

and 307–308 were finished, while many others were still under construction. The construction of the city took more than forty years, and only by the early 2000s were both wings completely built up.

The standard apartment building contains between 50 and 120 apartments on six stories—the older buildings in the *superquadra* rows 100, 200, and 300 usually have 48 apartments. The outer super-blocks sometimes have only three-story buildings. The buildings were generally made from high-quality materials. Apartments varied in size, but most were significantly larger than tower block apartments in France or the Soviet Union. Costa proposed sizes of 89, 107, 134, and 178 square meters[5]—huge in comparison with the 44 square meters of a two-room flat in a Russian Khrushchev-era building. The most common typology for residential buildings was the seven-story block with six stories of apartment space that rest on pilotis over a free ground floor. It can be found in the *superquadras* 100, 200, 300, and 400, and occasionally too in some of the 700 blocks and in the Cruzeiro and Octogonal neighborhoods.[6] The buildings are characterized by clear geometrical forms and austere design. The façades were plastered and sometimes adorned with glass mosaics. More recent buildings display crenellated and sometimes curvilinear profiles and protruding balconies—the ascetic slab form of the 1950s with rectilinear forms, brise-soleils, and glazed façades were gradually abandoned in favor of more bulky and more individualized designs.

Brasília's slab buildings are much more differentiated than those that were built in France or the Soviet Union at the same time. The building regulations, particularly in the early period, aimed at harmony but not standardization, and Costa's plan encouraged architectural creativity. The apartment design, too, did not live up to the goal of socialist equity. Units within the same building differed in size and level of comfort, and most were designed for ownership rather than tenancy. Already on the first completed *superquadras*, SQS 107 and SQS 108, most buildings had elevators, service entrances, and maid's rooms, and thus catered to the wealthy Brazilian middle class, where maids and in-house nannies

5.5
Superquadra South 105
(Richard Williams)

are the rule. In 1965, most apartments in the Pilot Plan were made available on the open market, forcing even middle-class inhabitants to relocate, including many lower-income civil servants.[7] The obvious designation of apartments for certain classes led to a particular social stratification even within the Pilot Plan.[8]

Architectural differentiation was eased by the fact that the construction of the new capital did not go hand in hand with an industrialization of the building industry. In contrast to those in France or Germany, Brazilian apartment blocks were mostly designed by individual architects and built one by one, employing bricks, plaster, and concrete.[9] There had been investigations into the standardization and industrialization of construction processes, but they had not been developed beyond select experiments.[10] The ongoing abundance of cheap labor made rationalized construction less urgent, and the industry in Brazil stayed in the hands of smaller regional companies.

Repeated changes in the building codes reinforced the social differentiation. The original code from 1960 was revised in 1967, 1989, and 1998. Even by the first of these revisions, attention was being paid to the ongoing gentrification of the Pilot Plan, introducing requirements for service elevators and service entrances in the larger apartments.[11]

The 1989 building code mandated the preservation of Costa's original plan, which by then had acquired a historical cachet. In 1998, differentiation was further increased. In line with neoliberal politics, private developers were granted greater liberties and architectural requirements were reduced. With these modifications the groundfloor spaces between the pilotis were gradually privatized: In 1967, entrance halls and superintendents' apartments were authorized, in 1989 security guard houses and bicycle storages, and in 1998 even party rooms.[12] The 1960 code, ironically, had not even mandated parking garages, and most older buildings do not have them, despite the fact that Brasília from the very beginning was based on car ownership. Mandated first in the 1967 code, the number of parking spaces per apartment grew steadily, from around 50 spaces in some late-1960s slabs to more than 100 in the apartment buildings carried out at the turn of the twenty-first century.[13] These newer buildings followed the general housing block type design, but were nevertheless different from the ones carried out in the 1960s and 1970s.[14] They were designed with larger balconies, glass-clad façades, and tile ornaments—an example is the *superquadra* SQN 211. Instead of 11, 14 buildings per *superquadra* were now being built, thus restricting the available space for communal facilities. The new buildings were partially being set up diagonal to the street pattern. Most had nine instead of seven stories. The additional space was used for larger maisonnette apartments or sometimes for recreation rooms with roof terraces or barbecue spaces.

Egalitarian dreams in a polarized country

The social differentiation of Brasília's mass-produced apartment blocks, which increased over the years, from the very beginning contrasted with the egalitarian rhetoric among both designers and politicians. According to these statements, serial buildings were to express a classless society decidedly different from the socially polarized colonial lifestyle that had been determining Brazil for centuries. Comments such as a 1958 article in the official Novacap journal expressed the great modernist hope for a revolution through architecture. Brasília's slabs were to promote civic humanist values and inspire a democratic egalitarian society without racial or social discrimination:

> The apartment blocks of a *superquadra* are all equal: same façade, same height, same facilities, all constructed on pilotis, all provided with garages and constructed of the same material—which prevents the hateful differentiation of social classes; that is, all the families share the same life together, the upper-echelon public functionary, the middle, and the lower.[15]

The rhetoric caught on, despite the fact that it blatantly contradicted not only the social reality in the newly founded city but also the foundations of leftist theory—convinced Marxists cringed at the idea of establishing a socialist space within a capitalist system.[16] The popularity of the strategy "equity through architecture" was also evidenced in the ongoing laments about an alleged betrayal of the original ideas, in light of the thousands of impoverished and poorly housed in the metropolitan agglomeration a few years after Brasília's foundation.[17]

Brasília's peculiar reality as a "housing project for the rich" reflected the symbolic dimension of an egalitarian society that was hoped for rather than real. Equity as an objective has always stood in stark contrast with the country's "social apartheid." At the turn of the twenty-first century, those who can afford what would be considered a middle-class lifestyle in Western Europe or North America—a decent house or apartment, possibly a car, and access to health-care and education—make up less than a fifth of the total population in the Brasília metropolitan area and stand against an overwhelming majority of poor.[18]

The egalitarian dreams were rooted in the context of urban development and social policy in Brazil during the 1930s and 1940s. At that time, the country witnessed a growth in the number and visibility of a social group that was not as wealthy and influential as the traditional elites of agricultural landowners and bourgeois merchants, but aspired for a similar lifestyle. Like no other era before, the short-lived democracy between 1945 and 1964 favored this fledgling middle class. Since eventually this group turned out to be less influential than many had hoped, one could say, in a slight oversimplification, that Brasília evolved from this period as a middle-class city without a middle class. It was conceived as a prototype for standards of living that were a clear luxury at the time, but that the architects' and politicians' stern optimism expected to soon become the average. This included education in the same way as running water or automobile ownership. Unlike in France, Germany, or the Soviet Union, however, social housing never made it to the top of the political agenda in Brazil. Given that lack of a comprehensive development policy in the following decades, very few of the original promises were kept.

The Brazilian discourse on workers' accommodation, which was emerging in the 1930s contemporaneously with Roosevelt's New Deal in the United States and the social housing policy in France, was comparatively small. Like in many European countries, it sprang from a contradictory mix of protective state involvement and authoritarian rule. At that time, the Brazilian economy, which for centuries had relied on the export-based production of coffee, sugar, and minerals, changed toward partial industrialization. Cities grew immensely through the influx of migrants from rural areas, and the country, which before had been predominantly rural, became predominantly urban. The 1930s and 1940s also marked a change in the way most Brazilians lived. Social polarization had been extreme since colonial times, but its spatial structure changed in the mid-twentieth century. Before the Second World War most urban working-class Brazilians had been housed in investor-built rental abodes in the inner cities, but by 1960 large parts came to live in *favelas*, informal and often self-built settlements on the periphery.[19] The shortage was visible, and the calls for a state-supported housing policy became louder.[20]

The changes took place under Getúlio Vargas, who ruled Brazil from 1930 to 1945 and again from 1951 to 1954, alternating between democratic mandate and dictatorship. During the period of the so-called Estado Novo, which lasted from 1937 to 1945, he dissolved the parliament and established a conservative authoritarian regime. Vargas, who came from a family of cattle-farming landowners from Rio Grande do Sul, nevertheless promoted the interests of the urban bourgeoisie, thus creating a counterweight to the old elite of agrarian-based oligarchs that so far had determined the country's political life. He supported both industrial development and liberal reforms, including labor legislation. Over the course of his political career, Vargas increasingly followed a state-interventionist policy paralleling that of Franklin D. Roosevelt, which among his supporters earned him the moniker "father of the poor." It was the time when Brasília emulated European schemes of modernist urbanization based on CIAM principles. An example was the Cidade dos Motores (Motor City), situated 30 miles from Rio de Janeiro. The Soviet-style industrial new town was planned for 25,000 people and building began in 1945 after a design by Josep Lluis Sert and Paul Lester Wiener.[21]

Housing policy under Getúlio Vargas was in many respects paradoxical. The regime persecuted communists, and at the same time took a number of measures that one would rather expect from a leftist regime, such as the restriction of landlords' property rights. The most consequential law was the 1942 Lei do Inquilinato (Tenancy Law), which froze housing rents, and which its critics see as the one measure that determined the future course of urban development in Brazil, in particular the flagging of private housing invest- ment and the massive increase of informal settlements.[22] In the following years, various institutions built social housing. Among the most significant were the social security providers IAP (Instituto de Aposentadorías e Pensões—Institute for Retirement and Pension Funds). Most IAPs were founded in the 1930s and specified according to different groups of workers; most of them soon became state institutions. The IAPI (Instituto de Aposentadorías e Pensões dos Industriários—Institute for Industrial Workers' Retirement and Pension Funds) stood out as the most active commissioner of housing and most vigorous promoter of modernist urban design.[23] The Vargas regime's housing policy spawned numerous projects, including the Conjunto Residencial de Realengo in Rio de Janeiro (1939–43, design: Carlos Frederico Ferreira, 2,300 units) and the Conjunto Residencial "Prefeito Mendes de Moraes," known as Pedregulho (1947–53, design: Affonso Eduardo Reidy, 330 units).

It has to be pointed out, though, that the diverse and sometimes contradictory regulative measures taken under Vargas and his successors cannot be deemed a consistent housing policy. This distinguishes the Brazilian case from, for example, France or the United States. The 1942 Tenancy Law, the additional laws that regulated use, sale, and lease of real estate, and the creation of regional housing authorities, were based on a commonly shared conviction that the state had a certain responsibility for the provision of housing, but at the same time derived from the most diverse theoretical backgrounds.[24] Taken together, the measures proved to be insufficient to fight the housing crisis. The output was minimal, not only in comparison to the actual housing need, but also to the number of members of the social security associations—the IAPI and the others. In the five years from 1946 to 1950, apartments were built in Brazil for only 0.6 percent of the IAPs' members.[25] Since housing production fell far short of need, the few state-subsidized compounds soon turned into residences for the privileged. The poor increasingly built their own dwellings, and the massive construction of *favelas*, according to some scholars, was an unsatisfactory yet far more effective solution to the housing shortage than the numerous state-supported programs.[26]

"City of Hope" and modernist dystopia

The perception, significance, and social configuration of Brasília's slabs was heavily influenced by their image in the media, which from the very beginning was particularly strong and could hardly be separated from the actual buildings. Few cities have attracted a similar amount of coverage. The international appeal of the metropolis built from scratch spawned countless reviews, dissertations, newspaper articles, and coffee table books, and has barely waned in the five decades since the city's foundation. These reviews betray the widespread fascination with success and failure of modernism's most alluring dream: a city, if not on a hill, then at least on a plateau, a futurist egalitarian community in the middle of a wilderness, built from shiny housing blocks that espoused artistic mastery with scientific innovation.

That Brasília is more important as an idea than as a real city was reiterated over and over, particularly in the early years. The grandeur and daring of the plan was the designers' most valuable resource. Kubitschek and his supporters took great effort to disperse Brasília's fame before it was even built, celebrating the scope and boldness of the enterprise to mobilize popular support. In 1956, the construction firm Novacap started the monthly journal *Brasília*. Other important publications included the *Coleçao Brasília* (Brasília Collection, 1960), a government-sponsored 18-volume documentation, and the books *Quando mudam as capitais* (When Capitals Move) by José-Osvaldo de Meira Penna (1958) and *Brasil, capital Brasília* by Osvaldo Orico (1960)—both authors were also politicians and diplomats. Most importantly, the famous art critic Mario Pedrosa in 1959 organized the Congreso Internacional Extraordinário de Críticos de Arte.[27] At this event, which took place in São Paulo and Rio de Janeiro half a year before the official inauguration of Brasília, the most renowned architectural critics in the world were introduced to the new city. Participants included André Bloc, Bruno Zevi, Carola Giedion (architect and wife of the historian Sigfried Giedion), Eero Saarinen, Françoise Choay, Gillo Dorfles, Jean Prouvé, Meyer Shapiro, Tomás Maldonado, and of course the most important Brazilian architects and critics, including Lúcio Costa and Oscar Niemeyer. In his opening speech, Costa set the guidelines for the significance of the new capital, stressing that Brazil from now on "does not only export coffee, sugar, and cocoa, but also contributes a little to the universal culture."[28] As a result of this conference, Brasília was firmly anchored in the international architectural discourse. In the following year there was no major journal that did not present the concrete blocks under the glaring Brazilian sunlight. Editorials and interviews by Juscelino Kubitschek and Oscar Niemeyer appeared in such great number that one wonders if the two had any work to do other than catering to the international press.[29] With unabashed optimism they reiterated the city's main themes: courage and determination, a gargantuan enterprise to fight underdevelopment, poverty, and corruption, and the rebirth of a forgotten Third World country from the spirit of national cohesion. Both praised the frontier town feel, where laborers and engineers lived side by side and suffered the same hardships, and presented it as a portent of the future egalitarian society.

Foreign visitors joined the eulogy. The Modern Movement's most eminent historian, Sigfried Giedion, praised Costa's "unbroken courage for innovation,"[30] the American geographer David Snyder cheered that "behind the notorious political intrigues and fiascoes is a vocal Brazilian people imbued with the vision of a great destiny for their nation,"[31] and the Swiss member of parliament Willy Stäubli enthused about "the nativeness, originality, and perfection" of the design.[32] The daily life in the new capital was also celebrated. The French architectural critic Lucien Hervé praised "a life, stripped of luxury, but refined,"[33] and the German journalist and Brasília resident Henry Moeller was taken by the affability of his new neighbors, who "completely lack any kind of class conceit."[34]

Brasília was seen as a big counterpoint to the "colonial Portuguese" life in the old capital Rio de Janeiro, which was often presented in architectural terms and in contrast to Brasília, as in the popular magazine *Manchete*:

perimeter block houses, the permanent predomination of stone, the two-wing door, the stairs, the balcony, no garden . . . And outside, the street corner, the street fair and the bodega, the passage and the alley, the Lady of Mercy and the pillory . . . the fear that divides and connects the people that are separated by so many fences.[35]

A German visitor, more bluntly, celebrated the break from a lifestyle where "bureaucrats do not start what they call work until 11:30 am, have lunch between 1 and 2, and a coffee break afterward."[36] The new capital's modernist forms, thus, were conceived as a conscious cutoff.

As mentioned at the beginning of this chapter, there was no abrupt swing of opinion or any particular moment when the once widely celebrated project fell into discredit. Acknowledgment of Brasília's successes and criticism of its shortcomings always existed side by side. In the early 1960s, this ambiguity reflected the zeitgeist. At the peak of modernist planning practice in Europe and North America, its underlying principles were increasingly questioned. Although, particularly in Brasília's early years, the architectural world was generally enthusiastic about the idea of building a new capital, critics from the very beginning voiced their disappointment with the many unsatisfactory particulars. Given the city's iconic status, they often formulated these opinions as statements on modernism as such and thus challenged the idea of a "City of Hope"—the term coined by the French Minister of Culture, André Malraux, which was much quoted. Discomfort and uneasiness was particularly widespread among the many foreign visitors who had accepted the inconvenience of a trip across the globe to see the fulfillment of modernism's hopes and had arrived at a dusty construction site. They lamented not only that the city was far from being completed, but also that it differed from its plans in some fundamental aspects. The social housing on the Pilot Plan's edges was not being built, and neither was the central area, with cafés and theaters at the crossing of the principal axes.[37] However, only very few were as blunt as Jean-Paul Sartre, who felt he had been catapulted onto "the moon's backside,"[38] the anthropologist James Holston, who analogous to the "sarcellitis" in the Paris suburb of Sarcelles, detected the pathology of "brasiliaitis,"[39] or the sociologist Gilberto Freyre, who spoke of an "abstract city where no one wants to live."[40]

Most early reports were clearly ambivalent. They reflected the tension between the designers' self-understanding as audacious visionaries and their declared enemy—narrow, everyday life.[41] Enthusiasm for the bold enterprise, the monumental architecture, and the orderliness existed alongside shock at the many half-finished buildings, the repelling coldness of the vast geometrical forms, the hostility toward pedestrians, and the dirt and chaos in the surrounding *favelas* where the workers lived.[42] The rigidity of Brasília's airplane-shaped plan was both celebrated as the incarnation of a new order[43] and denounced as cold and impersonal.[44] The impressiveness of Niemeyer's poetic city center was both praised as aesthetically impressive and censured for its "deadly dull weekends" and its complete lack of shopping and entertainment facilities.[45] Terms such as "surrealist town"[46] or "Wild West town"[47] expressed both admiration and estrangement. The RIBA journal in 1967 was one of the few publications that published non-heroic images of Brasília, betraying both beauty and ugliness. They showed the shabby but lively main street in the informal settlement of Cidade Livre, with its pioneer-town-style wooden billboards, and the few finished single-family homes, which were, like many in Brazil, surrounded by unkempt gardens, leaning lamp posts, and pot-holed streets.[48] Here, the "City of Hope" looked like a paradise lost, embodying both a romantic idea's glorious failure and the fair punishment of human hubris.

The contradictions between plan and reality, ironically, turned many of modernism's promises against modernism itself. This is most clearly evidenced in the account of one of the most famous intellectuals at the time: Simone de Beauvoir. She visited the city in 1960 together with Jean-Paul Sartre. Lamenting the absence of public life, human solidarity, or an egalitarian society, she used the very terms that abounded in Brasília's ostensibly favorable presentations, such as "human scale" or "towers of light and air."[49] In her description, the aspects that had often been quoted to underline the city's humanist potential—big scale, clear forms, a remote location, and vast open spaces—stood precisely for the lack of civic values.[50]

The "tower in the jungle"

Brasília's housing blocks inspired a powerful re-edition of the dichotomy between rapid modernization and the idyllification of pastoral life that had determined Western culture since the nineteenth century. Critics saw the surrounding landscape as one of Brasília's most eminent characteristics, and they construed the opposition between architecture and nature very differently from the Corbusian tower in the park or the greenbelts of North American housing reformers.

Remoteness from civilization was real, as the city was literally built in the middle of nowhere. When construction began in 1957, there were no roads or railroad lines within 60 miles, and all materials had to be airlifted. The 3,000-foot-high plateau on which the city was erected was an arid and mostly barren savannah; it was situated more than 550 miles from the country's major hubs of Rio de Janeiro and São Paulo. The uncultivated landscape and the vast open sky were thus dominant features from the beginning, embodied in the name of the president's palace in the city center: Palacio Planalto (Plateau Palace). Nature thus constituted a fundamental element in the reports of pioneer spirit and adventure—reiterated over and over by architect Oscar Niemeyer.

The main elements of Brasília's pastoral narrative were an architecture that embodied both noble simplicity and technological sophistication, and an unfathomable and un-domesticated natural environment. Such a description appears, for example, in the account of the distinguished British geographer Lawrence Dudley Stump before the Royal Geographical Society in London in 1962:

> We in Europe simply cannot visualize Brasília. If you'd like to take Whitehall and place it in the north-west Highlands of Scotland, you begin to get some idea of the distance involved; if you took everything to your new Whitehall by air, you would get a little nearer what has actually been done in Brazil.[51]

Fifty years later, the city is still presented in similar terms—for example in a photo report in the French magazine *L'architecture d'aujourd'hui*, in which the buildings disappear amid vast grasslands and glaring spots of red earth. The author, a Brazilian architect, celebrated Brasília's nature as an overwhelming and yet benign force in the built environment and cheered: "Grass of all species, overruns the buildings of the South Wing!"[52]

Along with the spirit of pioneer work and conquest there is often also a proto-colonialist undercurrent in this rhetoric, evident in formulations such as "the capital in the jungle." The awkward formula, which appears in the works of well-known architectural historians such as Kenneth Frampton and Manfredo Tafuri, first and foremost betrays their geographical ignorance, since Brasília was built thousands of miles away from the nearest rainforest.[53] Its appeal is nevertheless related to the spectacular juxtaposition of modernist order and the chaos of a natural environment, which in the works of these authors gave rise to both awe and compassion. It was a powerful re-edition of the machine-in-the-garden dichotomy that had been present in much of the Western discourse on modernization.[54] Construing a romantic image of the nature-based Third World nation on its path to progress, it entwined some of Europe's most cherished tropes into a civilizing success story.

Pilot plan versus satellite cities?

The shiny housing blocks of Brasília, both as an idea and as a built reality, have to be understood in relation to their less formally planned counterparts. The *cidades satélites* (satellite cities) evolved concomitantly with the Pilot Plan and are inseparable from it. At the turn of the twenty-first century, they are utterly diverse in terms of architecture, social structure, and level of formal organization, ranging from the wealthy middle-class suburbs of Águas Claras to the *favelas* of Santa Maria. In the collective imagination, the satellite cities are the Pilot Plan's prolonged shadow: they are alternately construed as modernism's limiting condition, as the glitzy capital's evil face of misery and deprivation, as the incarnation of an unruly Brazilian vitality, or simply as evidence of the triviality of everyday life, untouched by utopian promises.[55]

The division between Pilot Plan and satellite cities dates back to the pioneer days. When construction started in the Pilot Plan, the two existing villages in the area, Planaltina (founded in 1859), and Brazlândia (founded in 1932), proved too small to house workers and engineers. Makeshift camps were set up, and many of them lingered long after construction was finished. Some workers' accommodations—originally made from tents—were set up directly by the construction company Novacap, and some others resulted from negotiations between Novacap and the workers, such as Taguatinga (the first satellite city, established in 1958), the "engineers' town" Vila Planalto, and Velhacap (later renamed Candangolândia), which contained Novacap's administration and hospital.[56] Other new towns were set up over the following years: Gama (24 miles south of the Pilot Plan) and Sobradinho (14 miles northeast of the Pilot Plan) in 1960, Guará in 1967 (3 miles west of the Pilot Plan, now 115,000 inhabitants), and Ceilândia in 1971 (16 miles west of the Pilot

Plan, now 344,000 inhabitants). Numerous satellite cities grew from self-built shacks erected without permit by the thousands of migrants in search of work on the construction sites. An example is the *favela* Vila Sarah Kubitschek, which was founded in 1958 by settlers from the poor northeast and named for the country's First Lady, whose protection they hoped to attract. The difference between "official" *campamentos* (camps) and "unofficial" *invasões* (squats, literally "invasions") blurred over the course of the 1960s.[57]

The unplanned workers' towns were both necessary tool and bothersome obstacle for the designers' ambitions, and official policy treated them accordingly. The optimistic predictions that the workers would return to their home regions or find apartments in the Pilot Plan had been unrealistic from the very beginning, and state-driven efforts to eradicate "illegal" squats alternated with half-hearted activities to channel urban growth into a planned agglomeration.[58] The world's most comprehensively designed city thus developed amid the struggles between next-to-almighty top-down planners and informal settlers who challenged their authority.

Cidade Livre (Free Town, later renamed Núcleo Bandeirante) is a textbook example. Established by Novacap in the late 1950s approximately 3 miles south of what was to become the edge of the Pilot Plan's South Wing, it was designed as a temporary settlement to accommodate workers and provide commercial facilities while the Pilot Plan was still under construction. The settlement was laid out following most basic principles. It had a main street, three parallel cross streets, and makeshift one-to-two-story buildings on regular plots. It was Cidade Livre which inspired the early visitors' accounts of the "Wild West town" next to the unfinished modernist capital. The inhabitants of Cidade Livre subsequently waged a years-long war for their right to stay. The local resident organization Movimento Pró-Fixação e Urbanização (Movement for Establishment and Urbanization) won its great victory in 1961, when the National Congress legalized the colony as a permanent settlement. The decision, according to contemporary observers, was celebrated with a day-long street party on which allegedly more than forty oxen were grilled and eaten.[59]

Other squatters were not as lucky as the residents of Cidade Livre and often wrestled with the state authorities for decades to secure their right to stay. In the early 1970s, when the Brasília region grew at an increasing rate, forced relocations were frequent. At that time, the government started the Campanha de Erradicação de Invasões (Squat Eradication Campaign), whose acronym CEI lives on in the name of one of the largest satellite cities, Ceilândia.[60] It was founded as part of the CEI and, ironically, soon became the site of various informal settlements itself.

Defying the official efforts to neglect, ignore, or eradicate the unplanned settlements, the Pilot Plan and satellite cities retained a persistent equilibrium. When Brasília was inaugurated in 1960, half of the agglomeration's approximately 142,000 inhabitants lived outside the Pilot Plan.[61] Today, most satellites are larger than the planned city—in 2000, Ceilândia had approximately 340,000 and Taguatinga 240,000 inhabitants, compared to 200,000 residents in the Pilot Plan.[62]

The *cidades satélites* were fundamental in the discourse around the meaning of Brasília's housing blocks. From the very beginning, they were seen as evidence of the new capital's success or failure.[63] The first descriptions follow the image of the "other" that

5.7
Mixed typologies in the satellite city
Águas Claras. In the background
middle-class high-rise residences,
in the foreground the Setor
Habitacional Vicente Pires, a
middle-class neighborhood which
started in the 1980s as an illegal
settlement on agricultural land
(Augusto Areal, 2007)

complements and contrasts the Pilot Plan, be it as a boisterous and unconscionable workers' camp or as a dangerous den of vice. The opposition was also aesthetical. "Its ugliness," according to an early visitor to Cidade Livre, "could emphasize the pleasing qualities of the formal city."[64] While the insufficiencies of the plan to address the living conditions in the wider metropolitan area were obvious from the very beginning, there were few voices that openly contested the conception that saw the Pilot Plan as the real city and the satellite settlements as disturbances. The dichotomy thus remained unchallenged for more than a decade and only changed in the early 1970s, when scholars began to stress the qualities of informal settlements.

Today, the satellite cities embody an era of urban development that has little to do with the principles of Lúcio Costa and Oscar Niemeyer. The typological opposition between the Pilot Plan and satellite cities—shiny housing blocks here and ramshackle shelters there—has largely vanished. Large parts of the satellite cities are composed of formal buildings, and many are slab blocks similar to those in the Pilot Plan. But the satellite cities also contain pre-modernist and post-modernist structural principles. Only a few miles from the apartment blocks one finds a patchwork of single-family homes, low-rise apartment blocks, and self-built shacks.

Cidade Livre/Núcleo Bandeirante, for example, has long changed from provisional to permanent architecture. Many of the original wooden shacks were taken down in favor of concrete buildings. Basic construction ordinances were enforced, such as a continuation

5.8
The satellite city Cidade Livre, later renamed Núcleo Bandeirante. Established in 1956 as a workers' camp from wood and sheet metal huts and legalized as permanent in 1961, it inspired many of the early accounts of a "Wild West town" next to the unfinished modernist capital. It is now a city of 36,000 inhabitants, with many highly popular middle-class neighborhoods (Augusto Areal, 2008)

of the perpendicular street plan and a height restriction limiting the buildings to two stories in the small side streets. More and more streets were paved. The basic functions are nevertheless still mixed. Stores and workshops of mechanics and electricians stand next to private homes and offices. Inhabitants sometimes show great imagination in the decoration of their façades, including drawings, columns, and decorative arches. Some degree of neighborhood diversification can be found in the "spiritual center" in the south of the Avenida no. 3, where churches and temples for many different cults can be found in close proximity.[65]

Brasília's self-understanding as a metropolitan area that comprises both Pilot Plan and satellite cities took a long time to develop and has not yet come to full fruition. There is a clear functional separation to date. The Pilot Plan is reserved for administration and housing for high-paid administrative workers and government officials. The satellite cities are home to lower-paid employees and the working class. The stratification along the class line thus, ironically, turned out to be more marked in the allegedly egalitarian Brasília than elsewhere in the country. The class distinction led to a commuting pattern in which the spatial configurations of many historic cities in this book are reversed: the modernist tower-and-slab ensemble constitutes the "central city," while the mixed-use neighborhoods make up the periphery. Since the tower blocks are the destination of commuting workers, public transit is being used as a means of social control. Buses only circulate at certain hours, corresponding to the standard working times, and either do not run at all on the weekends or charge significantly higher fares, thus restricting the presence of the poor in the Pilot Plan to certain times of the weekday. The metro service is also limited to weekdays. The segregation is also reflected in the subway system (Metrô Brasília), which was inaugurated in 1998. Designed to connect Taguatinga, Samambaia, Águas Claras, Guará, and Ceilândia with the center of the Pilot Plan, the metro is still underused: at the turn of the twenty-first century, the number of users per subway kilometer was 0.4—compared to 10.1 in Tokyo, 6.3 in Paris, 3.1 in Berlin, and even 1.0 in Los Angeles.[66]

The satellite cities, though, have quite diverse structures. While a great portion of residents—some say the majority—still live in self-built huts, the centers of Águas Claras, Núcleo Bandeirante, and Taguatinga have long been converted into places of residence for the wealthy middle class. In all three cities, apartment prices are still lower than in the Pilot Plan, but have risen significantly in recent years, driving the lower middle classes to the poorer suburbs such as Ceilândia, Santa Maria, Gama, and Planaltina.[67]

On an administrative level, the relation between Pilot Plan and satellite cities is subject of an ongoing debate. The 1977 master plan finally acknowledged that both are inseparably connected and together constitute the city of Brasília, but the struggle over the specificities of a common framework is continuing. In the late 1980s, a group of urban planners based at the Universidade de Brasília and coordinated by geographer Aldo Paviani called for a substantial modification of Costa's plan, most notably for the decentralization of city-wide functions from the Plano Piloto, and the integration of informal settlements into the regional planning activities.[68] And in 1980 the anthropologist Gustavo Lins Ribeiro proposed including the satellite cities in Brasília's historic heritage, since they are a testimony to the pioneer spirit from which Brasília grew, and as such an architectural monument to a time when the construction of the new national capital was conceived as a collective enterprise that united laborers and engineers, rich and poor.[69]

An architectural comeback?

Social conditions in the Pilot Plan have changed significantly over the last sixty years. Rising apartment prices have gradually driven out less wealthy people, and the mass housing here has become highly exclusive. Most residents belong to the wealthy classes: 80 percent have a college degree, and 83 percent own their apartments. The household income level is twice the average of that of the Federal District and more than six times that of the poorest community in the area, Santa Maria.[70] Brasília's Pilot Plan has thus become more "normal"—more like most other Brazilian cities, which are highly stratified according to income level. As a consequence, the space in the *superquadras* has come to be increasingly determined by the preferences of the wealthy. Over the years, equal design and public facilities were increasingly modified according to a more individualized lifestyle.[71] Façades and interiors of the blocks were revamped according to different levels of quality and design, which reflected social distinctions. Communal park spaces were turned into private gardens. And the openness of the block, which was mandated by historic preservation, was limited by subtle systems of access restrictions, including the lack of public transportation on weekends, as already mentioned. Social life in the *superquadra* has been waning for various reasons. Since public schools in Brazil have a bad reputation, few middle-class parents send their children to the schools in the publicly owned *superquadra* but, rather, prefer to drive them to remote private schools.[72] The same applies for educational and sports facilities, which are mostly restricted to particular social groups and typically situated outside the *superquadra*.[73] Widespread car ownership, one of the city's fundamental planning principles, has thus further contributed to the demise of another basic principle—that of the self-contained neighborhood cell. In 1997, the Assambléia Legislativa of the Federal District of Brasília passed a law sanctioning the patroling of the *superquadras* by private security companies, the installation of surveillance cameras, and the setting up of bars prohibiting entrance to the public premises for foreign vehicles. While this clearly contradicts the idea of openness and accessibility—designer Lúcio Costa protested accordingly—at the same time the law prohibited the construction of walls and fences, quoting reasons of historic preservation.[74] Open access to the public land surrounding the buildings continues to be contested, but so far without the spatial consequences found in other Brazilian cities where the middle classes live almost exclusively in gated communities.

On the occasion of the city's fiftieth anniversary, the architectural critic Clifford Pearson prophesied an "architectural comeback."[75] Far from being outdated, he argued, Brasília's slab architecture might inspire cities such as São Paulo. Pearson's perspective is shared by many of his colleagues. Many aspects of Brasília's city planning that were criticized in the 1960s are now acclaimed. Recent observers have commended the "feel of Southern California" generated by the car culture in combination with outdoor living, and have even loved the "odd charm" of the numerous design failures such as the bombastic national cathedral.[76] There are also numerous new interprations of public life in the city. The art historian Jean-Louis Cohen called Brasília a "planning success story" and stressed that the stark black-and-white photographs on which the historical criticism of Brasília had relied are now being modified with "Brazilian color," embodied in open markets and ground-level stores that have opened up Costa's rigid separation of functions.[77] The historian Richard Williams has stressed that, contrary to the early visitors' Paris-inspired criticism, Brasília enables a certain form of civic life that reaches beyond the bourgeois tradition connected with the street café but is induced by a collective experience of monumentalism that in a positive way produces a sense of "shock."[78] The architect Matheus Gorovitz, on the other hand, has pointed out the existence of traditional forms of public life, as numerous locations, including churches and strip malls, have become the site of street celebrations related to soccer games, electoral campaigns, and carnival festivities.[79] His colleague Carlos Moreira Texeira has also stressed that rather than any form of civic performance, it is the landscape that constitutes the city's unique feel.[80] His argument is supported by the photographer Todd Eberle, who has celebrated the city's strange liveliness, as embodied on the one hand by the harsh geometry of the *superquadras* wedged between lush trees and a sky of spectacular clouds, and on the other hand by the visible dilapidations that give the city a humane appearance and soften the hard concrete edges.[81]

In Brasília the slab block paradigm is less eminent than sixty years ago. But unlike in Chicago, Paris, or Berlin, where mass housing developments are being demolished or redesigned, Brasília has followed a strategy of re-framing. Built with superior technology and protected by historic preservation laws, the Pilot Plan has attained the status of a European old town. Like the seventeenth-century quarters of Amsterdam and the palaces of Venice, it remains the city's most powerful symbolic image, despite having lost importance in everyday life. And like the old towns of Amsterdam and Venice, it is increasingly inhabited by the wealthy and educated. The city's attractivness might not only depend on its small size, temperate climate, and a crime rate seven times lower than that in São Paulo.[82] The inhabitants of the Pilot Plan, like those of Old Town Amsterdam and Venice, are also likely to value outstanding architecture and the daily experience of the past— in this case the history of the twentieth century rather than that of the early modern period.

While the openness of the site plan and the focus on accessible public spaces is still noticeable sixty years after the city's foundation, Brasília's apartment blocks have never lived up to the ideals of egalitarian mass housing. They were built along the lines of class division from the beginning, and over the years became more and more similar to the luxury condos in other countries such as Chicago's Millennium Center or Shanghai's Yanlord Gardens. They house the wealthy rather than the poor, they are situated in the city center rather than on the periphery, and they provide amenities far above the city's average. Among the privileged fifth of the population that does not have to live in substandard dwellings, the modernist slabs are more popular than ever. For them, however, they are no longer a symbol of hope for a better society, but merely constitute a rather mundane form of dwelling.

6 Mumbai—Mass Housing for the Upper Crust

The tower and the slum

Mumbai[1] challenges many preconceived ideas about serial mass housing. The city, which is a hotspot of tower block construction in India, provides an insight into the reciprocal relationship between the global concept of modernization and local conditions. The foremost feature here, compared to cities such as Paris or Berlin, is that, with very few exceptions, mass housing is inhabited by the privileged and not the marginalized. In a country where the overwhelming majority lives in utter poverty, privilege is of course relative. Any form of formal housing, much less facilities such as warm water or electricity, is accessible only for a minority. The standards of living enjoyed by the lower classes in Western countries, such as running water or a solidly built and self-contained apartment, are still out of reach for most Indians. The character of mass construction in Mumbai is determined by the fact that not even the cheapest formal house built by the state is affordable for the poor, since they are not even able to pay for the most basic maintenance. The great majority of the city's residents thus stand outside the housing market by definition, no matter how much it is subsidized. The modernist promise to provide equal housing standards for everyone was as prevalent in India as it was in the Soviet Union, Germany, or France. But unlike these countries, where the housing crisis was solved or at least mitigated as a result of state-driven programs, Mumbai's shortage is worse than ever. Demography played an important role. Unlike many cities in the north whose populations were stable or even shrinking, Mumbai's population has multiplied by almost ten since the 1960s.

Despite the numerous discrepancies, the discourses on modernization and mass housing that took place in these different cities are still comparable. India, like France or Germany, has a long tradition of state-driven response to the desolate conditions in which the majority is forced to live. Particularly in the decades following the country's

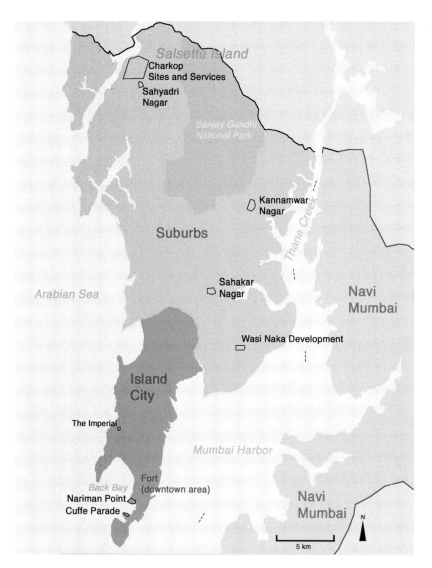

Salsette Island

Charkop
Sites and Services

Sahyadri
Nagar

Sanjay Gandhi
National Park

Kannamwar
Nagar

Suburbs

Thane Creek

Sahakar
Nagar

Arabian Sea

Navi
Mumbai

Wasi Naka Development

Island
City

The Imperial

Mumbai Harbor

Fort
(downtown area)

Back Bay

Nariman Point
Cuffe Parade

Navi
Mumbai

N

5 km

independence in 1947, socialist-inspired governments undertook repeated efforts to resolve the housing crisis and serial housing was part and parcel of this strategy. The main goal of improving the living conditions of the majority nonetheless clearly failed. Next to massive demographic growth and country-to-city migration that made the tower blocks appear like a drop in the ocean, the most quoted reasons are the lack of commitment among the political elites, the massive demographic growth, the high level of corruption, the power of the real-estate lobby, the inefficient bureaucracy, and global power relations hampering India's economic development. In light of these constraints, mass housing blocks attained a peculiar position within India's, and particularly Mumbai's, urban fabric. Symbolic of unfulfilled dreams about equity, they also stand for some of contemporary India's most salient challenges.

In Mumbai, unlike in Chicago or Paris, state-sponsored towers and slabs never fell from public grace—and at the same time never really succeeded. They never failed, since the better-maintained ones are continuously popular among the wealthier classes, and the worse ones, which actually look like Chicago's Robert Taylor Homes or Paris's Cité des Quattre-Mille—with leaking roofs, dysfunctional piping, failed elevators, and tenants below the poverty line—are still more solid than self-built huts or plastic sheets. On the other hand they never succeeded, since they barely mitigated the extreme housing shortage. Their impact in absolute numbers was nevertheless substantial. It is estimated that approximately 1 million individuals—around a tenth of the 10 million within Mumbai's city lines—live in the close to 200,000 apartments built by public agencies between 1947 and the early 1990s.[2] This might appear small in light of Mumbai's current 5 million plus inhabitants who live in informal housing, but it is still remarkable compared, for example, to the merely 20,000 public housing units built in Chicago, a city of 3.5 million, in post-war decades.[3]

Like in Paris, the policies that underlie Mumbai's serial housing were to a large extent inspired by the city's informal settlements, which residents, officials, and scholars usually refer to as slums. The proliferation of these encroachments in nearly every Mumbai neighborhood is one of the city's most striking features. Makeshift huts from wood and corrugated sheet iron seem to be everywhere, next to parks, industrial complexes, and railroad lines, and immediately adjacent to many middle-class buildings. Like in Paris or Brasília, there is also a direct relation to the tower blocks, since many slums started as temporary housing for construction laborers and later housed those who guarded and cleaned the towers. Mumbai's slums are highly diversified among the different layers of the urban underclass, but all types are growing. They were rare before independence, but have become ubiquitous since the 1960s.[4] Ironically, their growth was largest during the time when the municipal government attempted both vigorously and unsuccessfully to rid the city of them.

While the slum dwellers in the last thirty years have increasingly founded organizations to protect their rights, the government has displayed an ambiguous approach. There were many slum clearances from the 1960s onward, whereby inhabitants were driven out after promises to rehouse them in permanent structures that were never built. From the 1970s clearances continued, but the focus of official policy shifted on slum upgradation, whereby existing slums were improved through the provision of water, electricity, and trash service.[5] Given the disproportion between the number of slums and the amount of funding for these programs, the success was minimal and the great majority of slum dwellers were never affected. Other attempts to resolve the slum crisis by means of state control proved similarly ineffective, most prominently the cap on private land ownership, called the Urban Land Ceiling and Regulation Act (ULCA), which was valid from 1976 to 2007 and in theory provided for expropriations to build apartments for the poor, but was rarely enforced.[6] Next to the serial apartment block the slum thus constitutes Mumbai's other mass dwelling.

Mumbai—Mass Housing for the Upper Crust

6.2
The tower and the slum—
informal dwellings next to
upscale residences at
Nariman Point (Florian Urban,
2008)

A metropolis on seven islands

Mumbai, the state capital of Maharashtra, is India's largest urban agglomeration, with an estimated 12 million inhabitants in the greater city area and 19 million in the metropolitan region.[7] When India became independent in 1947, the Mumbai area counted approximately 2.8 million inhabitants and was relatively prosperous. The city profited from partition in the sense that it virtually held a monopoly on west coast shipping after the main competitor, Karachi, had become part of Pakistan. Next to the port, the city's main income was provided by the cotton textile industry, which employed half of the city's workforce in 1961 but has declined ever since—in 1996 only 40,000 of the one-time workforce of 250,000 textile workers was left.[8] Today's Mumbai is built more on information technology than manufacturing, and constitutes the country's financial hub. The city also supports the Bollywood movie industry, which is the largest in the world. The presence of both high-tech and low-tech industries makes Mumbai an extremely polarized city, even by Indian standards.

Construction policy is strongly influenced by the city's particular geography. Mumbai was originally built on several marshy islands off the coast of the Arabian Sea. They were gradually connected through landfills and now form a peninsula, which in its central area lies below sea level and is frequently flooded during the monsoon. The peninsula measures approximately 30 miles from its tip to the northern border of Greater Mumbai. The city center is situated in the southern part, on what used to be the original seven islands and is now known as the Island City. Here, the peninsula is only 1–5 miles wide. The part of the Arabian Sea (south)west of the Island City is called "Back Bay," although it is part of the open sea, in contrast to "Front Bay," the Mumbai Harbor that divides the Island City from the mainland. Historically, the center of Mumbai faced the harbor, but shifted to Back Bay over the course of the twentieth century. To the north, the peninsula broadens. Salsette Island, which is the northernmost portion of the Greater Mumbai city area and the connection between the Island City and the mainland, has an east–west extension of 12–15 miles and is separated from the mainland proper by the two branches of the Ulhas River that flow into the Arabian Sea: the Vasai Creek in the north and the Thane Creek in the east. The built area on Salsette Island—not one of the original seven islands—is commonly referred to as "the suburbs." The Mumbai city center is separated from the mainland by a bay, which is a continuation of the Thane Creek estuary and at its broadest part approximately 6 miles wide. The southern part of this bay is Mumbai Harbor. Although since the 1960s there have been proposals to link the city center with the mainland with a 6-mile-long-bridge, access to date is only possible through the bottleneck of the peninsula. Due to those geographical features, Mumbai had very limited options for growth. From the 1950s onward, the built-up area extended to the suburbs on Salsette Island. In the 1970s, there were numerous attempts at decentralization, and the city of Navi Mumbai (New Mumbai) was incorporated on the mainland across Mumbai Harbor. Today, the majority of the built-up area is on Salsette Island and on the mainland proper, and the old center on the Island City has a declining population rate. It nevertheless still houses the central business district and most commercial areas. This presents a continuous traffic problem. Real-estate prices in the Island City are skyrocketing, while masses of low-income workers are commuting from the suburban areas twice a day, bringing streets and railroads on the bottleneck of the peninsula to the brink of collapse. In most planning documents, the pressure of a booming population on Mumbai's limited land is deemed the main source of evil, accounting for the fact that the living conditions have been deteriorating steadily since 1939, when at least for the middle classes there had been more units available than tenants. Since the 1960s, it has been regularly stated that the city center is at its limit in terms of traffic and population and that decentralization is a major objective. An alternate view, espoused by planning bodies such as the National Commission on Urbanisation, points to the city's vibrancy and economic power, which have been both the source and effect of the demographic growth and deems it naïve to believe that migration could be stopped by political measures. Given the precariousness of the housing situation and the potential for high profits from land speculation, private developers and builders form a powerful lobby.[9]

As a result of the scarce land resources on the peninsula, Mumbai is unique in India with regard to its number of high-rises. Today there is barely a middle-class person who does not live in a multistory building. Before independence, heights were restricted to 23 meters, approximately the size of the nineteenth-century blocks in Paris or Berlin.[10] After independence, there were no specific limits to building heights, but during the era of state control residential buildings rarely exceeded five stories. This changed rapidly with economic liberalization and skyrocketing land prices in the 1990s. Currently, 50 stories are not unusual for classy apartment buildings in favorable locations.

Colonial precedents: the chawl and the apartment block

The history of mass housing in Mumbai goes back to the British colonial era and can be roughly divided into three phases. In the late nineteenth century, the city grew from a small trading post to an industrial hub and required the construction of cheap dwellings, which were provided by both private and public institutions. When India became independent, a state-driven housing policy was introduced, which with some modifications lingered on until the 1990s. During that period, public institutions built numerous mass housing projects for the low-income groups that shared many characteristics with the tower block estates in Paris, Chicago, and Berlin. With state control waning after the 1970s, India officially abolished the quasi-socialist economy, with its reliance on import subsidies and state planning, in the 1990s and paved the way toward a neoliberal market economy. The policy change paralleled Mumbai's development from a local industrial center to a global city and hub of India's thriving IT industry. The following subchapters will outline the characteristics of these three phases with regard to mass housing policy and introduce the most important developments spawned by them.

Mumbai's mass housing blocks grew from two different roots: the Western apartment block and the chawl. The former was first introduced in the 1930s with Mumbai's first modern housing in art deco style. Art deco sparked mostly four-story apartment buildings for the city's well to do, for example on the Back Bay reclamation area in the western downtown area. A typical development was the Shiv Shanti Bhavan compound on the Oval Maidan, which was started in 1934 and featured decorated façades. Art deco buildings also lined the 2-mile-long ocean-front boulevard on the Back Bay shore, which emulated Ocean Drive in Miami and was accordingly named Marine Drive (now officially N. S. C. Bose Road). They display simple elegance, combining steel, concrete, and brick. For the Indian elite, life in these representative buildings was a considerable adaptation to modern Western lifestyle. With regard to both style and program, art deco buildings were visible markers of the transition from Victorian city to modern cosmopolitan metropolis.

The chawls were the evil face of that transition. With the growth of the textile industry in the late nineteenth century, the city experienced an enormous influx of workers who settled in the overcrowded tenement neighborhoods north of the downtown Fort area. The chawls were the architectural response to the rapid industrial growth, and the Indian equivalent to the Glasgow tenement or the Berlin backyard building. They were one to four-story structures constructed from brick masonry and a load-bearing wooden framework and offering one-room dwellings with shared toilets and water cranes. Rooms were lined along a central corridor, as in a military camp. In fact, most chawl dwellers in the early years were single men from rural areas who shared rooms—the chawl only later housed entire families. Chawls were first built by private investors. By the turn of the twentieth century, occupation density rose to an appalling level, and state-built chawls became the British authorities' first public intervention in Mumbai's housing market. Two institutions commissioned the construction of chawls; firstly the Bombay Improvement Trust (BIT), founded in 1898 to improve poor hygienic conditions in the city after the bubonic plague epidemic, and secondly, the Bombay Development Department (BDD). Both became the most important players in Mumbai's city planning. Despite criticism of the soon overcrowded "trust chawls," which apparently offered no improvement on the desolate dwelling conditions of the working classes, the BIT continued its policy under different names throughout most of the twentieth century.[11] The Chandanwadi Chawls, built by the trust in 1904, are a typical example. Situated on the southern side of Chandanwadi Road in the working-class neighborhood of Kalbadevi, they consist of four-story brick masonry structures with courtyard spaces in between. Overcrowded as they still are, for Mumbai they continue to have a surprisingly large amount of open space. The BDD Chawls on GM Bhosale Marg in the Worli district north of downtown are situated in close proximity to numerous textile mills. Constructed in 1923, the buildings show an early form of industrialized construction: instead of bricks they are constructed from concrete blocks. The chawl typology continued to be used long after independence, and many of the state-built housing colonies of the 1960s featured similar one-room apartments with communal toilets lined up along long corridors. In the better cases, these buildings also had verandahs.

From independence to neoliberalism: housing in a mixed economy

Until the 1980s, economic policy in India had numerous similarities with socialism. Jawaharlal Nehru, Prime Minister from 1947 to 1964, in particular favored a high degree of state control over the economy and at the same time strongly supported industrialization. Economic objectives were formulated in five-year plans passed by the national Planning Commission. State-subsidized housing was part and parcel of this policy. With the Hindi slogan *roti kapda aur makaan* (food, clothing, and shelter), the national government declared its responsibility for the satisfaction of basic needs. Like many decolonizing nations, Indians had great hopes that misery and hunger would disappear along with the colonizers who had systematically destroyed the country's economic basis. Official documents of the 1950s abounded with commitments to progress and a human life, and many of these hopes were connected to rational planning. Alas, the hopes were not to be fulfilled. Along with state responsibility grew an inscrutable state bureaucracy fettered by increasing corruption. The

6.3
The Chandanwadi Chawls, built for industrial workers by the Bombay Improvement Trust in 1904 (Florian Urban, 2008)

approval of public housing was particularly slow—a contemporary observer complained that "a note must be signed by at least six officers before any worthwhile action can be thought of."[12] By the early 1960s, when the Nehru generation of state leaders who had led the struggle against the British left the political scene, the explicit commitments to equity and the greater good also quietly disappeared from the official rhetoric, and the younger generation became increasingly disappointed with their politicians.[13]

This was the time, however, when the housing programs that had been prepared and approved in the 1950s were first implemented. State control in India was never so tight as to allow for a comprehensive restructuring of the construction industry, as in the Soviet Union or East Germany. Rather, the government carried out individual social-housing projects whose scope was steadily declining—in 1947 housing investment consumed 7 percent of the state budget; in 1972 only 1 percent.[14] In Mumbai, this took place at various levels of government. The State Housing Board and its successor institution from 1976, the Maharashtra Housing and Area Development Authority (MHADA), were the largest providers—MHADA colonies can today be found all over the city. Much of its funding came from centrally directed national organizations, such as the Central Public Works Department. Public agencies such as Indian Oil, Indian Railway, or the Reserve Bank of India also regularly built housing estates for their employees.

The apartments built by the state authorities were mostly rental units. As in the Soviet Union, the People's Republic of China, or East Germany, India imposed tight rent control. In 1947, the rents were frozen at the 1940s level, and landlords had few possibilities to terminate a rental contract. As a consequence, private investment in housing plummeted, as did the amount of new rental contracts being concluded between private individuals. State organizations became the almost exclusive providers of new rental contracts.[15]

Housing projects in Mumbai, as in the whole of India, were specifically targeted to designated income groups. The government distinguished between "economically weaker sections" (EWS), "low-income group," (LIG) "middle-income group" (MIG), and "high-income group" (HIG). While EWS and LIG housing was built for industrial workers and daily-wage laborers, middle income group housing, still rather modest by Western standards, was typically inhabited by white-collar workers in government offices or private companies. Of the units built by the Housing Board/MHADA until 1986, 75 percent were for economically weaker sections (EWS) and low income groups (LIG).[16] In the 1960s, the state institutions that dealt with housing—Housing Boards, Municipal Corporations, Improvement Trusts, and Public Works Departments—developed numerous simple designs for LIG and MIG dwellings. The best were assembled in a publication by the National Buildings Organisation to guide future plans.[17] The four income group categories were distinguished mostly by square footage. Such serial design was hailed as an "intellectual principle" in the struggle against substandard housing.[18]

Even for the low-income group, the Housing Board/MHADA designed colonies with high planning standards. In the development Kannamwar Nagar (Kannamwar Colony), which was begun around 1970 in the northeastern suburb of Vikhroli, five-story buildings were assembled around a central square (*maidan* in Hindi). While there is an obvious similarity with the central square in Ebenezer Howard's garden city plan or Bruno

6.4
Kannamwar Nagar, built in the 1970s for "low income group" tenants (Florian Urban, 2008)

Taut's Horseshoe Colony in Berlin, the pattern can nevertheless be equally attributed to an Indian tradition. *Maidans* were laid out in Persian and Indian cities for centuries; the most famous Mumbai example is the Oval Maidan in the downtown Fort neighborhood. They are currently used for meetings, promenades, and, most importantly, for cricket games. In Kannamwar Nagar, the *maidan* has a circular shape and constitutes the colony's social and geographical center. The colony is separated from the rest of the city by the six-lane Eastern Express Highway, which has to be crossed on foot bridges to reach the Vikhroli suburban train station at about thirty minutes' walking distance. The geographical situation reinforces the feel of a secluded, self-contained neighborhood.

The quality of architecture and planning in Kannamwar Nagar and other colonies was high, and they offered significantly better living conditions than the slums in which the low-income groups usually lived. From the very beginning, this disparity created a pressure on the state's housing strategies. On the one hand it made the administration vulnerable to all kinds of corruption—theoretically the new tenants were supposed to be selected through a lottery. On the other, it created an informal housing market for the sale or passing on of rental contracts, and the developments that were originally conceived for industrial workers were gradually appropriated by middle-class residents, including government employees and other white-collar workers. In the late 1980s, it was discovered that of the approximately 75,000 dwellings that the Housing Board/MHADA built for "economically weaker sections" and "low-income groups" between 1952 and 1986, about 40 percent were occupied by higher-income groups who had bought out the original occupants. The transfer of a rental contract for money was technically illegal, but widely practiced, since particularly for poorer families in cases of financial emergency, apartments were often their only valuable good. The amount of money paid was comparable to the market price of a similar apartment.[19]

While the design and planning of these mass housing colonies was widely praised, maintenance became increasingly problematic. For the state authorities, it was politically unviable to raise rents, which upon completion of the colonies had been fixed at a more or less nominal level and which were never sufficient to cover even the most necessary repairs. The average resident of an old and dilapidated building in 2006 paid 100 rupees rent per month—2.5 US dollars.[20] The Housing Board/MHADA therefore constantly had to invest in maintenance, and still could not prevent progressive dilapidation.

Approximately one third of the Housing Board/MHADA's more than 90 colonies were conceived for the middle-income group from the beginning. An example is Sahakar

6.5
Middle-income-group home on Road No. 4 in Sahakar Nagar (Florian Urban, 2008)

Nagar I (Cooperative Colony I) in the southern suburbs, which is also known as the Shell Colony, because at some point apartments were preferentially allocated to Shell employees.[21] The development, which was begun in 1976, is composed of different building types, including one-story garden pavilions and mostly three-story apartment buildings surrounded by greenery. To date, it is mostly inhabited by government officials and middle-rank employees of large corporations, who cherish the quiet neighborhood, conveniently located ten minutes from the suburban train station. The colony has the feel of a European garden suburb.

An example of a low-income-group colony is Sahyadri Nagar, built by MHADA in the early 1990s and situated in the northern Charkop neighborhood. It was built for government-employed construction laborers who were migrants from the Satara district in Maharashtra.[22] Sahyadri Nagar was composed of five-story buildings with 30 or 60 units per building. Façade designs were similar to the middle-income-group developments, only the units were slightly smaller. Sizes varied between 24, 26, and 40 square meters.

Other public institutions built similar colonies, such as the Mumbai Port Trust Colony in Wadala (East)[23] and the Mudran Press Colony in Andheri (West).[24] Both are situated in the suburbs and were begun in the 1970s for employees of the respective agencies, who usually had to move out if they quit their jobs or retired. The former was reserved for lower-grade employees of the Mumbai Port Trust and the latter for employees of the printing company that produced state publications.

1993–present: the state as facilitator of housing

The early 1990s marked a change in Indian housing policy. In 1991, the state-controlled mixed economy was abandoned for the neoliberal New Economic Policy (NEP). Deregulation had slowly begun in the late 1970s and has continued to increase since then. The 1991 legislation was a consequence of a continuously deficient state budget, which had brought the country to the brink of bankruptcy. The new doctrine defined the state as a facilitator rather than a provider of housing, and private actors were assigned increasing significance. State power over private landholdings was gradually removed. In 2007, the aforementioned Urban Land and Ceiling Regulation Act (ULCRA) was revoked, which had limited the size of privately owned land and provided a legal framework for expropriations—critics had repeatedly pointed out that it had never been efficiently implemented. While construction increasingly followed market rules and building regulations became more investor-friendly, the government did not fully withdraw its responsibility for the housing sector, but rather retained its influence on various levels. It also promoted large-scale projects and negotiated private–public partnerships on all levels, from the development of upscale colonies to slum redevelopment projects. Rent control, the state's other major leverage on the housing market, has so far stayed in place, but has come under increasing political pressure.

In the following years, most state-subsidized housing projects, be they the MHADA colonies or the employee housing by public institutions such as the Mumbai Port Trust, were converted into housing cooperatives. The state thus indirectly acknowledged the main shortcoming of its rental projects—poor maintenance. Unable to keep up with the endless repairs resulting from shoddy construction, government authorities transferred ownership to Cooperative Housing Societies, of which the inhabitants became shareholders—basically tenant-owners. Being granted property almost for free, they were at the same time burdened with the high cost of maintenance, which turned out to be a multiple of the nominal rent that they had paid so far. Those who were unable to afford it had to sell their apartments. While many were forced to return to the slum dwellings that they had once escaped, they at least profited from the sales. The wealthier tenants who could afford to stay as cooperative members mostly decided to redevelop their colonies, meaning that the old buildings were torn down and new ones were erected instead. All of the colonies described earlier—Kannamwar Nagar, Sahakar Nagar, and many others—have recently been converted into cooperatives and will be redeveloped in the near future.[25] This could be financed through the high land prices. The new buildings are higher and denser, and, selling or renting the additional apartments at market rate, generate a considerable profit for the housing cooperatives. While often presented as a win-win situation for both the state and the tenants-turned-owners, the situation is better characterized as a win-much-or-win-very-little: the wealthier tenants who could afford to stay and profit from the redevelopment gained much, while the poorer ones who moved out gained significantly less. At the same time, this process was a flat rejection of the goals of equity formulated three decades earlier: reducing slums and providing similar housing standards for all.

Considerably more controversy was sparked by the new model of developer-based slum removal, which had been in preparation since the early 1990s, and whose most important institutional body was the Slum Redevelopment Authority (SRA), established in 1995. These projects are thus colloquially known as "SRA schemes."[26] A private investor is granted property and development rights to a slum and in return commits to providing free apartments to the slum dwellers. Of course this is only possible through densification—not only the substitute dwellings for the slum dwellers have to fit on the former slum plot, but also a number of additional units, mostly luxury apartments, that the investor sells at market rate and thus uses to finance the entire enterprise.

SRA schemes are made possible through what had already been introduced in 1967 and what is currently the most powerful substance of the state's role as a facilitator: the concept of the Floor Space Index (FSI). The FSI is the ratio between floors and space and thus characterizes how densely a certain area is populated. A high FSI is dependent either on the lack of open spaces or on particularly high buildings or both. In Mumbai, as in all booming cities, land is a scarce resource, and the shortage is exacerbated in the Island City. In a free market situation, investors would thus build as densely and as high as possible in the most desired downtown areas. The municipal authorities, on the other hand, restrict FSI in order to guarantee minimum standards of light and ventilation. The SRA schemes now grant investors additional FSI, and thus additional profit to be made from the extra apartments.

A typical example is the twin tower development, The Imperial, in the downtown Tardeo district, built on a former mill area west of Pandit Madan Moyan Malviya Road.

Mumbai—Mass Housing for the Upper Crust

Designed by the famous Hafeez Contractor for the Shapoorji Pallonji Group, the project is, on the one hand, comprised of two 50-story high-rise buildings with aluminum-swathed façades that include a swimming pool, a club, a carwash, nine levels of parking in the basement, and a supermarket, and, on the other hand, next to the towers, several austere six-story concrete blocks to house the 2,500 families that used to live in self-built huts on the plot.

The Imperial exemplifies another main characteristic of Mumbai's mass housing: in no other context are the two architectural types that grew out of modernist design—the luxury condo and the mass dwellings for the poor—so closely connected. While Chicago's Lake Shore Drive Apartments and Robert Taylor Homes are separated by 10 miles and an entire universe, in Mumbai there are often only a few feet between rags and riches. In both cities the separated worlds are economically connected. But in Mumbai, unlike in Chicago, the economic connection also entails spatial contiguity—a situation that many wealthy residents pragmatically accept for the convenience of having their drivers and housekeepers live close by. In their eyes, projects such as The Imperial also achieve the impossible: they house slum dwellers "for free" by relying on market forces without cost from the state and at the same time cater to the market segment that is currently growing fastest in Mumbai: residences for the wealthiest 5 percent of the population.

A brilliant solution to the housing crisis? Hardly. As valuable as a new apartment might be for a slum dweller, the new combination of high-end and low-end mass housing has numerous conceptual shortcomings. First and foremost, the strategy only works for selected downtown locations, where the land prices have been skyrocketing since the 1980s and are currently high enough to finance both redevelopment and rehousing the poor. In less favorable locations, where most slum dwellings are located, the model is unfeasible, because the home buyer is unwilling or unable to carry the added cost. Secondly, there are the deficiencies of a system where corruption is rampant and the power gap between a professional investor and an illiterate slum dweller is wide: there are no efficient controls to guarantee that all families who used to live on the plot really are rehoused, and many SRA schemes are overshadowed by debates about whether or not the slum dwellers really consented to the redevelopment. And finally, it is questionable from an equity point of view why the state, by granting additional FSI, should offer the opportunity for unequal profit—after all, a slum dweller receives a small apartment, while the investor's profit is incomparably higher. To counteract these side effects, critics propose self-redevelopment rather than investor-driven redevelopment—the slum dwellers, who are often highly organized, should form their own redevelopment firms and thus profit themselves from the additional FSI.[27]

In their new role as facilitators of housing, state authorities also introduced another tool: the concept of Transferable Development Rights (TDR). TDR are also an indirect subsidies involving a higher FSI, but unlike the increased density granted to the developers of The Imperial, they are, as the name suggests, transferable. That means that an investor who provides free housing for slum dwellers in return receives the right to develop a certain number of residential units at a higher FSI, which he can use anywhere in the city north of where the substitute housing is built. The north–south clause aims to decongest the Island City and increase density in the suburban north.

6.7
Wasi Naka Colony for
relocated slum dwellers
(Florian Urban, 2008)

The shortcomings of the TDR strategy are best illustrated by the Wasi Naka Colony in the Chembur district, which is sometimes referred to as Shastri Nagar.[28] Starting in 2002, the Anik Development Corporation began to build high-rise apartments for thousands of slum dwellers relocated from different parts of the city who had had to leave because of road construction. A total of 25,000 units was planned. For the developer, the investment paid off. Given that the Wasi Naka Colony is located quite far south on the peninsula, the Transferable Development Rights generated here can be used in some of Mumbai's most profitable locations, including, for example, the new business center, the Bandra-Kurla complex. For the slum dwellers, however, the new homes are a considerable burden. They are badly served by public transportation and far from most work places. In addition, it is safe to say that the new high-rises are worse abodes than most slum dwellings. The cheap megablocks, each with 8 stories and 64 units of 24 square meters each, are crammed together at a distance of less than 5 meters, to the extent that they block any light or ventilation. In the case of dilapidation, which is already noticeable, there is not even enough space to set up scaffolding. The inhabitants are barred from many of their traditional sources of income,

Mumbai—Mass Housing for the Upper Crust

since it is considerably more difficult to convert a high-rise apartment into a shoemaker's workshop or scrap yard than a corrugated sheet metal hut, and, probably the worst aspect, contrary to the developers' promises, most residents do not even have running water in their apartments and are forced to carry each and every drop up as many as six flights of stairs.[29] No wonder housing activists denounce the Wasi Naka scheme as inhuman and some would rather see it "dynamited."[30]

While the strengthening of market forces has so far not succeeded in alleviating the housing shortage that the planned economy had not been able to resolve, the goal of equity has been gradually abandoned. The most palpable architectural manifestation of the new polarization are the two types of tower blocks—high-rise condos such as The Imperial for the wealthy and zero-amenities blocks like the Wasi Naka Colony for former slum dwellers. While tower-and-slab architecture remains the prevailing paradigm, its modifications according to a more and more divergent class structure reflect the disappearance of the egalitarian ideas that had once triggered its creation.

"High-rise slums for the rich": the Back Bay land reclamation

Mumbai's most debated mass housing developments are at the same time its most famous ones: Nariman Point and Cuffe Parade, built on land that was reclaimed from the Back Bay. They are atypical in every respect: they were designed for the rich rather than the poor and they are situated not on the periphery but in the very center, on the western shore of the Island City's southern tip, facing the Arabian Sea. Beginning in the 1920s, Mumbai followed a policy of land reclamation to increase its limited downtown spaces. The Back Bay reclamation scheme was originally planned in the 1920s, envisaging the construction of a sea wall along the foreshore of Back Bay from Chowpatty Beach to Colaba Point.[31] It was halted in the 1930s and only resumed in 1958. By 1975, about 200 additional acres had been reclaimed, and two high-rise areas were developed with luxurious apartment blocks and office towers. Nariman Point was begun in 1967, at a time when the debate over the *grands ensembles* in Paris was in full swing and criticism of Berlin's tower blocks was about to start. Cuffe Parade followed in the mid-1970s. Nariman Point, a residential and business district composed of rectilinear slabs with concrete framing and glass infill, was soon known as "the Manhattan of Mumbai." Eventually more than 40 skyscrapers, averaging 15 floors each, were packed together in a small area. The only low-rise building was the National Centre for the Performing Arts. To date, the area features some of the city's tallest buildings, including landmarks such as the Indian Express Building (1967–70) by the Delhi-based American architect Joseph Stein, and the five-star hotel Oberoi. Next to office towers are consulates and luxurious condominiums. Cuffe Parade, situated half a mile south of Nariman Point across a small bay, consists of luxury apartment blocks crammed together with little open space in between.

Criticism was relentless from the very beginning. The area was called "India's biggest urban fraud,"[32] "a concrete jungle . . . [and] new hell for the nouveau riche to stew in their

6.8
Cuffe Parade (Florian Urban,
2008)

own juices," and a "symbol of rampant commercialism."[33] Some arguments against the mass housing project for the rich were particular to the Mumbai context. The Back Bay reclamation was called a "moronic metaphor of simulated occidental design"[34] and censured for using public funds for land reclamation that subsidizes the rich.[35] Other points of criticism paralleled those used against tower blocks in Paris or Berlin—mainly the lack of sensitivity for the context and the deficient planning. First, open space and traffic solutions were unsatisfactory. Observers spoke of an area "choked with an array of high-rises,"[36] and a "mushrooming monstrosity" where pedestrian circulation was neglected.[37] Second, the scheme was seen as being at odds with the decades-long efforts to decentralize the over-crowded Island City, which had culminated in the creation of Navi Mumbai. Critics remarked that the Back Bay reclamation merely extended the old business center and attracted 300,000 daily commuters to an area already at the brink of collapse, turning it into a "chaotic market place during the day and an eerie ghost town during the night."[38] Third, the elevator buildings with big glass façades were considered an obscene waste of national resources in the light of millions of slum dwellers, and scarily dysfunctional for a country with hot summers and frequent blackouts.[39] And fourth, the neighboring community was equally worse off. The shore between what was now Nariman Point and Cuffe Parade for centuries had been inhabited by fishermen (Koli), whose settlements ended up wedged in between the towers.[40] As a consequence of the ongoing criticism, it was decided in the mid-1980s to abandon further reclamation projects.[41] The popularity of the Back Bay high-rises among those who could afford them nevertheless remained untouched, and both Nariman Point and Cuffe Parade continue to be highly desired neighborhoods.

Why is there no prefabrication in India?

Among the most outstanding features of Mumbai's serial housing projects in comparison to those in Moscow, Berlin, or Paris is the almost complete absence of prefab construction. As in the whole of India, Mumbai's towers and slabs were almost all built in situ. Why is there no prefabrication in India? As a matter of fact, there is. But the reasons why it never became widespread can be found in a number of local factors.

During the 1960s and 1970s, prefabrication was repeatedly proposed as a means to accelerate and economize the production of housing for the masses and arrive at higher standards for the poor—more or less a line of thought similar to that was also at work among progressive European theorists.[42] There were even direct connections between slab-style prefab housing in Eastern Europe and India. In the early 1970s, the Ford Foundation financed the adaptation of a prefab panel system developed by the engineer Zenon Zielinski.[43] Born and educated in Poland, Zielinski had directed the Department for Design and Standardization of Precast and Prestressed Structures at the Industrial Building Research and Design Office in Warsaw from 1950 to 1962, the time when Poland embarked on the gargantuan enterprise to rebuild many of its war-ravaged cities with prefab structures. He emigrated in 1962 and became a consultant for the Ford Foundation in 1965. From 1967 to 1971, he developed prefab schemes in Calcutta and subsequently established the design firm UCOPAN in Montreal, Canada, where he produced panel systems for Canada, Indonesia, and Iran. Zielinski's UCOPAN (Universal Concrete Panel System) was first used by the Calcutta Metropolitan Planning Organisation for a new development in the city of Durgapur near Calcutta. Approximately 200 units were built for the low-income group. The dwellings were simple: one of the three types did not even have toilets inside the apartments. Zielinski's system was based on prefab panels of 292 × 90 centimeters with a maximum weight of 360 kilos that could be used equally for walls, roofs, and floors. The relatively small size compared with similar systems in Russia or France was specifically designed to facilitate their manual handling with low-tech levers and pulleys. This form of prefabrication also avoided the difficulties of transportation in a low-infrastructure country: the panels could be produced on-site.

6.9
Universal Concrete Panel System (UCOPAN), developed 1967–71 by Zenon Zielinski for the Calcutta Metropolitan Planning Organisation (Zenon Zielinski)

Prefabrication nevertheless remained an exception in India. There are three major reasons. First, there was no authority influential enough to implement a Soviet-style comprehensive industrialization of the construction industry. Second, and perhaps more important, the country abounded with cheap labor. Since there was never a shortage of labor in India, the need to economize was not felt. And third, India lacked technological infrastructure. M. B. Achwal, professor of architecture at the University of Baroda, in 1971 put it bluntly: Since construction in India is "not an industry but a chaotic trade . . . it will be a futile exercise to try to introduce too sophisticated materials and methods."[44] Currently, the transportation of prefab components exceeds the costs for an in situ building; the relation is exacerbated since an additional 15 percent tax is added if panels are cast in a centralized plant.[45]

Contrary to other countries, prefab construction is therefore used for the wealthy rather than the poor. Examples include the Amboli Cooperative Housing Society (1969) for

6.10
Prefab construction for luxury
apartments: Petit Hall (1967) in
the Malabar Hill district
(Florian Urban, 2008)

the middle-income group, a series of seven-story apartment blocks in the suburban Andheri (West) neighborhood, and two of the three upscale skyscrapers, Petit Hall (1967) in the posh Malabar Hill area. In both projects, prefabrication was chosen for its higher stability and better waterproofing compared to site-built buildings.[46]

As the chapter on Shanghai will show, the hesitant acceptance of prefabrication in India initially paralleled that in China. In both countries, site-built houses appeared as a consequence of low technology, abundance of cheap labor, shortage of resources, and a strong state. There were nonetheless significant differences. Once its infrastructure was improved, that is, from the 1970s onward, China began to make use of prefabrication. Since the country subsequently retained certain socialist aspects that made prefabrication profitable—namely large-scale planning and centralized decision-making—prefab construction was continued under market capitalism. In India, on the other hand, poor infrastructure and slow administration lingered. Prefabrication therefore offered no significant advantage in increasing construction efficiency but rather afforded higher quality. The very technology that was proposed as a means to house the poor became instead a constructive improvement for the rich.

Alternative approaches: sites and services

An account of Mumbai's mass housing would be incomplete without mentioning the efforts to house the poor in architectural types that were not serial apartment blocks. Since in the Indian context even Western-style affordable housing was not affordable for the majority, more pragmatic solutions had to be sought.

One of the more successful was the Sites and Services approach. Government authorities would provide slum dwellers sites—designated plots to build their own houses—and services—water, electricity, sewerage, paved roads, and trash service. The slum dwellers, then, could build their own houses according to their meager means—often also from bricks and corrugated sheet iron—but would be considerably better off than in their old informal houses.

Financed by the World Bank, the Low Income Group Shelter Program, usually referred to as the Sites and Services Program, was officially launched in 1985. Together with the Slum Upgradation Program, it was part of the World Bank's Bombay Urban Development Project. Influenced by an international discourse on informal abodes that was most prominently advanced by John Turner, Indian housing experts increasingly propagated incremental self-help solutions and the use of indigenous materials.[47] The World Bank program was started in 1985 and completed by 1994.[48] It provided 85,000 sites, each for one family. Typical examples are the Sites and Services projects in Charkop and Gorai, in Mumbai's distant northern suburbs.[49] Despite the usual difficulties with the choice of beneficiaries, the allocation of plots, and scarce revenues from new tenants that barely amortized the infrastructure cost, the project came to be widely viewed as a success.[50] The project had supplied a greater amount of units in a shorter time than most others before. However, it still did not meet the required scale to end slum dwelling in Mumbai, and land

6.11
Plan of the Sites and Services
project in the Gorai district
(courtesy of Collective
Research Initiatives Trust –
CRIT, Mumbai)

was becoming scarce even on the city's northern periphery. The World Bank thus chose to discontinue the program. Critics pointed to four main flaws. First, many considered one-story buildings a waste of space in a city with such scant land resources, and real estate developers pressured the state not to give slum dwellers land for free. Second, to many who did not pay attention to the paved roads and the site planning, the self-built neighborhood at first glance still looked like a slum. Third, the project received only lukewarm support from the state, partially because it lacked the glamour that both politicians and engineers needed—there were no big contracts to be signed. And fourth, even for the many families who had been fortunate enough to be allocated a site, their self-built dwelling did not become a long-term solution. Like the low-income residents of state-sponsored mass housing they were often forced to sell their dwelling in times of financial hardship, since it constituted their only valuable possession. While for those who could afford to stay the Sites and Services projects continue to be thriving communities, the state authorities increasingly trusted the market to relieve the ongoing housing shortage.

Standardized upscale dwellings

In Mumbai, unlike in Chicago, Berlin, or Paris, the image of modernist apartment blocks has remained generally positive ever since the first buildings were completed. To a large extent, this has been a consequence of the country's extreme economic polarization. The large majority of the population is too poor to live in formal dwellings at all, and even the wealthy have hardly ever experienced an alternative to multistory dwelling. There is little evidence of preferences connected with a certain architectural type. Differentiations are based only on apartment size and amenities, the quality of construction, and the location—the most desired neighborhoods lie in the downtown area on the western shores of the Island City with a view to the sea.

In Mumbai, there has been nothing comparable to the "old town renaissance" in Western countries, despite the fact that the city features a considerable number of early-twentieth-century buildings, particularly in the downtown area.[51] Some of the upper-class Victorian houses continue to be home to wealthy people, but as a rule of thumb, whoever can afford it, moves into a high-rise apartment—the higher the better.[52] The most exclusive ones stand in Malabar Hill and Cumbala Hill, both located on the western shore of the Island City. Buildings with thirty stories and more offer a broad view over Back Bay. The area has the city's highest real estate prices and is home to Mumbai's wealthy, including a number of Bollywood celebrities.

The Indian story is still related to other countries. The changing international discourse on modernist mass housing was also noticeable in Mumbai, albeit with less emphasis. From the 1960s onward, one read about the hope-inspiring "scale of the new construction" and the trust in Corbusian vertical buildings and comprehensive plans to order the chaotic growth.[53] Many of these ideas were as utopian as their counterparts in Europe and North America. In the same way, the anti-modernist criticism that in the late 1960s tore to shreds St. Louis's Pruitt-Igoe development and West Berlin's Märkisches Viertel reverberated in India, where it was uttered with an undertone critical toward Western approaches. In a 1982 response to Peter Blake's famous anti-modernist pamphlet "Form Follows Fiasco," Indian author Abu Nadeem drew numerous parallels with the modernist fiascos in India.[54] The author censured the "uncritical imitation" of Western modernism—particularly that of the "un-Indian" skyscraper that "destroys human interaction" and does not pay due to India's realities marked by a low level of motorization and modern technology. The only solution, for him, is a rediscovery of traditional Indian architecture—a parallel to the calls for strengthening local traditions in Europe and North America from the same period. Others lamented the unimaginative layout of the state-sponsored developments in the 1970s and the lack of concern for the living environment in what they deemed the city's "new slums."[55] And the struggle against forced relocations of slum dwellers often fed into a wholesale refutation of top-down planning and "Western plans" that paralleled similar lines of criticism in the West.[56]

Why, then, one might ask, did the criticism not lessen the popularity of modernist mass housing? The first reason for the ongoing lure of the towers is Mumbai's socio-spatial continuity over the decades. The textile industry left the city in the 1980s, but unlike in New

York, Berlin, or Paris, the late-nineteenth- and early-twentieth-century working-class neighborhoods continued to be overcrowded and inhabited by poor people. A Mumbai developer would have a hard time refurbishing an early-twentieth-century chawl in the way that his counterparts did with a New York loft or a Berlin tenement. He would not be able to evict the inhabitants who over the generations have been entangled in a maze of subtenancies and are still protected by effective rent control laws. He also would hardly find a wealthy person to live in such a renovated chawl—few who have a choice would opt for a noisy, filthy neighborhood clogged with hagglers, vegetable mongers, and *vada pav* stands and few would like to share the narrow road space with endless crowds of trucks, taxis, push carts, and ox drivers.

Second, as in many poor countries, modernist architecture in India lacked its technological *raison d'être* and was thus rather read as a signifier of lifestyle. Simple geometry and standardized parts could not be justified by the argument that they lead to greater efficiency due to the use of machines. Given that labor was cheap, India's skyscrapers were built with a minimum degree of industrialization and a maximum use of manual labor. In the words of an Indian architect writing in 1971:

> the simplest mechanical aids are unknown. Bricks are carried to the fifth floor by women workers in a basket on their heads. Human labor is cheap and a donkey or bullock is still the most economical mode of transport . . . Material manufacturing, stock and supply [are] always uncertain. Time is of no importance since there is plenty of it.[57]

Many specificities of modernist mass housing are therefore a product of design rather than technological rationalization and retain their attraction on aesthetic terms.

Third, the semantic framework that tied modernism to a national project was particularly strong and is, albeit less predominantly, still noticeable. Starting with the 1930s art deco buildings, Mumbai's modernist dwellings implicitly carried an anti-colonialist message. In contrast to the orientalizing buildings with domes and pseudo-Indian ornamentation that the British built at the turn of the twentieth century, modernism was connected not only to progress and development but also to national freedom and recognition as an equal by the Western world.

As a result of the failure to mitigate the housing shortage, mass housing in Mumbai never housed the masses. Even the poorly maintained MHADA colonies with their crumbling façades, leaking roofs, and failing water pipes are the home of a comparably privileged minority. The idea of equal housing, inherent in India's serial apartment blocks as much as in those in Paris or Berlin, never ceased to clash with the country's extreme social inequality. At the same time, the country was always spatially mixed to an extent unimaginable in Europe or North America—in none of the cities portrayed in this book are the rich and the poor living in such close proximity. With the effects of state-sponsored homogenization neutralized by demographic growth, bureaucratic inefficiency, and a powerful real estate lobby, Mumbai did not experience the painful end of its welfare-state housing policy—in a way, it had never seen its beginning. This holds true even despite the fact that in India, as in China and Russia, and unlike the US or Brazil, a significant degree of state influence over the housing market was retained even after the turn toward market-driven policies. While the majority of Mumbai residents continue to be housed informally, the two distinct types that grew from the modernist dream of housing the masses—the cheap apartment block and the luxury condominium—serve the different strata of the new Indian upper class.

7 Prefab Moscow

The industrialization of the Soviet construction industry

A classic view of mass housing apartments is shown on Russian television every New Year's Eve. In Eldar Ryazanov's 1975 movie *Ironia sud'by* (Irony of Fate), a man wakes up in what he believes to be his bedroom and finds himself in the company of a woman he has never seen before. It turns out that after a vodka-soaked night and an unplanned flight he has mistaken his Moscow tower-block apartment for a similar one in Leningrad, which happens to be situated on a street with the same name. The film is a typical comedy of errors and a not-too-subtle satire on drab standardized apartment blocks, where not only streets, buildings, and entrance doors are of the same type, but equally bathrooms, furniture, and apartment keys. The film ridicules the state-sponsored, one-size-fits-all architecture in a far more open way than one would expect to be tolerated under a socialist regime, and at the same time offers a tongue-in-cheek portrait of the average Soviet living environment.

Standardized housing blocks were indeed more widespread than any other building type, following an unprecedented wave of residential construction started by the Khrushchev administration in the 1950s. The new buildings were almost entirely assembled from prefabricated parts. In the 1970s, the Soviet authorities proudly declared that half of the industrialized housing construction in the world was carried out in their country.[1] When the Russian Federation in 1991 emerged from the disintegrated Soviet Union, mass-produced prefab buildings constituted half a billion of its 2.8 billion square meters of housing.[2] Like in other socialist countries, the shabby apartment block, decaying almost since its completion, not only stands for the Soviet Union's peculiar housing policy but also for daily life under the "dictatorship of the proletariat."[3]

When the ambitious Soviet construction program kicked off, there was a dire need for housing. Since the nineteenth century the urban population had risen steadily. By the

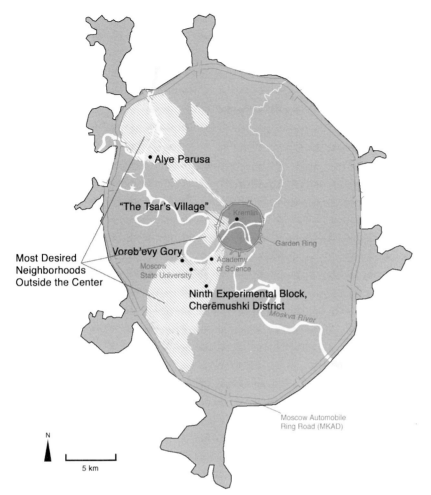

1950s, the living space for the average Soviet city dweller was less than in the 1920s, and the country was facing a housing shortage that is unimaginable in most industrialized countries today.[4] The square meters per capita decreased from 8.2 in 1926 to a lamentable 7.4 in 1955.[5] Given that these figures represent a national average and included kitchens, bathrooms, and corridors, many had much less personal space. For the Soviet leaders, there was only one solution to this situation: increase the efficiency of construction at all costs. And they were intent on restructuring the entire industry to achieve their goals.

The Soviet Union had been among the pioneers of industrialized construction. In the 1920s, architects such as Moisei Ginsburg, Andrei Burow, and Boris Blokhin carried out numerous projects, and Stalin's oppression of the architectural avant-garde from the early 1930s did not completely stifle experiments with this new technology.[6] During the Stalinist era, however, residential construction was mostly carried out in a traditional manner. Neoclassical multistory buildings with thick brick walls, spacious apartments, and orna-mented façades were built for a privileged few and did little to relieve the exacerbated housing shortage among average citizens.

It was Nikita Khrushchev who triggered the turn toward industrialization. In 1951, when he was still the party leader of the Moscow region, he promoted the incorporation of the Architectural Planning Directorate, where a consortium of architects developed low-cost construction.[7] When he succeeded Stalin as Head of State in 1953, he pushed housing to the top of the agenda. On the basis of sheer need, he bluntly rejected calls for higher standards and famously asked: "Do you build a thousand adequate apartments or seven hundred good ones? And would a citizen rather settle for an adequate apartment or wait ten to fifteen years for a very good one?"[8] In that respect, Khrushchev's mass housing program was a conscious trade-off: apartments were distributed more widely among the population, but at the lowest possible quality.[9] In December 1954, the Moscow Union Conference of the Construction Trade promoted type-based construction under the motto "better, faster, and cheaper."[10] A year later the Central Committee passed a resolution in which it called for a "Soviet architecture of natural simplicity, austere in its forms, and economical" and criticized the Stalinist buildings as too ornate and too costly.[11] And at the Twentieth Party Convention in February 1956, where Khrushchev promoted de-Stalinization, he also established the *Gosgrazhdanstroi* (*Gosudarstvennoye grazhdanskoye stroitel'stvo*—State Committee for Civic Construction), which was to control a process of standardization.[12]

The first *domostroitel'nyie kombinaty* (DSK, state-owned residential construction companies) were set up in the late 1950s, starting the production of serially prefabricated homes. The design schemes had been produced since 1951 in the Architectural Planning Directorate instigated by Khrushchev.[13] The engineer Vitali Lagutenko (1904–67), chief engineer of the planning directorate and a zealot of prefab design, guided Khrushchev's efforts to increase construction efficiency.[14] Lagutenko designed several series of mass-produced housing types that were subsequently built in large numbers all over the country. He thus made new apartments available to a large share of the Soviet population for the first time. In 1962, 98 percent of Moscow's new apartments corresponded to the Directorate's specifications and showed a distinct aspect.[15] They were five-story apartment buildings, composed of repetitive sections that could be combined to form buildings of any length. Each section had a stairwell to access four apartments per landing—there were no long corridors. One of the most famous creations that followed that type was the K-7 series, a five-story walk-up. In these buildings, a two-room unit had 44 square meters and included a small entrance hall, a 6-square-meter kitchen, and a cubicle bathroom with a 1.2-meter-long "sitting bathtub" that was assembled at the factory and only had to be connected to the main pipes on the construction site.

The mass-produced, five-story walk-up of the 1950s and 1960s, and particularly the K-7 buildings, is known as *khrushchëvka* (Khrushchev building, plural *khrushchëvki*). In the beginning, they were made from bricks, but the most popular construction method soon became the on-site assemblage from prefabricated concrete panels, known as big panel construction. According to Lagutenko's schedule, such a *panyel'ny dom* (panel house) could be assembled without mortar and topped out in 12 days. Construction was designed to be shoddy, mainly because the buildings were meant to be temporary and demolished in the following decades when the Soviet government was supposed to provide its citizens with better apartments. For the so-called *snosimye serii* (disposable series) a life span of 25 years was projected. There were also the longer-lasting *nesnosimye serii* (non-disposable series), but even these structures were built from comparatively cheap, low-quality materials. Given the continuing need for housing, many of these buildings of course linger to date.

The motto "better, faster, and cheaper" hardly left any room for debates over high-rise versus low-rise, mixed use versus functional separation, or historical versus modern buildings. It seems that both politicians and architects were happy about every additional square meter of residential space. In light of rising demand, the building size was increased as much as the latest technology permitted. By the end of the 1960s, the average apartment block had 11 stories.[16] Built under the Brezhnev regime, these newer and higher apartment towers, often with balconies, elevators, and separate toilets, are also known as *brezhnevki*. In a country as sparsely populated as the Soviet Union, high-rises were a matter of

7.2
Khrushchëvka in Moscow, Ulitsa Malye Kamenshchiki, Building no. 18 (Natalya Soukhova, 2008)

technological efficiency rather than economy of space. Under the system of production set up by Lagutenko and his colleagues, heat, piping, and sewerage were most economical in large buildings, and construction used least resources if carried out in large quantities and using standardized forms. These decisions were hardly based on long-term calculations, as evidenced in the much-ridiculed single-pipe heating: to save materials, radiators were usually connected in one continuous system, making it impossible to regulate the temperature in an individual room other than by opening the window. In the long run, the waste of energy by far surpassed the initial savings on pipes. Following this logic of instantaneous efficiency increase, brick walk-ups advanced to prefab ones and later to 11-story high-rises. Increasing standardization and growing building heights went along with a tendency to build bigger developments.

The Khrushchev era thus marked the end of the Stalinist compact city, in which the historical center had still retained its significance as a structural point of reference. Now development mostly took place on the fringes of the city. The housing shortage only occasionally allowed for Western European or American-style urban renewal in the inner city—as much as many party officials would have liked to replace "obsolete" historical buildings. It became the rule that new residential buildings were jointly constructed with communal facilities such as schools, grocery stores, nurseries, and sports fields to form a *mikrorayon* (residential compound).

7.3
Brezhnev-era building in Moscow on Mosfil'movskaya and Minskaya Ulitsa (Martin Schwegmann, 2008)

In Moscow, the areas of increased residential compounds in the 1950s included the southwestern Cherëmushki, southeastern Kuz'minki, northwestern Khoroshevo-Mnëvniki, and northeastern Izmaylovo districts.[17] One of the first large estates to accommodate ordinary families was the Ninth Experimental Block in the Cherëmushki district in southwest Moscow (1956–58, design Natan Osterman) with *khrushchëvki* apartment blocks for 3,000 tenants, food stores, a day nursery, a kindergarten, a school, and a movie theater. The development featured self-contained two- to three-room apartments and kitchen and bathroom amenities far above the average at the time.[18]

Soviet ideologues frequently expressed their enthusiasm with the new type of urban environment. Already in the 1920s, the avant-garde had deemed architecture a key force in

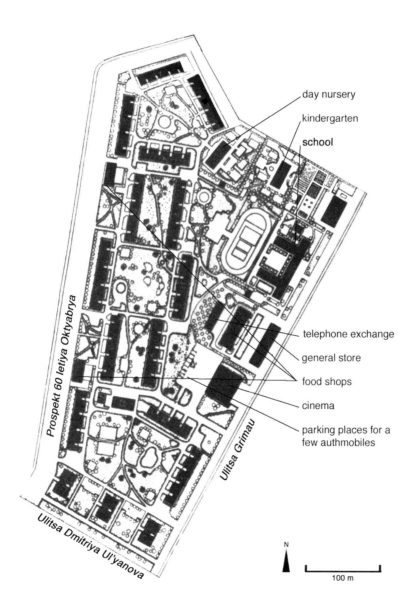

day nursery
kindergarten
school

telephone exchange

general store

food shops

cinema

parking places for a
few authmobiles

N

100 m

7.4
An ensemble of
khrushchëvki—the Ninth
Experimental Block in
Moscow's Cherëmushki
District (1956–58, design:
Natan Osterman) (Florian
Urban on the basis of a plan
from *Devyatyy kvartal:
Opytno-pokazatel'noye
stroitel'stvo zhilogo kvartala v
Moskve,* Moscow:
Gosstroiizdat, 1959, 17)

the construction of a new society. Ever since, new dwellings with modern facilities were not only considered the reward of an allegedly superior political system, but also inseparably linked to the promise of a socialist "new man." While experimental architectural discourses were muted during the Stalinist purges, the prefab *mikrorayony* of the post-war era were nevertheless a faint reflection of this hope for social change through new buildings. The compounds of apartment blocks, nurseries, schools, stores, and sports fields were seen as the cradles of a socialist society. The *mikrorayony* were aimed at creating the particular living condition that socialist scholars deemed to be inherently collective.[19] They were defined as combining "both familiar and societal character."[20] Soviet urban planners stressed the residents' activities in the complex, particularly regarding "cultural, educational, and ideological work among the inhabitants . . . neighborly help, care of the green spaces, cleaning of buildings and open spaces, [and] small repairs."[21]

While the effectiveness of architecture to enhance collective life remained unproven, the reality of the *mikorayony* was shared by more and more people. When Khrushchev was removed from power in 1964, his successor Leonid Brezhnev continued the policy of increasing construction, and repetitive *mikrorayony* mushroomed all over the country,

7.5
Khrushchëvka in Tomsk, Kulagina Ulitsa (Wikipedia Commons)

becoming the most common form of housing. By 1980, 70 percent of Moscow housing was constructed from prefab parts.[22] At the time, standardized towers and slabs were built with similar regularity in the Kazakh steppe and on the shores of the Arctic Ocean.

Oxygen for the housing market

The reaction of Soviet citizens to the mass construction program was mixed. The cheap Khrushchev-era blocks that originally had been designed for a nuclear family with one or two children were often filled with six or more people. Hence they were soon ridiculed as *khrushchëbi*, from *krushchëvka* (Khrushchev building) and *trushchëba* (slum).[23] Popular jokes also jeered that having successfully advanced sanitary technology toward producing combined shower/bathtubs, the relentless progress of Soviet architecture would soon yield apartments that increased efficiency further by merging floor and ceiling.

The far-reaching goals of a collective education through architecture contrasted with the fact that, according to a 1982 survey, 60 percent of the residents of a Moscow residential compound had no contact with their neighbors.[24] It also stood against the drab reality of unkempt greenery and dilapidated entrance halls, which were mostly unlit due to frequent lightbulb theft. Rumor has it that to date one can cheaply buy blown lightbulbs at Russian open markets, for the exclusive purpose of pilfering functioning bulbs from public spaces by replacing them with blown ones.

However, both the state ideologue's rhetoric and the critics' facetious cracks stood aside from what, in the eyes of the inhabitants, was the foremost quality of their new homes: in contrast to the small output of the Stalinist construction industry, the Khrushchev- and Brezhnev-era buildings successfully relieved the most urgent need. They provided self-contained apartments for a greater share of the population than ever before. They were the true modernizers of popular life. Not only did Soviet children increasingly experience collective education in compound kindergartens and schools, they also enjoyed modern comfort: by 1975, 98 percent of the Moscow housing stock was supplied with central heating and 79 percent with running hot water.[25] This was significantly more than, for example, in capitalist West Berlin, where in 1970 only 43 percent of the apartments had a modern heating system and not a coal stove, and only 75 percent had a hot water supply.[26] For families who before had had to share a room or even an *ugol* (curtained-off corner) in a *kommunalka* (communal apartment, inhabited by several families), a narrow prefab apartment was a considerable improvement. Many first-generation residents perceived these buildings as a new kind of freedom and as signs of enormous progress for Soviet workers.[27] According to the official statistics, the share of Moscow citizens living in *kommunalkas* decreased from 60 percent in 1960[28] to 30 percent in 1974.[29] While the exact number of units completed during the 1950s and 1960s is debated due to the lack of reliable statistics, all authors agree that Khrushchev's program significantly relaxed the precarious housing situation in the Soviet Union.[30] For large parts of the population it was virtually a dose of oxygen.

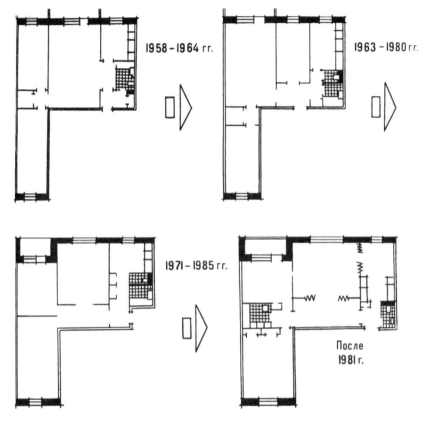

7.6
The development of the standard three-room prefab apartment in Moscow between 1958 and 1981 (source: Ya. Dikhter, *Mnogoyetazhnoye zhilishchye stolitsy*, Moscow: Moskovskiy rabochiy, 1979, 52)

1958 – 1964 гг.

1963 – 1980 гг.

1971 – 1985 гг.

После 1981 г.

Stratifications of a socialist metropolis

In the Soviet Union, housing was always regarded as a social good rather than a commodity. Acceptable housing had been one of the most fundamental goals of the workers' movement since the nineteenth century. In 1928, the Soviet Union prided itself on fixing the lowest rent tariff in the world for residences, and the right to housing was later codified in the constitution.[31] There was also a particular ideological quality of tower-and-slab buildings related to their making. Standardization and mass production responded to an ideal that since the times of Friedrich Engels determined socialist thinking: the quality of housing should be uniform, and the size of accommodation only related to the inhabitants' need. Of course under all socialist regimes this noble principle was often undermined from the very beginning, and in the Soviet Union privileged groups were always allocated better housing. Sometimes these differences were officially recognized as rightful, as in the case of artists and architects, who were granted more space to carry on their profession, or deserving workers, party officials, and veterans, who were rewarded with larger apartments for their merits.[32] In other cases, a spacious apartment was simply the result of individual power and personal connections. Especially during the late Stalinist period, the preferential treatment of the socialist elite could be read from the residential architecture. Many of

Moscow's most representative buildings, which featured solid workmanship, high ceilings, large rooms, and ostentatious façades, were officially designed for high-ranking members of the nomenklatura. This includes the Kaluzhskaya Zastava (Kaluga Gate) apartments for KGB officers, the apartments on Leninskiy Prospect for senior academicians, the residential skyscraper on Vosstaniya (now Kudrinskaya) Square, and the luxurious buildings on the radial Leningradski, Kutuzovskiy, and Leninskiy Prospects.[33] The mass-produced housing of the Khrushchev era modified this visible distinction. While the members of the elite were allowed to hold onto their privileges and often continued to live in Stalinist apartments, the newly constructed panel homes now conformed to the rhetoric of similar housing for everyone. At least new construction became more equal.

Did the new housing equality in all but a few central neighborhoods eradicate the differences between neighborhoods? Certainly not. Despite several decades of state-supported sameness, Soviet citizens continued to distinguish between "better" and "worse" neighborhoods and thus indirectly between more and less desirable mass housing. The slabs were hence differentiated according to numerous indirect factors, such as number of park spaces in the neighborhood, access to public transportation, and proximity to workplaces, and social and cultural facilities.

Perceived differences between uniform mass housing developments were particularly strong in Moscow and Leningrad, where the small groups of privileged Soviet citizens were concentrated. Historians agree that the two Soviet metropolises were incomparably more homogeneous than capitalist cities of the same size.[34] The differences, however, were more remarkable since they contradicted not only the officially stated goal of equal housing standards, but in the cases of desired mass housing neighborhoods, also the apparently similar architectural features. Class specifications are difficult to establish in a socialist society. But a comparison of the percentage of residents with a higher education degree shows that in Moscow, for most of the late Soviet period, educated people concentrated in the city center inside the Sadovoye Kol'tso (Garden Ring) and in the northern and south-western districts close to Moscow State University near the Lenin Hills (now Vorob'ëvy Gory, Sparrow Hills). These areas also offered the most spacious residences in relation to the number of inhabitants.[35] The working classes tended to live in the east and southeast.[36] The distribution roughly correlated with that of square meters of housing per capita—people in the center and in the west had more spacious apartments.[37]

A similar geography could be found with regard to desirable neighborhoods, although individual preferences remained mostly unspoken during a period when very few people could even think of choosing their place of residence. From the 1970s, however, when the most serious housing shortage was overcome, mass housing was increasingly diversified according to location—the idea of a better or worse neighborhood became more palpable. Soviet scholars slowly recognized the existence of such a class differentiation, despite the fact that it contradicted the tenets of socialist ideology, and started surveying the phenomenon. Since the use of questionnaires required an official permit that was difficult to obtain, in many cases they examined the openly accessible *zayavki* (classified ads for apartment exchange) and drew conclusions on the desirability of certain neighborhoods.[38]

In the eyes of the inhabitants, Moscow's most desirable areas were the neighborhoods west of the Kremlin around the Kalininskiy Prospect (now Novy Arbat), between Gertsen (now Bol'zhaya Nikitskaya) Street in the north and Kropotkin (now Prechistenka) Street to the south. This neighborhood, dubbed "the Tsar's village," had already been popular among the pre-revolutionary elites but was now built up with different building types, including mass-produced blocks. Other desirable areas include a sector in the northwest along Leningradskiy Prospect and Leningradskoye Chaussee, and a long wedge from Oktyabr'skaya (now Kaluzhskaya) Square past Gor'kiy Park and Moscow State University, and further to the periphery at Tropar'yevo and Teplyy Stan near the Moscow Automobile Ring Road (MKAD) that constituted the 1960 boundary of Greater Moscow.[39] The *khrushchëvki* and the *brezhnevki* in the sleeping areas outside the Garden Ring were significantly less popular. The least desirable areas lay in the southeast, east, and northeast, where a lot of heavy industry was concentrated.[40]

This estimation remained rather stable and continued into the post-Soviet era. At the turn of the twenty-first century, the most desirable and most expensive apartments are found in the center inside the Garden Ring and on the Western periphery. They are either situated in the small share of surviving pre-revolutionary buildings or the spacious Stalinist blocks.[41] Examples include the neighborhoods on the bank of the Moskva River or the elite developments on Tverskaya Street, Leningradskiy, Kutuzovskiy, and Leninskiy Prospects that have already been mentioned. The poorer parts of the population tend to live in slab neighborhoods outside the Garden Ring, with the worst located in the eastern periphery. The most undesirable neighborhoods are situated outside the Moscow Automobile Ring Road (MKAD).[42]

The studies of both distribution of privileged groups and desirable neighborhoods show that Moscow largely retained its pre-revolutionary social geography; this was even reinforced during the Soviet and post-Soviet eras. Historically, a similar distinction between a bourgeois west and a working-class east could be found in almost all great cities of the northern hemisphere, where the predominant winds blow industrial fumes eastward. With regard to the stability of these distinctions, Moscow is different from many European metropolises, where the geography of desirable and less desirable neighborhoods was repeatedly reconfigured over the course of the twentieth century, and where the privileged groups alternatingly favored the inner city or the suburbs. Perhaps the most striking difference to Western metropolises was the absence of ethnic neighborhoods. In cultural terms, Moscow was surprisingly homogeneous, despite the fact that the Soviet Union was home to more than two hundred distinct ethnic groups. The percentage of non-Russians among Moscow residents oscillated around only 10 percent, and there is no evidence that they concentrated in certain areas.[43]

The geography of desirable neighborhoods only to some extent correlated with the proliferation of pre-revolutionary and Stalinist housing typologies, which abound in the historic center but are much less frequent in the northern and southwestern districts. The same modernist mass housing units were thus more or less desired according to the neighborhoods in which they were built, and the different perception was to a large extent based on urban factors, such as access to public transportation, proximity to work, and "quality of environment."[44]

With regard to individual buildings, modern mass housing nevertheless fared worse than its predecessors. The average Soviet citizen's dream home in the 1970s looked much more like a Stalinist neoclassical building than like a *khrushchëvka* or *brezhnevka*: it should have a room for each person plus a living room, it should be located centrally in a brick or stone building with high ceilings and a balcony, and it should have all modern conveniences, such as gas, hot water, an elevator, and a telephone. The flat should be located on an upper floor—but not the top because of possible roof leaks, and not on the first two floors because of noise and the danger of burglary.[45]

Why were the mass-produced housing blocks of the Khrushchev and Brezhnev eras seen as acceptable rather than attractive? First, there was the low material quality. A case study in St. Petersburg showed that when it came to deciding whether to buy a rented apartment, *khrushchëvki* tenants were most hesitant—more so than tenants in the better-equipped and less-decayed Brezhnev-period apartment blocks, and far more than inhabitants of more solid Stalin-era and pre-revolutionary buildings.[46] Second, the tiny apartments with low ceilings accounted for the fact that they were frequently ridiculed as *khorëvniki* (kennels, from *khorëk*, meaning "polecat"). Third, inhabitants complained about the monotony in the standardized block developments, and intellectuals censured the *kvadratno gnezdovoye stroitel'stvo* (square block building) as being all-too-symbolic for the majority's uninspired way of thinking. In 1974, a third of the respondents to a Moscow survey disapproved of the "addresslessness" of their homes, a criticism that matched not only the confusion of the film characters in "Irony of Fate" but also corresponded to the reactions in other socialist countries such as the German Democratic Republic.[47] And third, the slab buildings were less common in the city center: those districts in Moscow which since the 1980s had been sought after by privileged groups for their "social microclimate, rhythm of life, and prestige"[48] were also the location of most Stalinist and pre-revolutionary buildings.[49]

The low regard for the modular high-rise relates not only to its typological features. Moscow—as St. Petersburg—is unique in Russia because of its large number of high-quality pre-revolutionary and Stalinist buildings in the city center, which are often situated in favorable locations and offer spectacular views. The vicissitude of architectural and other qualities is evidenced by the nineteenth-century buildings in St. Petersburg's center: if they are divided into *kommunalki* with shared kitchen and bathrooms, they are among the least desired abodes and far less popular than prefab buildings; if they are rented out as a whole, they suddenly become part of the city's most elite housing.[50] The perception of the towers and slabs is thus highly contextual: they are accepted as decent abodes under conditions of shortage, but quickly jilted whenever there is a better option.

Privatization and differentiation

The significance of prefab towers and slabs can only be understood in relation to the particularities of the housing market in the countries of the former Soviet Union, and especially in Russia. Like in most socialist countries, freedom of movement did not exist under Soviet rule. In 1932, Stalin introduced the *propiska* (registration) and required citizens to remain at the residence where they were registered—similar restrictions had already existed under the tsarist regime.[51] Registration in a different municipality required an official permit, which was usually only granted in the case of marriage, study, or a job offer. In the Soviet Union, big cities were better off than rural areas in terms of material supplies, cultural life, and educational opportunities, creating a city–countryside dichotomy that was far more pronounced than in most Western European countries.[52] Moving to Moscow or Leningrad was therefore particularly attractive and at the same time unimaginable for most small-town residents—there were many cases of pro-forma marriages to obtain the treasured permit. The *propiska* system was also an attempt to prevent further growth in the Russian metropolises, where the waiting lists for an apartment were already too large for the authorities to handle. The *propiska* was formally abolished in 1993 and replaced by the *registratsia po mestu zhitel'stva* (registration at the place of residency). The exclusionary system nevertheless lives on in a number of practices that, particularly in Moscow, deny unregistered citizens certain state benefits, which might include housing, pensions, or medical assistance. Unregistered citizens are also more likely to suffer from homelessness, unemployment, and police harassment. In addition, valid registrations are most difficult to obtain for certain ethnic minorities—particularly Caucasians—and for the poor.[53] Under Soviet rule, however, there was also a positive side that went with the restrictions of free movement. Soviet citizens who had been assigned a state-owned apartment were in a much more stable situation than tenants under capitalism. They had to pay extremely low rents, and they could hardly be evicted—both amenities that many now fondly connect with mass housing units.

In 1990, the last year of the Soviet Union, 67 percent of the apartments in Russia were state rentals provided by municipalities, state enterprises, and government agencies; 4 percent were cooperatives, often run by state-owned companies for their workers; and only 26 percent, mostly rural dwellings, were individually owned.[54] Already in the late Soviet period the government started a kind of privatization. In December of 1988, a decree was passed that permitted each tenant to purchase his or her apartment from the state. This meant that against a token processing fee the tenant was granted the right to use the apartment for life, pass it on to their heirs, pay no rent, and in return become responsible for the cost of maintenance.[55] With the introduction of market capitalism in the 1990s this meant that the new owner could also sell these rights and in this sense sell the apartment. Thus a housing market comparable to that in Western countries was created. In Moscow the new housing market started to emerge as early as 1993. By the late 1990s, about 25 percent of Russian households had "bought" their apartments, while another 25 percent already lived in private homes.[56] As a rule, neither the land nor the communal portions of the building, such as cellars and corridors, changed ownership; to date the state or the municipal authority remains the official owner.[57]

Of course this measure did not go without criticism, since those who occupied the most prestigious apartments benefitted most. Many high-ranking party officials were given spacious luxury apartments in the center of Moscow practically for free, while the less privileged were eligible for a tiny flat on the outskirts, if anything at all. Residents who lived "illegally" at their apartments (that is, without a *propiska*) went away empty-handed. During the wild years after the end of the Soviet Union there were also many opportunities for swindlers to trick dupable tenants out of attractive apartments. It has to be pointed out that a consistent legal framework for this growing private housing market is yet to be completed. Privatization nevertheless continues.

At the turn of the twenty-first century, 47 percent of the apartments in Moscow were on the new housing market—that is, the rights of their use could be bought and sold.[58] In turn, 50 percent of Russian households still hold rental agreements from the Soviet period and have not yet made use of their right to privatize. Most of them still occupy their apartments on the basis of *sotsial'nyy naëm* (social tenancy).[59] They pay very little rent and, unlike tenants-turned-owners, do not have to bear the expense of maintenance. For the state authorities, this constitutes a problem, since the low rents do not pay for necessary renovations, and even during Soviet times investment in the buildings tended to be poor. At the same time, the municipal authorities still keep a long list of those who wait for their turn (*ocheredniki*) to move into such an apartment, although vacancies are very rare and basically only occur in the case of a tenant's sudden death—in all other situations, he or she is likely to make use of the privatization right and sell the apartment. There is also *kommercheskiy naëm* (commercial tenancy), in which, contrary to what the name suggests, the tenant enjoys some form of rent control, but does not have a right to sell. But these municipally owned flats are also rare. In general, Soviet and post-Soviet privatization granted a significant portion of the population the security that they already enjoyed under Soviet rule, that is, low-cost housing and protection against eviction. For the rest, however, the situation has became precarious. Anybody who is from out of town or too young to hold a rental agreement from the Soviet period has to depend on the free market and face a rent level that in the large cities is far out of reach for the average wage earner.[60] This situation is particularly grim for the weakest groups on the housing market: migrants and refugees. Homelessness, which was limited under Soviet rule, is on the rise.[61]

The housing situation reflects the general development of Russian society. Since the end of the Soviet Union, there has been an increasing gap between a small number of very rich and a large number of very poor. Although between 2001 and 2005 the average monthly salary almost tripled from 112 to 302 dollars, this barely allows a standard wage earner to survive in Moscow, which ranks among the world's most expensive cities.[62] A considerable number of Russians live in deep poverty.[63] On the other side of the social divide are the so-called "New Russians," the winners of capitalism and subjects of the same kind of popular jokes that were once told about the party elite. Their total number is the subject of much speculation; most probably they constitute less than 5 percent of the total population.[64] They nevertheless are concentrated in Moscow, where their presence sets the parameters of the housing market and accounts for an increasing segmentation. In light of this development, tower-and-slab buildings are emblematic for the post-Soviet society. They are a safe harbor for many poor who at least own their apartment and are thus not threatened by home-lessness. At the same time, the very structures that afford this refuge for some sharply exclude others who are equally poor and also in need of housing. Either way, slab buildings are among the aspects of socialist heritage which most strongly influence daily life in post-socialist Russia.

Panel buildings in Russia today

In contemporary Russia, prefab high-rise blocks are not viewed as negatively as they are in Western Europe. One reason is their ubiquity: the five-story *khrushchëvki* alone still make up half a billion of the 2.8 billion square meters that constitute Russia's housing stock.[65] Other reasons are particular to any country with limited resources and strong state involvement over decades: unlike in the capitalist West, panel buildings in Russia are not the home of the marginalized, but socially mixed environments.[66] And unlike in many other countries, they are far from being considered obsolete. The Russian state is continuously involved in the provision of apartments. In the late 1990s, state authorities and former Soviet enterprises still owned 40 percent of the housing stock.[67] Cities continue to operate state-owned construction companies to maintain them. And the country spent approximately 3 percent of its gross domestic product on housing and utility subsidies—far more than on its military.[68] Soviet-style housing complexes with schools and daycare centers are still being planned too—with apartment buildings often constructed by private companies.[69]

The priorities have nevertheless shifted since the end of the Soviet Union. This is most evident in Moscow, where the wealth of Russia is concentrated and where soaring real estate prices create an immense pressure on the housing market. The city administration plans to replace especially the "disposable" *khrushchëvki* with more soundly built, higher, and denser blocks.[70] They also plan to demolish all five-story *khrushchëvki* from the P-32, P-35, and 16-AM series and from Lagutenko's famous K-7 series—a project that carries the potential for large profit margins.[71] The Soviet promise that the *khrushchëvki* are meant to last no longer than 30 years, ironically, has become a mandate of the market—albeit in a very different way to what the planners foresaw. Instead of increasing the housing standards for the entire population, demolition leads to a greater social polarization. The city administration announced that they would provide substitute apartments for the displaced tenants, but even if these promises are kept the new homes are likely to be situated in less attractive neighborhoods.[72] On the other hand, the city of Moscow is still looking for cheap methods to provide housing. It has launched a pilot program to recycle the panels from demolished *khrushchëvki* and use them, technically modified, for new construction. A handful of prototypes have been constructed according to this method.[73]

Moscow, like Mumbai, Chicago, and many other cities in recent years has also seen the construction of high-end apartment blocks. The peculiar lavish condominiums constitute a very different type of mass housing than the prefab panel buildings of the Soviet era, but they follow the same typology of a repetitive tower in a park. They are built from bricks and reinforced concrete, they feature richly decorated façades with expensive finishing, and the apartments are adorned with neoclassical elements. Some of these buildings were constructed on the site of demolished *khrushchëvki*, others on newly developed land on the periphery. Two famous examples from the late 1990s are Vorob'yëvy Gory (Sparrow Hills) in southwestern Moscow near Moscow State University and Alye Parusa (Scarlet Sails), northwest of the city center.[74] They are located in prominent locations near the Moskva River; Vorob'yëvy Gory is also relatively close to some of the luxury compounds that were erected in the 1980s for members of the party elite.[75] Both are gated communities with their own infrastructure and services. They comprise 24–30- story brick buildings with load-bearing structures from reinforced concrete. Façades are decorated with color panels, ceramics, and natural rock. The apartment prices in such compounds are among the highest in the world, and appear even more extreme considering the country's average monthly wage of around 300 dollars. In 2007, a 140-square-meter apartment in Alye Parusa was advertised for 7,500 US dollars monthly rent.[76] The fortunate residents enjoy many qualities that are also found in Stalinist housing: a sound brick structure with neoclassical decorations, spacious rooms with high ceilings of up to 3.2 meters, and large balconies with scenic views. Other amenities are particular to the post-Soviet age: underground parking, supermarkets, a water park with artificial surf, a Turkish bath and sauna, soccer and track fields, and a yacht club. The difference in perception between the nouveau riche tenants on the one hand and some foreign critics on the other could hardly be more extreme. The former enjoy the buildings to the extent that they are willing to pay the exorbitant rents, while the latter see them as the epitome of bad taste. Interestingly enough, the critics who deride the "vulgar Florentine nightmares" blur the boundaries between cheap and expensive forms of mass housing.[77] The liberal German newspaper *Süddeutsche Zeitung*, for example, censured Alye Parusa, technologically incorrect, as a *Plattenbau* (slab building), and thus equaled it with the unloved socialist prefab towers in East Germany. Claiming that two-thirds of Moscow's new residential construction consists of such "slabs," the author lumped modernist socialist prefab blocks together with fancy post-socialist luxury condos, and interpreted them as evidence for an all-encompassing Russian tradition that is only capable of producing despicable serial mass buildings.[78]

While in contemporary Russia there is no negative view of mass housing in general and of residential towers in particular, close attention is paid to their specific variations. The buildings from the Soviet period are judged according to material qualities rather than typological differences. Moscow's ten-story *brezhnevki*, for example, fare better than some of the "disposable" five-story *khrushchëvki*. Older buildings, where repairs have been delayed for decades, are less popular than younger and less-deteriorated ones. And high-quality Stalinist buildings are more sought-after than low-quality apartment blocks from the 1950s and 1960s. Some scholars thus detect a binary opposition in public perception based on building quality. On the one hand, there are the cheap panel blocks, and on the other hand the prestigious Stalin-era homes, whose eclectic neoclassical façades are now frequently copied in newly built upscale developments.[79]

Generally, the Soviet-period slab buildings are subject to a contradictory policy. On the one hand, the Moscow municipality is eager to sell dilapidated panel buildings in attractive areas to private firms for demolition and redevelopment—in many cases these transactions involve corruption or dubious practice.[80] On the other hand, the city shows a certain degree of responsibility toward the inhabitants who, in most cases, cannot afford free market rents, and negotiates the provision of substitute apartments with the developers. This responsibility, though, is diminishing. Until 2006, Moscow obliged developers to construct a certain number of substitute apartments for every demolished *khrushchëvka*. Now they only have to pay a lump sum, and it is up to the city whether or not to invest these funds in housing. In those cases where substitute buildings are being provided, the distribution is clear: cheap and low-quality panel buildings are constructed for (poor) renters; brick buildings for (wealthy) buyers.[81] While the proportion of those who are able to choose between different housing types has increased since the end of the Soviet Union, the great majority of Muscovites are stuck in their Soviet-era mass housing apartments. This situation is maintained by economic constraints. Since the tenants cannot afford to move, they adopt a rather pragmatic view on the blocks. To conceive of a city without these buildings seems to be out of the question; in public perception this impossibility forestalls any desire for a different form of housing. With the few rich living elsewhere, prefab towers and slabs continue to be the dwellings of ordinary people—a situation that is not likely to change any time soon.

8 High-Rise Shanghai

The Shanghai skyline

Shanghai's most popular postcard image shows a skyline of glitzy high-rises that has seemingly grown overnight on the marshy right bank of the Huángpǔ River. To an extent that is only matched by New York City, public imagination equates China's second city with tall housing blocks. They comprise a vast range of variations: in the classy upscale compounds near the financial district on the riverfront one is greeted by a security guard at the gate, parks one's car in an underground garage, and saunters through immacutely cut lawns into a marble lobby from where an elevator takes one to a spacious apartment overlooking the river. In less prestigious developments, one pushes one's bicycle through a rusty iron gate and walks up several flights of badly painted concrete stairs into a narrow studio where kitchens and bathrooms have to be shared with the neighbors.

Mass housing is ubiquitous. As a result of unprecedented construction efforts, by the turn of the twenty-first century the majority of Shanghai residents live in serially built multistory buildings, and seemingly without resentment. The apparent acceptance of mass housing among Shanghainese of all social classes stands in clear contrast to the controversial perception of these buildings in many Western countries. This can only partially be attributed to the city's physical particularities—namely an overpopulated area where many people have to share a relatively small space—and an incessant traffic congestion combined with a limited subway system, which both make suburban life unattractive. To a significant degree, the perception of Shanghai's tower blocks was shaped by social and cultural factors, and the specific ways in which the Shanghainese appropriated this architectural type.

The Shanghai story is characterized by several particularities. First, high population density and limited space have been predominant features of China's cities for centuries. Many pre-modernist dwellings, including the famous *lǐlòng*, which will be described below,

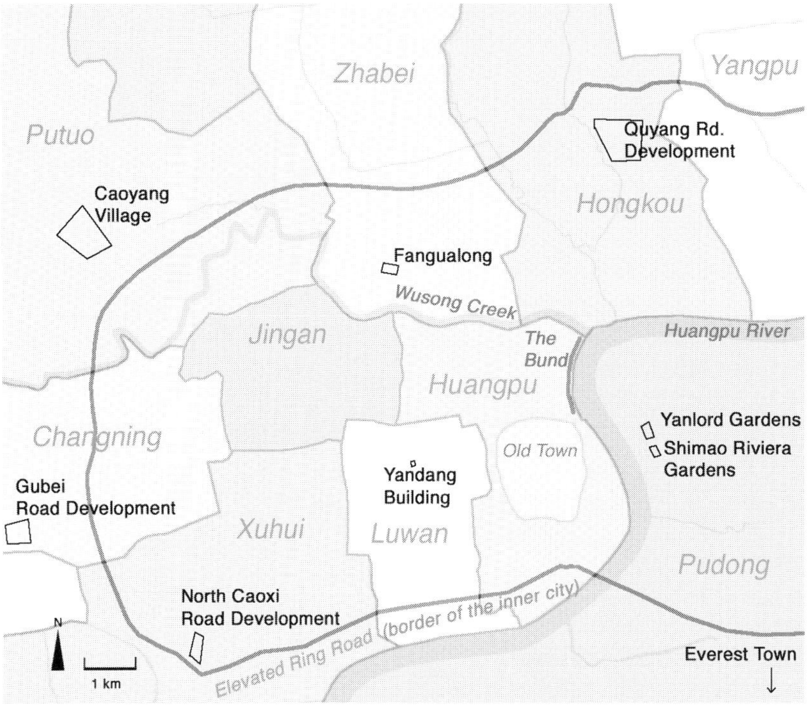

Map labels: Zhabei · Yangpu · Putuo · Quyang Rd. Development · Caoyang Village · Hongkou · Fangualong · Wusong Creek · Jingan · The Bund · Huangpu River · Huangpu · Changning · Old Town · Yanlord Gardens · Shimao Riviera Gardens · Gubei Road Development · Yandang Building · Xuhui · Luwan · Pudong · North Caoxi Road Development · Elevated Ring Road (border of the inner city) · Everest Town · N · 1 km

can therefore be considered precursors of contemporary mass housing. In the decade before the Second World War, Shanghai was one of the first cities in Asia to build several types of multi-family homes with modern amenities: the hybrid new *lǐlòng*, which integrated balconies and showers into a traditional Chinese typology, and also a great number of European-inspired apartment buildings. Second, throughout most of the twentieth century Chinese state authorities maintained a high degree of control over many details of their citizens' daily lives. A powerful state was not particular to the period of planned economy and in many respects lingered on after the structural reform. Housing was part of the *tiě fàn wǎn* (iron rice bowl), the state-organized satisfaction of basic needs, and government intervention was always taken for granted. Although it played out differently at different points in time, its basic tenets were never challenged, let alone openly debated. State instruments for the organization and control of residential life were not limited to housing policy but included, for example, the tight surveillance of personal life by the *dānwèi* (work unit) to which every Chinese citizen belonged, and the system of *hùkǒu* (registration) that will be discussed later in this chapter. Third, compared to the forced cohabitation of several families in the same space that was the rule in the early decades of the People's Republic, the self-contained apartment in a mass housing block appeared to be considerable progress to many and effective protection against conflicts with neighbors, bad rumors, and denunciation. And fourth, the Chinese rulers did not voice the goal of equal housing standards for everyone as emphatically as those in other socialist countries. In no planned economy did allocation practice live up to its ideals, but in the People's Republic of China housing was never meant to be egalitarian. The square meters to which Chinese citizens were officially entitled followed a hierarchical system, depending not only on marital status and number of children, but also on age, profession, and position in the company hierarchy. The close connection between social position and housing was thus more obvious in the People's Republic of China than, for example, in the Soviet Union. In addition, Chinese mass housing never became a prominent tool in the organization of socialist society as it did with the Soviet tower blocks, and construction was neglected for decades in favor of other industries, such as coal and steel production.

Shanghai takes pride in a long history of multistory housing. In the 1930s, the city pioneered high-rise construction in Asia. Among the numerous art deco skyscrapers from the 1930s are not only banks and office towers, but also prestigious residences such as the 12-story Peace Hotel on the waterfront boulevard Bund, which was erected in 1926 to serve as the weekday home of the city's richest merchant, Victor Sassoon. The nearby Park Hotel, built in 1934 with 22 stories, remained the highest building in the Far East until the 1980s. The tradition of building high was interrupted only in the first two decades after the foundation of the People's Republic, when political and economic hardships hampered the evolution of tower architecture. Housing in Shanghai was subsequently dictated by the different stages of politics and by a demographic growth of the urban agglomeration from approximately 5 million in 1950 to almost 13 million in 2000.[1]

In the late twentieth century, one can roughly distinguish four phases: the foundation years of the People's Republic (1949–66), Cultural Revolution (1966–78), experimental market economy (1978–92), and fully fledged market economy (since 1992). When the People's Republic was founded in 1949, China was an underdeveloped country ravaged by wartime destruction. Shanghai, which until the 1930s had been the basis for foreign powers exploiting China's resources and at the same time a location of intense encounters between Western and Eastern cultures, was still one of the six most populous cities in the world, but had largely lost its economic significance. The first two decades of the communist regime saw major man-provoked disasters: the 1959–61 famine triggered by the collectivization of agricultural production and forced establishment of heavy industry during the Great Leap Forward (estimated death toll: 20 million people), and the Cultural Revolution, which lasted from 1966 to Mao Zedong's death in 1976, and entailed an economic downturn, a brutal persecution of real and imagined dissidents, and an unprecedented destruction of cultural heritage. From the 1970s onward, China experienced a period of relative political and economic stability, and high-rise construction again became one of Shanghai's unique selling propositions. While civil rights remained precarious and political opposition continued to be oppressed, the national product grew at rising rates. A market economic system was gradually introduced from 1978 onward. At the same time, the socialist government remained in power and set the terms of the market economy. Further legislative amendments were passed in 1992, and the freedom of business now nearly equals that in Western countries. By the turn of the twenty-first century, two-digit growth rates turned the country into an economic superpower.

Until very recently, living conditions in Shanghai, as in other Chinese towns and cities, were determined by a housing shortage unimaginable from a contemporary point of view. In 1958, Shanghai inhabitants statistically could dispose of only 3.8 square meters of "net dwelling space" per person (not including kitchens and bathrooms), a number that increased only marginally until the 1980s.[2] That is, the average Shanghainese had less personal space than an American king size bed would occupy (3.92 square meters). Even for a socialist country this was lamentably little—the average Soviet citizen in the 1950s lived in more than 7 square meters.[3] Between the mid-1980s and 2007, per capita dwelling space in Shanghai multiplied by four, and presently oscillates around 20 square meters.[4]

The 1950s: standard design, individual construction

In the People's Republic of China, modernist mass housing was introduced in two stages. In the 1950s and 1960s, serial apartment blocks were erected on a comparably small scale. Compounds of buildings were constructed according to standardized design, but employing traditional methods. At that time too select experiments with prefabrication and industrialized building were undertaken, but not until the late 1970s were they produced in larger numbers. The 1950s nevertheless changed the dwelling conditions particularly of the former middle and upper classes. Private dwellings were nationalized and once-privileged groups were forced to share their homes with strangers. The housing shortage, exacerbated through country-to-city migration, was now felt by all parts of society, and privacy became a rare commodity.

From 1953 onward, China pursued an economic development policy modeled on the Soviet Union's mode of industrialization. There was nevertheless a fundamental difference. In China, the expansion of heavy industry was given clear priority over urban accommodations and services, a policy that was backed by premier Zhou Enlai (1898–1976) and referred to as "production first, livelihood second."[5] In the architectural realm, this translated into a commitment to "function, economy, and, if conditions allow, appearance (beauty)," a motto from the 1950s that is often attributed to Minister of Construction, Li Xiufeng.[6] The Chinese version of Stalinist architecture that was pursued in the early 1950s—traditional "big roofs" with decorative elements from both vernacular Chinese and Western contexts—was soon abandoned in favor of austere modernism. In contrast to the Soviet Union, which in the 1950s started the mass production of prefab apartment blocks, housing remained of lower priority in China, and investment into residential construction dropped significantly over the course of the 1950s.[7] Experiments with large-panel construction were not continued beyond select pilot projects.[8] One can only speculate as to the reasons for the decades-long hesitation of Chinese officials to promote prefabrication. Most likely, they were the same as in India: the lack of infrastructure necessary for production and transportation of large concrete panels, and the availability of cheap labor.[9] An official report from 1960 stated that the construction cost for prefab developments was clearly higher than for brick buildings, and suggested that it could be lowered if the construction industry was further industrialized.[10] But since the Chinese leaders were unwilling to promote such structural change, industrialized buildings remained an exception.

In this early period, the "modernization" of Chinese housing was thus limited to the design. Apartment blocks were constructed according to standardized plans—the first were carried out under the guidance of Soviet engineers.[11] From 1955 onward, the Ministry of Urban Construction directed the development of standard designs for the entire country. Aiming at the improvement of Soviet models, the ministry tried to capture the housing needs of one of the world's most geographically diverse countries in six different proposals, corresponding to six regions: northeast, north, northwest, southwest, central, and southeast.[12] Saving resources was crucial. Units were built from brick and concrete. They had a standardized floor plan and could be combined to form different buildings, mostly with two stories and five units per story. [13] The reference design referred not only to form and structure but equally to heating, lighting, and piping. Although not industrially produced, these buildings looked similar to the Soviet *khrushchëvki* (Khrushchev-period buildings). Over the course of the 1950s, the standards were repeatedly adjusted to the new policy of frugality and the space per inhabitant was further and further reduced.

Modernist "new villages"

Although in the 1950s and 1960s mass housing ranked low on the political agenda, the Shanghai authorities nevertheless promoted a number of prestige projects that were to demonstrate the achievements of the new regime. Among the most famous were the Cáoyáng and Fánguālòng developments, which will be introduced here.

Both followed a particularity of Chinese residential design that has remained unchanged since the pre-modernist period and possibly contributed to the widespread acceptance of Shanghai's apartment blocks. Housing is built in compounds. This form of organization can be found, with certain modifications, in the back alleys of the prewar period, the modest four-story apartment blocks of the 1970s, and the glitzy skyscrapers of the 1990s. In all these types of construction, a fenced-in residential area is accessed from the main street through a gate. Each compound is guarded by a concierge, who in the more modest developments does not take visitors' names but denies entrance to peddlers and beggars. Inside, the individual buildings are communicated through a system of interior streets that are barred from through-traffic and might contain park spaces, fruit stands, kindergartens, and small stores. This outlay of the compound turns inside streets into a semi-private space for hanging the laundry, repairing one's bicycle, chatting with neighbors, and allowing children to play. It thus fosters a sense of community and enclosure. Numerous residential compounds were built in the first decades of socialism, referred to as *xīncūn* (new villages). In contrast to the developments in the Soviet Union and other socialist countries at the time, they were rather small and rarely contain more than a few hundred inhabitants. Whenever larger areas had to be developed, they were subdivided. Thus the Chinese authorities established a spatial hierarchy. Kindergartens might be situated inside each residential complex, while larger communal facilities such as schools, workers clubs, hospitals, or supermarkets catered to several compounds.

The most famous housing compound in post-war Shanghai was Cáoyáng Xīncūn (Cáoyáng New Village), designed by Wang Dingzeng and Jin Jingchang. Both contributed an international perspective. Wang had trained at the Illinois Institute of Technology in

8.2
Cáoyáng New Village,
designed by Wang Dingzeng
and Jin Jingchang, 1951–53
(Florian Urban)

Chicago, while Jin had studied at the University of Darmstadt, Germany. Built between 1951 and 1953 as a showcase project, the original compound comprised 48 buildings with 1,002 units along Cáoyáng Road in the northwestern Pŭtúo district.[14] The loosely assembled buildings of the first stage are mostly two to three stories high. They were constructed from bricks rather than prefabricated parts, but they followed a repetitive design. The residential area of approximately 95 hectares, measuring 1,200 meters from edge to edge, provided park spaces in between—a considerable luxury in a city as densely built as Shanghai. Cáoyáng New Village was an expression of the communist promise to spread the benefits of progress and modernization among China's industrial working class. With public buildings erected in the center, the whole neighborhood was well integrated in its surroundings. In other aspects, the economical was presented as ideologically appropriate: as in the Soviet *kommunalkas*, each family was allocated one room, and several families had to share a common bathroom and kitchen. As in other residential developments, public facilities were integrated, including schools, kindergartens, and a cultural and commercial center.

Cáoyáng New Village was the first stage in a program designed by Shanghai municipal authorities to address the housing shortage and introduce a particular form of mass housing. Until 1958, approximately 20,000 units were completed, most of them in the Cáoyáng area, extending the first compound with eight other ensembles of residential buildings. The output, as massive as it might seem, was still a drop in the ocean in a city of over five million people, which was growing at a breathtaking pace.[15] Although not a high-rise development, Cáoyáng New Village was the Shanghai authorities' first step toward mass-produced housing. The standardized floor plans, materials, and building designs allowed for rationalized construction, and although floors and stairs in the first compound were built individually from wooden planks, they looked the same in all buildings. Floorage per person was considerably higher than the deplorable national average, and residents enjoyed a quiet neighborhood with a large amount of greenery.[16]

Another famous mass housing compound is Fánguālòng near Shanghai's railroad station in the Zhábĕi district.[17] The development for 9,000 people was built 1963–65 as a prestige project. It consisted of 27 5-story buildings with standardized floor plans and unit sizes averaging 19 square meters dwelling space proper (34 square meters including corridors and kitchens). Buildings were designed as both point blocks and slab blocks. As in the Cáoyáng development, two to three units had to share a kitchen and bathroom. Like Cáoyáng Village, too, Fánguālòng formed a compound of semi-public alleys secluded from the main roads; it included schools, stores, a health care center, and carefully landscaped green spaces.

The Shanghai authorities proudly presented Fánguālòng development as an example of a slum-clearance policy by which "courageous architects with a creative mind" removed overcrowded substandard huts. The Fánguālòng area was one of the poorest neighborhoods in pre-revolutionary Shanghai, inhabited by manual laborers and rickshaw pullers, and an increasing population of poor immigrants from the northern Jiāngsū province. In the late 1940s, approximately 20,000 people here lived in shacks and straw huts.[18] The new Fánguālòng development was a prestige project, allegedly offering more than double the amount of dwelling space of the huts. Official publications stated that the "slum residents" were allowed to move into the new dwellings.[19]

8.3
Fánguālòng (1963–65), a prestige project built on a cleared slum site (picture c. 1965, source: *Shanghai Kexue Jishu Wenxian Chubanshe 1951–1996 – Housing in Shanghai 1951–1996*, Shanghai: Publisher for Documents of Science and Technology, 1998: 222)

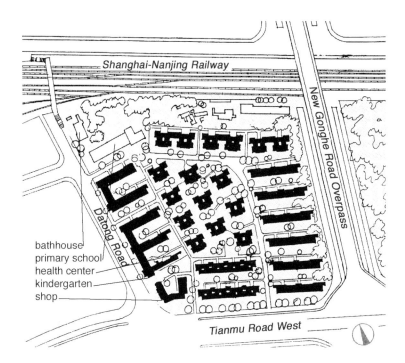

The Chinese slum clearance policies were and still are directed against two different building types. The wooden huts of the pre-1949 era, which Fánguālòng and similar developments aimed to replace, are called *pín mín kū* or *péng hù qū*. Next to these shanty-towns, most of which have long disappeared, there are neighborhoods of informal but solid buildings, which continued to grow under socialist rule. These tiny houses often have two stories and a tiled roof. They are called *wēi péng jiǎn wū* (dilapidated houses), a term which is also translated as "slum," although it does not carry the negative connotations of its English equivalent. To a Western eye, the "dilapidated houses" with their pitched roofs, terraces, and clotheslines look rather quaint. Chinese authorities, however, unanimously shared and continue to share the conviction that they have to go, and many a mayor or party official has built his career on spectacular "slum clearance" programs.

In this context, Fánguālòng is an example of how Shanghai's mass housing projects served as an architectural strategy of re-education.[20] School classes were taken to the new neighborhood to admire the advancement of their socialist society. The compound—at the time one of the most modern in Shanghai, with electricity, a water supply, and flush toilets in every apartment—was presented as a revolutionary holy land inhabited by steadfast supporters of the communist regime; their past, as embodied by the slums, was homogenized as a lesser stage of being and prelude to the communist present. For a long time, a number of the old shacks were preserved and shown as a daunting example, in order to teach elementary school students about the progressive construction policy of the communist regime. Through this propaganda effort, the Fánguālòng apartment blocks became an effective tool in promoting the legitimacy of the state.

8.5
Low-rise buildings with
integrated small businesses
on Shàngwén Road in
Shanghai's Old Town. Such
houses are considered slums
by the local authorities
(Florian Urban, 2008)

Showcase projects such as Cáoyáng New Village or Fánguālòng nevertheless remained exceptions. The forced industrialization of the economy during the Great Leap Forward of 1958–61 concentrated the country's resources on steel production. When the Cultural Revolution was proclaimed in 1966, housing construction in Shanghai and other great cities came almost to a complete halt. With large numbers of China's youth invested in the violent dissemination of Marxist ideology, urban housing again took a back seat. Large numbers of urban professionals were forced to move to rural areas, and construction in the cities stalled. Pressed-earth-wall houses, built mostly in rural contexts, came to embody the spirit of self-reliance, hard struggle, and low standards.[21]

Prefab experiments

Among the few early experiments with prefabrication in Shanghai, one is particularly noteworthy. The Mǐnháng Road development exemplifies a brief period when the government attempted to establish satellite settlements outside the city. It was started in 1959 at the peak of the economic crisis provoked by the Great Leap Forward. Situated on the southwestern periphery adjacent to an industrial area, this development was designed as a self-contained satellite city with its own center, about 20 miles from Shanghai's Old Town. Thirteen apartment blocks with four to six stories were erected along ample, tree-lined streets. The complex included stores, restaurants, a post office, a park called Red Garden, and a theater. The ground floors of many residential buildings were designed for commercial use—a novelty in China at the time. Buildings were mostly constructed from slabs measuring 1.4 × 2.4 meters.[22] Clear-cut, white, and unadorned, they resembled the aesthetics of Le Corbusier or the Bauhaus architects.

The history of industrialized mass housing in Shanghai nevertheless took a different course than in other parts of the world. In most countries of both the Eastern and Western Blocs, it reached its peak at a time when the respective politicians most vigorously stated their commitment to social democratic ideas and an egalitarian society. China's political leaders, however, started to promote them on a broader scale when the most radically leftist doctrine was about to lose momentum. In Shanghai, apartment blocks were rediscovered at the end of the Cultural Revolution in the early 1970s. The new policy was nevertheless an outcome of that period of radical politics, when housing was construed as a fundamental political task to transform society.[23] Shanghai, which was the base of the "Gang of Four" who headed the Cultural Revolution, came to be a hotspot of this development.

In 1973, the Cáoxī Běi Lù (North Cáoxī Road) development in the Xúhuì district was begun, the tallest prefab residential development at the time. Apartments in the 13–17-story blocks averaged 60 square meters and were accessed through interior corridors; all of them had individual kitchens and toilets.[24] North Cáoxī Road was the first large development from prefab slabs, and many were to follow. Over the course of the 1960s the use of prefabricated elements such as floors, staircases, balconies, and lintels had increased steadily, and prefab construction from concrete blocks had been used.[25] By the time North Cáoxī Road was begun, long-cherished arguments against high-rises had begun to lose their impact. A typical opinion was published in 1981 by architect Zheng Naigui, who powerfully refuted allegations about the detrimental effect of high-rises on children and elderly, and pointed to the ongoing popularity of high-rise construction in England and France. For Zheng, tall buildings were most functional for saving land and public utilities and thus guaranteeing rising standards of living.[26]

Structural reform: privatization and polarization

The character of mass housing in China was profoundly changed as a result of "structural reform." China's path toward capitalism began in 1978, two years after Mao's death. In December of that year, the Chinese leaders initiated economic reforms and set the course for an era of unprecedented economic growth. Starting what became known as the "Beijing Spring," they also overcame the country's political isolation and for a brief period relaxed the harshest repressions on dissidents.[27] With regard to housing and real estate, state

socialism in China began to erode in May of 1984, when the Sixth National People's
Congress called for the commercialization of urban housing, the establishment of a real
estate sector, and the collection of taxes and rents for land use in the city. Half a year later,
in October 1984, the Communist Party established guidelines for a "planned commodity
economy." Although these guidelines still stressed public ownership and did not speak of
purchase and sale, they nevertheless lay the groundwork for a series of contracted
responsibilities, which in many respects equaled rights of landownership. Over the
following years, these rights were continuously extended. In 1985 it was permitted to
bequeath and inherit such rights; a year later they were secured in the constitution.[28] Prime
Minister Li Peng also promoted the idea of a free housing market, stating that apartments
should not be treated differently from refrigerators and bicycles. Starting in the 1980s, real
estate development and construction was increasingly transferred from state-sponsored
institutions to profit-oriented companies. Ever since, landownership has been officially in
the hands of the state, but de facto private. Holding a "state lease," the private owner retains

the right of land use for 70 years, and can buy, sell, or inherit this right. The difference to ownership in the pure capitalist sense, however, exists only on paper. The first "state leases" will expire in the 2050s, and hardly anyone expects a future government to challenge the status quo. Most observers thus saw this policy as a strategic move by market-oriented leaders to escape criticism from socialist ideologies.[29] China's path to fully fledged capitalism was uninterrupted by the period of political repression that followed the Tiananmen massacre of 1989 and was largely completed in 1992, the year that is remembered as the beginning of a new economic era. Pushed by Head of State Deng Xiaoping, the Communist Party on its 14th National Convention decided to establish a "socialist market economy." Most regulations that had restricted the freedom of business were removed. The country's national economy subsequently experienced unprecedented growth rates—even by 1993 the GNP had increased by 13 percent.

With respect to mass housing, the privatization had three major consequences. First, residential construction increased dramatically. Some sources speak of more than 150 million square meters per year, or about ten times the amount that was completed during the years prior to 1979.[30] Since the 1980s, the share of GNP that China invested in housing was one of the largest in the world—8.14 percent in 1985, compared to 2.1 in the US or 5.7 percent in West Germany (1980 figures).[31] The focus lay on high-rise mass housing, which the government supported as beneficial for densely populated cities and whose height kept increasing.[32] Before 1979, the highest residential buildings in Shanghai did not exceed the pre-socialist maximum of 20 stories. By 1990, this number rose to 33 stories, and by 2000 to 60 stories.[33] The real estate industry also grew enormously.[34] Second, along with higher technological standards, modern amenities such as kitchens and bathrooms inside the apartments became the rule, as evidenced in the newly introduced planning concept of apartment unit. And third, the hierarchies in Chinese society became far more pronounced. The gap between privileged and disadvantaged groups widened, and, like in capitalist societies, both were now determined by their income difference. Industrial workers, as a rule of thumb, were no longer favored as under Mao, and the political influence of intellectual and business elites rose.[35] Along with social polarization, the standards, plans, and designs for mass housing were increasingly diversified.

In general, certain groups profited more from the construction boom than others. Far into the 1990s, the bulk of new housing—82 percent in 1990—was built by employers rather than private developers, and designed for their employees. This included the workers at large state-owned companies, national administrative offices, and universities but not, for example, schoolteachers or employees at small enterprises, who were therefore disadvantaged.[36]

While the large cities turned into economic growth poles and centers of wealth, another instrument of state control accounted for increasing polarization: the system of *hùkōu* (registration), the Chinese equivalent to the Soviet *propiska*. Each Chinese is registered at his or her parents' place of registration at birth.[37] Changing the *hùkōu* involves serious bureaucratic effort and is usually only granted in the case of marriage, for business reasons, or for certain qualified job offers. It is particularly difficult in sought-after cities such as Beijing or Shanghai. Like in Russia, this form of social restriction survived the introduction of capitalism nearly unaltered. At some point, the *hùkŏu* was also intended to keep country-to-city migration low, a goal that since the 1990s has proved to be less and less effective. The obligation to register does, though, impose severe distress upon the millions of rural poor who are forced to look for jobs in the big cities. Since it is unlawful to live and work in a town or city without registration and at the same time registration in big cities is next to impossible to obtain for migrant workers, they are legal offenders *per se*. This double bind makes them particularly vulnerable to all sorts of blackmail and exploitation. The outlaw status also bars them from most social services—until very recently, even from the right to send their children to school in Shanghai. Scholars compare the position of these "illegal" migrants with that of undocumented immigrants in the United States.[38] A recent study of Chinese cities has shown that while even under capitalism the rich and the poor live in much closer proximity than in British or American cities, residents of different *hùkŏu* status continue to be sharply segregated, and central neighborhoods tend to be inhabited by long-tenured residents.[39]

Along with the economic reforms, the housing system was also radically changed. Until the 1980s, with the exception of single-family homes, most urban housing was owned by the state and assigned to the citizens almost free of charge. Before 1990, the monthly rent for a small state-owned dwelling unit was less than the price of a pack of cigarettes, and the average household spent less than 1 percent of its income on rent.[40] The difference to the sales price on the increasingly free market, however, was enormous. Low rents stood in sharp contrast to astronomic prices for ownership.[41] Since the late 1980s, apartments began to be "privatized" in the sense that the state offered the transfer of property rights.[42] Housing, which so far had been provided by the state, now involved monetary wages. This led to a two-tiered system: the old system stayed in place for the middle- and lower-income classes and a market economy of owned housing was established for the wealthy.[43] For the lucky ones who continued to live in a state-owned apartment, the rent level increased very moderately, but the availability of such flats shrunk progressively.[44] By 1996, already 46 percent of Shanghai apartments formed part of the free market economy.[45]

Over the course of the 1990s, too, a great share of the middle and lower middle classes came to own their apartment.[46] Tenants became owners in various ways. First, like in the Soviet Union during the late 1980s, China's formerly state-owned apartments were given away to the tenants for only a symbolical fee.[47] Others were given apartments because they had to leave their homes for municipally sponsored construction projects. And a third group received apartments from private investors who, in return for obtaining the right to redevelop a formerly city-owned plot of land, committed to re-housing the inhabitants of the buildings to be demolished. As a result of this policy, by 2007 the homeownership rate had risen to 68 percent in China and to over 70 percent in Shanghai.[48] Within a decade and a half, therefore, a city of renters had become one of owners. The bargain, though, was offered to a limited few. Only those who were officially registered in Shanghai were allowed to profit. The masses of migrant workers, who never had a realistic chance of attaining legal status under the restrictive system of registration, were left out. Equally left out were those who at the time of the privatization were too young to hold a rental contract; they now have to rely on the rising free market.

Along with gradual privatization and the economic upturn, investment into housing rose steadily. By the mid-1990s the worst of the housing shortage was over. Living space per capita in Shanghai increased from 4.5 square meters in 1978 to 9.3 in 1997 and 15.5 in 2005.[49] The foremost problem now became the polarization of the housing market, which reflected an increasing gap between rich and poor. Already in 1985, a quarter of urban households could dispose of the unusually large amount of 14.8 square meters per capita, while the remaining 75 percent had to get by with only 4.4 square meters.[50] The fact that the winners of the new market economy tended to invest their savings in apartments, which then often remained vacant, exacerbated the situation.[51] With large numbers of market-rate housing idle for speculation, housing is still in short supply for middle- and lower-income groups.

High-rise apartments for the privileged and for the masses

The political change gave rise to a new type of residential tower that would significantly influence the perception of mass housing: the upscale apartment block. Shanghai's luxury condominiums are not as clearly distinguishable from simpler towers as those in the United States or Russia, since there are infinite variations of more and less expensive dwellings. But even the most luxurious compounds must rightfully be called mass architecture, since they often comprise several thousand units.

The first residential tower officially designed for privileged groups was constructed in the 1980s by a Chinese-foreign joint venture.[52] The Yàndàng Building in the Lúwān district is a cruciform, 28-story-high point block with a reinforced concrete skeleton. It contains 197 apartments and looks unspectacular to contemporary eyes, yet it nevertheless offers comparatively luxurious amenities. Yàndàng is situated in the city center, about ten minutes' walking distance from the town hall and People's Park. Each apartment has two bathrooms and a spacious kitchen, and those in the southern portion overlook Fùxīng Park.

The chic Àijiàn development on the corner of South Wǎnpíng and Línglíng Roads was also the result of a Chinese-foreign joint venture. It consisted of four 15-story buildings that were erected in the mid-1980s in the Xúhuì district.[53] Àijiàn consisted of point blocks with eight apartments per floor. They were built using reinforced concrete skeleton technology. Since the cruciform plan resembled the Chinese character 井 for "well" (pronounced jǐng), architects spoke of a "well shape." Building materials were superior and included marble tiles. Interiors were equipped with stainless steel sinks, hot water boilers, and phone lines. The 2.9-meter ceiling height and the apartment size of 96 square meters were also far above the Shanghai average.

Both Yàndàng and Àijiàn were designed for "overseas Chinese" (hǎiguī—returners)—expatriates who had returned from Taiwan, the United States, or other countries. A regulation that was valid until 2001 allowed only certain apartments to be acquired by foreigners.[54] Built especially for a wealthy clientele, they featured higher standards, larger apartments and park spaces, and a more extensive security service. The architectural forms, however, remained similar to those for normal Shanghainese. Affluent expats also lived in mass-produced, six-floor apartment blocks built from a standardized design.

To put the increasing diversification according to social class in context, one has to take into account that far into the 1980s modern housing facilities were the privilege of a tiny minority. A 1986 nationwide housing survey found that only 24 percent of urban dwellings—approximately 40 million urban households were surveyed—consisted of "complete" units, meaning that they accommodated one household and consisted of a living room, bedroom, kitchen, toilet, and an aisle or porch. While almost 98 percent of urban units had electric light, only 57 percent had their own tap water and another 16 percent shared tap water. Only 24 percent had independent toilets, 10 percent shared toilets, and the rest used public toilets on the streets. Only 63 percent of urban households had their own kitchens, another 6 percent shared kitchens, and the remaining used makeshift kitchens, for example in the corridors.[55]

Next to the upscale high-rises, a great number of tower-and-slab buildings for less wealthy families were built the 1980s. One of the largest is the Qūyáng development in the northern Hóngkŏu district, which was started in 1979.[56] Built for 30,000 inhabitants on an 80-hectare site, it comprised more than 1 million square meters of floor space. The development was divided into six different residential compounds, which almost look as if they belong to different developments. Each is entered through a separate gate. The developers took pride in the sophisticated arrangement of the public buildings. A hospital, schools, kindergartens, stores, and sports facilities are planned according to a strict three-level hierarchy, with the highest level catering to the entire development, the medium to the residential quarter, and the lower to the housing cluster. The goal was to avoid, wherever possible, pedestrians having to cross the wide thoroughfares. The administrative center at the northeast corner of Qūyáng and Yútián Roads included the neighborhood committee, several administrative offices, a police station, and Shanghai's first large shopping center. The Qūyáng development mixed different building types and floor plans. For the exterior, colored concrete was used, often adorned with mosaic murals. Compounds comprise both Cáoyáng-style 5-story slabs and cruciform 12-story point blocks; the 12-story buildings were among the highest in Shanghai at the time. In each building there are eight two-bedroom apartments per floor, each with its own kitchen and toilet. There are also several slab buildings with apartments spanning over three floors. Served by stairs inside the apartments, living rooms and kitchens are situated on the middle floor, while bedrooms and toilets are on the upper and lower floors. Its architects had also promoted the economical setup of the development. Skip-floor elevators only stop at every third floor, reducing costs. For new inhabitants who had previously had to share kitchens and bathrooms with their neighbors, an apartment in the Qūyáng development was a significant improvement. In 1989, the municipal authorities declared the development one of the ten best architectural projects in Shanghai since 1949.[57]

There was a clear hierarchy in Shanghai's mass housing, and the ranking of apartments was commonly agreed upon. For a 6-story building, for example, it was: 3rd floor (most desirable), then 4th, 2nd, 5th, 1st, and finally 6th (least desirable). Decisive factors were the number of stairs to climb, heat (unbearable under the roof) and humidity (worst on the first floor).[58] The preferable direction for windows was south or north—in subtropical Shanghai, the sun shines almost in the zenith on a summer noon, and south-facing windows heat up the apartment least. The unreliability of elevators—they were often operated manually by personnel who worked only certain hours—further detracted from living too high up. Over the years, however, floor plans, insulation, and elevators were improved, and these factors ceased to be relevant.

Tower block compounds versus historic alleys?

In the 1990s Pǔdòng Xīnqū (New Area East of the River) was developed across the Huángpǔ River from the Old Town—it was the time when glossy magazines worldwide started portraying Shanghai as a hip metropolis. The marshy Pǔdòng district, until the 1990s a largely rural zone where vegetables were grown for Shanghai's markets, now features the city's most impressive skyline. Next to the pink Oriental Pearl Television Tower stands Skidmore, Owing, and Merrill's 88-story Jīn Mào office skyscraper, the World Finance Tower, which once was to become the world's fourth largest building, and other landmarks. The mind-blowing construction boom was not limited to offices. All over the city, residential high-rises cropped up at a breathtaking rate, often on the site of demolished old buildings. Given so much construction one can understand why, according to the *New York Times*, China in recent years consumed 54.7 percent of the world's production of concrete and 36.1 percent of steel.[59]

A very different aspect of residential life can be experienced in those parts of Shanghai's Old Town that so far have been spared the Chinese equivalent of urban renewal. However, unlike in many European and North American cities, the relation between traditional and modern multi-family dwellings and the respective values that are placed on one or the other seem to be more of a variation than a dichotomy. Shanghai's pre-modernist residential buildings are mostly *lǐlòng,* a term that literally translates into "system of alleys." It denotes a particular type of residential compound that is much denser than, for example, the traditional *sìhéyuàn* (courtyard buildings) in Beijing. The back alleys (*lòng*) are accessed through a small gate from the main street and run like a grid through the inner parts of the block. The individual buildings are two to three stories high with pitched roofs and built in rows like English terraced housing. They are accessed from the back alleys, except for the ones that look toward the main street. The back alleys form a semi-public space, in which children play, elderly chat, and women dry their laundry; sometimes hawkers also sell their goods here. The kitchen, often at the ground floor of a row house, has to be shared by several families; individual gas stoves and water cranes nevertheless ensure that each family only pays for their own consumption. While older *lǐlòng* lack any modern sanitary facilities and chamber pots have to be emptied every day into the communal sink in the alley, the so-called "new *lǐlòng*" that were built in the 1930s feature inside piping, toilets, and often small balconies. *Lǐlòng* are nonetheless modern buildings in the sense that they constitute a decidedly urban typology that responded to the city's fast growth in the late nineteenth century. The oldest surviving *lǐlòng* dates from 1878;[60] the bulk was built in the early

8.7
Lǐlòng at 303 Pénglái Road, built in 1925 and renovated in the 1980s. The buildings on the left are the *shíkūmén* type (stone gate houses) (Florian Urban, 2008)

twentieth century. A particular form of *lǐlòng* architecture are the *shíkūmén* (stone gate houses). Here, each individual row house building is accessed from the back alleys through a tiny courtyard sheltering the entrance; one enters the courtyard through a richly ornamented stone gate. *Shíkūmén* are indigenous to Shanghai. Many regard them as a synthesis between traditional Chinese architecture and English terraced housing. Originally each *shíkūmén* was built for one family—a luxury that belongs to bygone times. It is still quite common that on each floor a family of parents and one or two children sleep in the same room; sometimes grandparents also bunk on the sofa. Street life is the result of sheer need. Grandpa is forced to drink tea or play cards on the street whether he likes it or not, since at home there is no space for him during the day. And for the son who exits the communal shower with a towel wrapped around his hips, greeting five neighbors on his way back to the apartment is often more of an annoying necessity than a sign of deeply felt community spirit.

For decades, the authorities aimed at removing the *lǐlòng* and replacing them with modern housing. The rhetoric was the same as in the West: modernization, increased hygiene, and removal of "obsolete" dwelling conditions. The methods, though, were different than, for example, in Berlin. The demolition of the *lǐlòng* was driven exclusively by a market economy. The high-rise buildings were seen less as an incarnation of a modernist dream, and more as the most efficient method of piling up a large number of people in an area where land prices were skyrocketing. Contrary to the formerly state-owned multistory buildings, which over the course of the 1990s were mostly handed over to former tenants for a nominal fee, the *lǐlòng* to date remain in the hands of the state. The row houses were simply too small to be divided up among the families that inhabited them. For this reason, the addition of toilets and bathrooms was also only possible in rare cases. Since the municipal owners did not have the means to relocate half of the population and thus increase the dwelling space for the remaining inhabitants, the city took to demolition and rebuilding as the most efficient way to increase dwelling standards. The *lǐlòng* were sold to a developer who demolished them and provided the inhabitants with financial compensation or substitute apartments, either on the site of the demolished *lǐlòng,* or, more commonly, on the out-skirts where real estate prices were cheaper. The method was comparable to the Slum Redevelopment Authority schemes in Mumbai. The city did not have to pay for renovation, the developers profited from any square meter they were able to build in excess of those needed by the displaced *lǐlòng* dwellers, and the former tenants became homeowners practically for free. As a result of this policy, during the 1990s and early 2000s thousands of square meters of the traditional homes have been bulldozed to make way for high-rise housing blocks. Only one-third of the *lǐlòngs* that existed at the end of the Second World War, when they had housed approximately 70 percent of Shanghai's population, has so far survived the demolitions.[61]

Since the mid-1990s, however, preservationists have been gaining ground. The destruction of entire blocks can still be witnessed, but their number, according to observers, is diminishing.[62] There are signs of a changing attitude among the municipal authorities. The *shíkūmén* in particular are increasingly valued as an important part of the city's architectural heritage. In 1991, China adopted legislation for historic preservation, and since 1994 entire areas can be listed as monuments.[63] This status nevertheless means only very limited protection in practice. Of the four categories of historic preservation, two allow for a modification of the entire building except for load-bearing structures and façade. And even in the preservation areas, only a small number of buildings are protected against demolition.[64] The denomination currently applies for 12 areas in Shanghai, including the entire Old Town and parts of the former French and British Concessions. Demolition of historic buildings continues in these areas, often because of permits that were issued before the preservation status was adopted.[65] Zheng Shiling, the director of the Shanghai Committee for the Preservation of Historical Areas, nevertheless observes a decline in demolition. He points to the statement made by Xi Jingpin, Shanghai's new Party Secretary, soon after his appointment in 2007, that old buildings must be preserved—a statement that ten years before would have been unimaginable.[66]

The proponents of *lǐlòng* preservation nevertheless face an uphill battle. Not only do they have to defy the interests of a powerful real estate industry, but equally the opposition of the *lǐlòng* dwellers. Those involved in *lǐlòng* preservation suggest that contrary to the residents affected by Mumbai's slum redevelopment schemes in the 2000s or Berlin's urban renewal in the 1970s, most *lǐlòng* tenants eagerly await the destruction of their homes.[67] According to the observers, they suffer most from overcrowding and a complete lack of privacy—the same condition that in European and American tenements a hundred years before supported the case of modernist mass housing. In a three-meter-wide *lǐlòng* alley there are no secrets even for the most discrete neighbors, and at the dinner table, so a saying goes, one has to be careful not to stick one's chopsticks in the rice bowl in the neighbor's house by mistake.[68] The wariness of overly close contact with neighbors might also reflect the many periods of repression in recent history, when a rumor or accusation could threaten

8.8
Demolition of *lǐlòng* on Dàjìng Road in Shanghai's Old Town (Florian Urban, 2008)

one's life or future. Also, compared to Mumbai's slum dwellers, their situation as legal tenants makes it more likely that they will be provided with a substitute apartment after their eviction. Whether or not the desire to move holds true for all *lǐlòng* dwellers—some of the elderly seem to be uneasy about leaving[69]—there is little evidence for tenants' resistance to demolition. This cannot exclusively be attributed to fear of repression and the absence of independent media, since there are cases where an Old Town dweller's fight against the bulldozers has made it to the newspapers—but all refer to individually owned homes.[70] In any case it is uncertain to what extent the lifestyle of street vendors, makeshift corner kitchens, and children playing on the streets will linger in Shanghai's inner city.

8.9
Rén Héng Bīn Jiāng Yuán (Yanlord Gardens) near the riverfront in the Pǔdòng district (1997–2003), one of the most expensive residential developments in Shanghai (Florian Urban, 2008)

Shanghai: future capital of tower block housing?

While few Shanghainese deliberately live in *lǐlòng,* the city's most prestigious apartments are situated in high-rise blocks. One of the most expensive, the Rén Héng Bīn Jiāng Yuán development (English name: Yanlord Gardens), is located in the Pǔdòng district on the right bank of the Huángpǔ, across the river from the Bund.[71] The compound, which was built 1997–2003, consists of 11 glitzy high-rises with 1,940 units. In many respects, it is the antithesis of a *lǐlòng.* Between the buildings, women walk their dogs across impeccable lawns and youngsters frolic in the swimming pool. The development is fenced in; security guards deny access to anyone without an invitation. Few Old Town dwellers could ever aspire to move into this well-kept urban paradise. A square meter in one of the spacious maisonette apartments overlooking the river costs approximately 60,000 yuan (4,000 US dollars); the security guard who takes care of them is likely to make no more than 120 dollars per month. And yet, these high-rises offer many of the amenities that are also found in the *lǐlòng.* Both are standardized homes for large numbers of people, sheltered from the noise and the dust of the 16-million metropolis, both enable intense public life between the dwellings, and both are situated in the middle of the city.

Rén Héng Bīng Jiāng Yuán and the nearby Shì Mào Bīng Jiāng Huā Yuán (English name: Shimao Riviera Gardens), a compound of high-rises between 49 and 60 stories high, represent the upper end of Shanghai's new new mass housing.[72] There are, however, also abundant offers for the middle class. The Sān Lín Yuán development was started in 1994 in the Pǔdòng district. It consists of seven-story buildings with moderate façade ornaments and slightly pitched roofs. They were designed for tenants who were displaced for the construction of municipal infrastructure; a portion of the apartments was also sold on the free market. Sān Lín Yuàn was designed to form a community. Buildings are grouped around a multipurpose clubhouse and a big public square. Individual buildings are assembled in groups of three to form little open courtyards; they have common functional spaces such as bike storage rooms on the ground floors of each building.[73]

One of the largest developments, Zhōng Yuǎn Liǎng Wān Chéng (English name: Brilliant City), was built in 2000 on the north bank of the Wúsōng River, a tributary of the Huángpǔ, in the Pǔtuó district.[74] The spectacular design makes Brilliant City one of Shanghai's most photographed new developments—the views of endlessly repetitive high-rises narrowly crammed together and the reflections of their silhouettes in the Wúsōng River resemble mass dwellings in Hong Kong. The shiny 36 towers were erected on a rather small plot of 0.5 million square meters, comprising a total floor area of 1.6 million square meters. The prestigious state-run architectural firm East China Architectural Design and Research Institute worked out the design. The buildings are 100 meters high and 100 meters long. The area has a floor–area ratio of 3.0, and only 15 percent of the area is built up, enabling a fair amount of green spaces despite the density. The apartments are accessed through interior corridors.

Like many new developments of the 1990s, Brilliant City was built on sites that were cleared from low-rise buildings, either the quaint self-built houses classified as slums, or historic *lǐlòng* compounds. Current observers acknowledge that this privately sponsored

urban renewal produced high-quality dwellings that the city would not have been able to supply, but at the same time are critical of the fact that the new high-rise developments furthered the gentrification of entire neighborhoods and destroyed the lifestyle connected with the traditional city. Instead of socially mixed neighborhoods, the number of upscale gated communities and monofunctional office parks increased.[75]

     The authorities still assume ample responsibility for the repair and improvement of state-owned buildings. In 2000, the city of Shanghai started a program to set up pitched roofs on modernist mass dwellings. Popular opinion claims that the mayor wanted to give a more historic impression to those who approach the city by plane. The true objectives, however, were the repair of leaks in the flat roofs and the improvement of insulation against heat and cold.[76] In numerous buildings, kitchens, bathrooms, and elevators were also added. Egalitarian goals have not totally vanished from the public agenda either: in order to increase

8.10
Zhōng Yuǎn Liǎng Wān Chéng (Brilliant City), consisting of 36 towers for comparatively wealthy inhabitants (2000) (Florian Urban, 2008)

the dwelling space for lower market segments, in 2006 the city started to force private investors to design at least 70 percent of their newly built apartments smaller than 90 square meters.[77]

High density is still official policy, although the standards now provide for slightly lower buildings than a few years ago. Outside the inner ring of elevated highways the floor–area ratio is now 2.0 for residential buildings and 3.0 for office buildings; before 2003 the respective numbers were 4.0 and 7.5. Inside the inner ring, the technical building ordinance suggests 9–12-story buildings; the cap is at 80 meters height, which approximately corresponds to a 20-story building. Buildings are also not supposed to be broader than 80 meters.[78]

8.11
Chīn Lǐ Chéng (Everest Town), a prefab development under construction in the southern part of the Pǔdòng district (Florian Urban, 2008)

The ongoing popularity of high-rise construction among the Shanghainese of all social classes has also led to the rediscovery of an architectural type that in France or Germany has come to epitomize architectural failure: the prefab high-rise. Under the socialist planned economy, prefab construction in China was never as widespread as it was in Russia or other Eastern European countries. Now, after the introduction of the market economy, it is mostly large construction firms that aim to profit from the economic advantages that prefabrication provides for large-scale projects. An example is the development Chīn Lǐ Chéng (English name: Everest Town), which is currently being constructed by the developer Vanke in the southern part of the Pǔdòng district, approximately 10 miles from the city center.[79] Colorful signs promise integrated living in the midst of a lush park. The brown 20-story buildings recall images from Stockholm-Vällingby or Berlin-Marzahn, although the building materials appear to be of better quality. A total of 280,000 square meters of dwelling space is planned. Since state regulations require the provision of infrastructure, commercial space, and public buildings such as schools and nurseries, this latest result of Chinese capitalism actually has quite a lot in common with a socialist dwelling complex. The company takes pride in its slab technology: "Standardization secures quality" is written on a sign with which Vanke advertises a corporate expertise that spans from design to completion. Their long-term goal is to develop prefab high-rises for all segments of the market.[80]

In Shanghai, high-rise buildings seem to be more a subject of discussions about freewheeling capitalism rather than social setting and physical qualities. The buzzing market leaves little space for Western-style debates on community values and neighborhood structures in low-rise buildings. Similarly, preservationist attempts to fight the effacement of the city's history, as embodied in the *lǐlòng*, find themselves under increasing pressure from a housing market that offers far greater profits for multistory housing.

The real estate market in China's largest metropolitan agglomeration nevertheless works quite differently from that in London or Chicago. Shanghai's high-rises sell, and life in the tall mass housing blocks has a degree of normality inconceivable in western cities. The preference for living high up is independent of the inhabitants' social class: the most prestigious apartments with a river view cost more than a villa with a garden on the outskirts. Living in the city center continues to be popular, and some of the amenities offered by Shanghai's *lǐlòng*—a central location, a secluded space, and the possibility of neighborly encounters in a semi-public sphere—are offered by many high-rise compounds in the same way. Given the high degree of acceptance of high-rise housing among the Shanghainese and the ongoing economic boom, towers and slabs are likely to remain one of Shanghai's most popular types of dwelling.

9 Global Architecture, Locally Conditioned

Adapting the mass housing block to local conditions

In the last sixty years, allegedly egalitarian mass housing blocks have yielded more differences than their creators could have ever imagined. An architectural type that like few others was developed to provide equal living standards for everyone developed into a wide array of unequal variations. Serially produced apartment blocks were built as low-rises and high-rises, on individual lots and large estates, by public or private developers, from bricks and prefab slabs, in the city center and on the periphery, as housing projects or luxury condos, with tiny one-room apartments and spacious maisonettes, with austere modernist and lavish neoclassical façades, crammed on paved grounds and surrounded by lush gardens. Their inhabitants are equally diverse. They house the middle class and welfare recipients, the privileged and the outcast, long-term residents and recent immigrants. How was a building type that on the surface appears so similar able to generate so much difference?

About a century after modernist architects and planners started to propagate equal dwelling conditions it is obvious that their goals are likely to remain utopian. Although many countries are now economically better off than fifty years ago, the world, alas, has become increasingly unequal. Formerly communist Russia and China are now highly polarized societies, and even in countries such as France or Germany, where the living conditions of the rich and the poor had begun to converge during the 1960s and 1970s, the gap is widening once again. In all these countries serial mass housing assumed a particular role in the new inequality.

As a rule, the design of the housing blocks tended to adapt to societal conditions rather than shaping them, but at the same time showed a certain degree of resistance. This is particularly evident in Brazil, where the goal of egalitarian housing clashed strongly with a highly polarized society. Instead of favoring the formation of a middle class as its designers had hoped, Brasília's tower blocks were adjusted to an individualized environment marked by social difference: parks, public spaces, and communal facilities were gradually privatized and design, amenities, and maintenance became more and more unequal. The impact of the designers' egalitarian goals nevertheless came to be reflected in what observers frequently celebrate as the particular ambience of Brasília compared to Rio de Janeiro and São Paulo—an egalitarian spatiality that harsh social polarization has not been fully able to obliterate. The city's obstinately different form of public life is part of this architectural originality and was, ironically, supported by the historic preservation movement, which for example forbade access restrictions to the *superquadras*.

All around the world, local variations in mass housing relate to three factors: a diversification in the conceptual background, the internal differentiation of the respective societies, and the different architectural context into which mass housing was introduced. First and foremost, two conceptual fundamentals—egalitarianism and state intervention—were interpreted very differently in the respective cities. Both cultural dispositions and political realities, including demography and migration, shaped the definition of the target groups for the policy goal of "equal living conditions for everyone," and at the same time determined how much the various national economies were willing to invest. This applied to the influence of Chicago's real estate lobby on size, form, and location of the local housing projects in the same way as for China's "production first—livelihood second" strategy that in the 1950s led to a withdrawal of state resources from the residential construction industry. State-sponsored egalitarianism had a different meaning in every sample city. In Shanghai's communist-era housing compounds it referred to a hierarchically organized state organism that collectively embarked on the path to progress and development. In Brasília, it meant a new solidarity between the tiny middle class with their less wealthy neighbors. The battle over modular apartment buildings in Germany, France, or the US was primarily concerned with an assessment of the state's role in promoting egalitarianism and at the same time regulating citizens' daily lives. The abandonment of large-scale housing programs in the US was the first step in the state's withdrawal from a form of social policy that it had never fully supported, and a successive reliance on the market. In countries such as France, Germany, Russia, China, or India, where interventionist policy was not completely jettisoned, it went along with a redefinition of the state's tasks and objectives amid a new array of private and public players.

Second, throughout the world a "modern lifestyle" never became universal. Modernized living diversified according to income, which in turn generated significant modifications of the housing block type. Not everywhere were the categories formulated as bluntly as in India, where plans and façades were officially designated to high-, middle-, and low-income groups. But in many countries a hierarchy between the different kinds of apartment blocks soon became apparent. The mass housing project is to the high-end condominium what the farmhouse is to the country-style mansion that imitates rural life. Both housing project and condominium derive from a common typology, but seriality and height are pragmatic necessities for one and stylistic principles for the other. In the high-end blocks one finds brick walls, spacious floor plans, and luxurious finishes, and in the cheap mass buildings, prefab panels, tiny apartment sizes, and low ceilings. While the former are built in the city center, the latter can be found predominantly in less desirable areas on the periphery. The luxury version of mass housing proliferates in Shanghai, Mumbai, Moscow, Brasília, and to a certain extent also in Chicago, yet is much more rare in Paris and Berlin. These differences are rooted in both legislation and cultural preference. In both Paris and Berlin, high-rise construction is restricted in the city center, both cities have spectacular pre-modernist buildings that are held in high regard, and Berlin's slumping economy generates a comparably small demand for high-end dwellings.

Third, the significance of mass housing was determined by the local context, and thus to a large extent the contrast with different forms of non-modern dwellings. Modern architecture and planning was formulated as an explicit counterproposal to the existing city. Hence the semantic vicissitude of the new and the old, the tower block and the tenement, the modern dwelling and the slum was decisive for the perception of the respective urban environment and changed if the context was modified. When the large tower block estates went up in the Paris *banlieue*, they were the beacon of progress sticking out of the huts and shanties that surrounded them. When the shanties had disappeared a decade later, the cheaply built towers appeared as inferior dwellings compared to the lavish nineteenth-century abodes in the city center. In Brasília's founding period, the half-empty modernist homes appeared hostile compared to the bustle of the self-built workmen's quarters; a decade later they connoted an urban order endangered by the despair in the proliferating *favelas*. Architectural resistance to surrounding social conditions, as previously mentioned, nevertheless lies in its potential to offer alternative views and reinterpretations: Brasília's soundly built and centrally located middle-class blocks were eventually accepted by both inhabitants and visitors, and even in the comprehensively discredited tower block neighborhoods in Paris or Berlin there are clear distinctions between higher- and lower-quality dwellings.

The local context includes socio-cultural conditions that accounted for a different course of events even in those cases where the overall development was similar—such as a deteriorating image over the course of the 1960s and an increasing association with marginalized minorities. For example, the decline of mass housing was framed very differently in the United States, France, and West Germany. In all three countries the apartment blocks had originally been planned for the majority population and later were increasingly inhabited by immigrants or African Americans, and in all three countries they suffered from a sudden and very extreme swing in public opinion. In France and West Germany, however, first- and second-generation immigrants only moved to the housing blocks on a large scale in the 1970s, approximately a decade after the buildings had been completed. In the United States, the focus of the housing programs shifted toward minorities before the largest developments had even been planned and built, and projects such as Chicago's Robert Taylor Homes were conceptualized for black residents. In West Germany, the share of minority groups (immigrants) among mass housing dwellers to date rarely exceeds 25 percent, whereas in France the percentage is much higher, and in many US housing projects nearly all residents are black. In both European countries the sudden swing in public opinion started at a time when the buildings were still dominated by the ethnic majority—in Paris in 1959 and in West Berlin in 1968. In the United States, public opinion has never been fully supportive but started to deteriorate massively in 1965, at a time when housing projects were already predominantly associated with African Americans. Thus even in Western countries, population shifts and public perception did not follow a common pattern.

Hardly anywhere did the standardized modern lifestyle connected with the mass developments become the exclusive form of living, and often it turned out to be just one among many. In Mumbai, the "pre-modern" life in huts and shanties is still a sign of economic disadvantage, but has become an intrinsic part of the modern metropolis and a labor pool for a booming urban economy in which slums and apartment blocks are connected by mutual dependency. In Paris or Chicago, the tower blocks became precisely the mass dwellings from which the wealthier groups distinguished themselves. But here too the economic ties between housing blocks and other building types are re-enacted every morning, when thousands of service workers, whose low-paid professions were once deemed obsolete by the theorists of a modern classless society, leave their tower-block homes to guard or clean the abodes of the wealthy. The significance of the serial blocks as homes of the privileged or the marginalized was therefore tied to the proliferation of a modern lifestyle and often manifested in their spatial situation in the city center or on the fringe. In this respect, modern mass housing channeled the development of modernity in the respective societies and cast it into a specific social geography.

Ambiguous effects, contextual perception

Were the numerous mass housing programs a success or a failure? Of course this question cannot be answered without a critical examination of the values that underlie such a judgment. Given the preeminence of a normative discourse around these developments in many countries it is nevertheless revealing to take a closer look at some common patterns in these debates and contrast the outcome with the goals that the theorists of mass housing had once formulated.

The comprehensive regulation of the housing market by state authorities in Shanghai, Paris, or Berlin has largely yielded positive results on a very basic level. In those cities, dwelling conditions for society's lower strata has improved significantly over the last fifty years. Even in Mumbai, where the project of housing the masses was largely foiled by poverty, demographic explosion, bureaucratic inefficiency, and the incapacity to secure long-term building management, the tower blocks succeeded in providing solid homes and running water for a sizeable share of the population. In Brasília or Chicago, on the other hand, where state intervention was significantly smaller, housing is only slightly less polarized than half a century ago. Market-oriented approaches have nowhere succeeded in providing acceptable apartments for all parts of society, and even in highly liberalized economies there is a continuous need for state intervention to limit the proliferation of substandard dwellings and homelessness. The 2008 crisis of the two largest private mortgage financers in the USA, Fannie Mae and Freddie Mac, and their subsequent takeover by federal authorities evidenced the shortcomings of the free market. Fannie Mae had been formed under Roosevelt's New Deal in the 1930s as a government agency holding the monopoly of the second market with mortgages—its privatization in 1968 was much criticized by interventionist politicians. The re-nationalization in 2008 has not heralded a new era of intensified state control over the housing market in the US, but shows the failure of free market policies to provide long-term stability even for the middle class. While state intervention did not succeed in providing quality housing for the entire population, the absence of state regulation almost everywhere led to an increase in catastrophic living conditions for the disadvantaged.

The debates over the success or failure of mass housing that were fought out in many countries were highly contextual. They depended on demographic factors in the same way as on the availability of alternative forms of dwelling, on local class differentiation in the same way as on the respective city's level of wealth, which both made a mass-produced apartment a form of accommodation far above the average, as in Mumbai, or far below, as in Paris. Among the examples in the book, only in Chicago, Paris, and West Berlin did the tower blocks trigger persistent debates, and public opinion deteriorated over a surprisingly short period of time. What was at stake in these places were the strategies the state used to determine people's living conditions. With regard to minorities such as African Americans in Chicago and North African immigrants in the Paris region, housing came to be inter-twined with identity politics. The shortcomings of the paternalistic state, which never lived up to its claim of impartiality and whose care was always a form of control at the same time, were particularly obvious in those cases in which, like in Chicago and Paris, special interest groups openly stood against one another. There, the tower blocks became focal points for social conditions that were not necessarily related to buildings but forcefully manifested in the local housing geography. The introduction of basic comfort, central heating and running water was therefore canceled out by the social exclusion inherent in the housing blocks.

Generally, the reputation of the tower blocks in those cities was unrelated to their effectiveness in resolving the housing crisis. The question of success versus failure was hardly ever guaged against the original promises of providing modern standards of living and resolving the housing shortage. Otherwise the result would have looked quite different. In Paris and Berlin, two cities where public opinion for a long time was and still is stalwartly anti-tower block, the balance was largely positive. Utter poverty comparable to that of the early twentieth century has largely disappeared in both cities. The same applies for Shanghai, where mass housing was never publicly debated. Here, housing programs were successful in meeting the challenges of modernization and significantly mitigating a dwelling situation that for decades afforded less than 4 square meters of private space for the average citizen.

The evolution of mass housing developments largely reflected social and political configurations that were already in place before the apartment buildings were erected. In China, the egalitarian theme was interpreted on the basis of a local pattern of hierarchical stratification that had already existed under the regime of planned economy and became more evident with the new class differentiation in the decades after structural reform. When towers with special amenities were first designed for the wealthy "overseas Chinese" and later for the domestic winners of the market economy, they still reflected a society built on collective values and hierarchical organization, but presented the differences between certain social groups in a far more pronounced way. They thus corresponded to the Chinese reality characterized by the ongoing tension between authoritarian state rule on the one hand and economic liberalization on the other. In India, the tower blocks were the products of a society that had always been extremely polarized, but which concomitantly with market liberalization experienced a growth of the urban middle class. In contrast to Shanghai, property and land use in Mumbai were negotiated by a much more diverse array of interest groups that included not only state institutions, developers, and real estate owners, but to some extent also slum dweller associations. The tower blocks were built following the city's extreme spatial mix, placing high-rises in close proximity to the slum dwellings. Here, the concept of state-sponsored mass housing with minimum standards was voided by the fact that throughout the twentieth century the masses had never been able to afford any type of formal apartment, a situation which lingered under the quasi-socialist mixed economy and became even more problematic under the conditions of market liberalization.

Flexible meaning, inflexible architecture

Next to the local economic, social, and political forces, there were also architectural variations that influenced the course of the debate. Most important were location and quality of construction. Wherever tower blocks were constructed near cultural and economic hubs—not necessarily in the city center—their reputation was much better. Very rarely did tower block neighborhoods themselves become new centers. And wherever they were built with spacious plans and high-quality craftsmanship they were more sought-after.

Apart from these basic aspects, arguably the most important architectural deficiency of the tower blocks was their relative inflexibility. The one-size-fits-all design from the very beginning carried a high potential for conflicts between a modern lifestyle and alternative models. This is most spectacularly conveyed in popular tales about former farmers keeping cattle in their sixth-floor apartments or former nomads dismounting fixtures before leaving their new homes never to come back, but is equally palpable whenever extended families have to split to fit the standard two bedrooms or when part-time workers unsuccessfully try to convert a dining room into an office or studio. Inhabitants have a hard time adapting their apartments to different lifestyles and requirements, and the dependence on good management is high. That the buildings prevented any form of self-help was particularly noticeable in those contexts in which a poor population depended on limited state funds. The results, from dysfunctional elevators and heating systems to clogged trash chutes and leaking pipes could be found in Chicago in the same way as in Mumbai and contributed significantly to the buildings' bad reputation. But even in well-managed developments the inhabitants had few possibilities for shaping their environment. The textbook example is the East German slab-building apartment, where the heating in designated bedrooms often by default was set a few degrees lower than that of designated living rooms, thus forcing cold shivers upon anyone who wanted to spend a day working or playing with their children in the wrong room. The rigid organization of daily life in the mass housing development included the communal facilities from the schools and daycare centers in the Soviet *mikrorayony* to the state-sponsored neighborhood associations and youth clubs in Paris and Berlin—as useful as these amenities were at a certain point, they all too often proved to be too inflexible to adapt to changing needs. This became evident when a community of young families turned into a community of elderly, and daycare centers could not be converted into nursing homes, or when the nuclear family with two kids and the breadwinner working outside the home ceased to be the rule. The programmatic strictness, so much cherished by regimes that believed in central organization and the social power of the exact sciences, was one of the main criticisms against the tower blocks of the 1960s and 1970s, before a new generation of architects aimed at developing more flexible apartment plans.

While the parameters of the discourse on mass housing developments were diverse and only to some extent related to architectural features, its effects were substantial. In many Western countries, including the US, France, and to a certain degree West Germany, the tower blocks had been planned for the majority population, and later became home to disadvantaged minorities—African Americans in the US, immigrants from Southern Europe and North Africa in France and Germany. The swing in public opinion preceded the population exchange and not vice versa. That is, in both France and Germany the reputation of the tower blocks first deteriorated among the better off who could afford to move and then these buildings became the home of the marginalized. In Chicago, the situation was more complicated, since, at least from the 1950s onward, the social housing programs that had once been planned with the white middle class in mind were more and more directed toward poor African Americans. But also here one can detect a similar pattern: once public opinion turned, those African Americans who were better off moved out and left the projects to those who had virtually no choice.

With regard to the near future, mass housing is far from having run its course, despite the well-deserved criticism of the social exclusion in the French *banlieues*, the American housing projects, and elsewhere. Despite its historical successes on many levels, direct state intervention into the housing market is declining in many countries. Tower block construction, however, is not. Rising popularity of tower block housing can be predicted with mathematical precision: with the exception of the shrinking cities in Europe and North America, urban life in the future will be determined by demographic growth and increasing urbanization, combined with congested streets and rising energy costs that make long commutes unattractive. Both Mumbai and Shanghai are exemplary in this respect: the middle classes live in apartment blocks rather than in single-family homes and enjoy not only proximity to the centers of urban life but at the same time stores, restaurants, and recreational facilities tailored to their needs. It remains the subject of speculation what new types of architectural creativity in apartment block design legislative control and consumer preference will yield, but one can expect that multistory homes will be increasingly accepted throughout the world.

Interview Partners

Banerjee-Guha, Swapna (geographer, Tata Institute for Social Science, Mumbai), Mumbai, June 9, 2008

Contractor, Hafeez (architect), Mumbai, June 3, 2008

Deshpande, Lalit (economist, professor emeritus at the University of Mumbai), Mumbai, June 6, 2008

Feldman, Roberta, (architect, professor at the University of Illinois at Chicago), April 10, 2007

Huang Yiru (urban planner, professor at Tongji University), Shanghai, August 29, 2007

Hunt, Bradford (Professor of Social Science, Roosevelt University), Chicago, April 10, 2007

Jiang Jiang (architect, Shanghai Municipal Housing, Land, and Resources Administration Bureau), Shanghai, August 29, 2007

Joshi, Pankaj (architect, preservationist), Mumbai, June 10, 2008

Li Zhengyu (architect, professor at Tongji University), Shanghai, August 24, 2007

Mahajan, Sulakshana (urban planner, Mumbai Transformation Support Unit, All-India Institute of Local Self Government), Mumbai, June 5, 2008

Manohar, Prathima (architect, journalist), Mumbai, June 9, 2008

Mehrotra, Rahul (architect), Boston, April 14, 2008

Patel, Shirish (civil engineer), Mumbai, June 2, 2008

Paul, Anirudh (architect, professor at the Kamla Raheja Vidyanidhi Institute of Architecture, Mumbai), Mumbai, June 10, 2008

Phatak, Vidyadhar (former head of the Town and Country Planning Division, of the Mumbai Metropolitan Region Development Authority), Mumbai, June 11, 2008

Prabhu, Chandrashekhar (architect, former president of the Maharashtra Housing and Area Development Authority), Mumbai, June 7, 2008

Reyes, Damaris, (executive director of the community organization Good Old Lower East Side) New York, October 9, 2007

Shetty, Prasad (architect, environmental planner with the Maharashtra Metropolitan Region Development Authority), Mumbai, June 4, 2008

Wakeman, Rosemary, (urban historian, professor at Fordham University), New York, October 10, 2007

Ye Ang (architect), Shanghai, August 27, 2007

Zhang Lixin (civil engineer, Shanghai Municipal Housing, Land, and Resources Administration Bureau) Shanghai, August 29, 2007

Zheng Shilin (Director of the Committee of the Preservation of Historical Areas and Heritage Architecture, Shanghai Urban Planning Commission, Director of the Institute of Architecture and Urban Space, Tongji University), Shanghai, August 28, 2007

Notes

1 Social Reform, State Control, and the Origins of Mass Housing

1   Unless otherwise noted, all translations are by the author. Floor counting follows the American pattern even when referring to French, German, or Indian buildings—the story above the ground floor is called the second and not the first floor.
    Tony Garnier, *Une cité industrielle* (Paris: Auguste Vincent, 1917).

2   See, for example, Nicholas Bullock, and James Read, *The Movement for Housing Reform in Germany and France, 1840–1914* (Cambridge: Cambridge University Press, 1985).

3   Robert von Halász, *Industrialisierung der Bautechnik* (Düsseldorf: Werner, 1966), 2. See also Carlo Testa, *Die Industrialisierung des Bauens* (Zurich: Verlag für Architektur, 1997), 9, and Christine Hannemann, *Die Platte* (Berlin: Schelzky und Jeep, 2000), 26.

4   H. Vergnolle, "La Préfabrication chez les Romains," *Technique et Architecture* 9 n. 7–8 (1950), 11–13.

5   Ibid., 15.

6   On the influence of Ford's production methods on Walter Gropius see Winfried Nerdinger, "Walter Gropius – Vom Amerikanismus zur neuen Welt," in *Der Architekt Walter Gropius,* ed. Bauhaus-Archiv Berlin (Berlin: Gebrüder Mann Verlag, 1985), 9–12.

7   See description of the new concrete technology in *Deutsche Bauzeitung* 5 n. 30 (1871), 236–238. See also Gustav Haegermann, *Vom Caementum zum Zement* (Wiesbaden and Berlin: Bauverlag, 1964).

8   Christine Hannemann, *Die Platte* (Berlin: Schelzky und Jeep, 2000), 36.

9   Kurt Junghanns, *Das Haus für alle. Zur Geschichte der Vorfertigung in Deutschland* (Berlin: Ernst und Sohn, 1994), 20.

10 Grosvenor Atterbury, "Model Towns in America," *Scribner's Magazine* 52 (July 1912), 20–35.

11 Kurt Junghanns, *Das Haus für alle. Zur Geschichte der Vorfertigung in Deutschland* (Berlin: Ernst und Sohn, 1994), 21–22.

12 Karl Kiem, *Die Gartenstadt Staaken* (Berlin: Gebr. Mann Verlag, 1997)

13 Ibid., 23, Frank Werner and Joachim Seidel, *Der Eisenbau* (Berlin: Verlag für Bauwesen, 1992), 35–36, and Christine Hannemann, *Die Platte* (Berlin: Schelzky und Jeep, 2000), 34–36.

14 Hannes Meyer, "Über marxistische Architektur," in *Bauen und Gesellschaft – Schriften, Briefe, Projekte* (Dresden: Verlag der Kunst, 1980), 94 [written in the early 1930s].

15 Ibid.

16 Walter Gropius, "Der große baukasten," *Das neue Frankfurt* 1 n. 2 (December 1926), reprinted in *Ernst Neufert, normierte Baukultur im 20. Jahrhundert*, ed. Walter Prigge (Frankfurt: 1999).

17 Kurt Junghanns, *Das Haus für alle. Zur Geschichte der Vorfertigung in Deutschland* (Berlin: Ernst und Sohn, 1994), 160–163

18 Ludwig Mies van der Rohe, "Industrialized Building," *G* n. 3 (Berlin, 1924), reprinted in *Ulrich Conrads, Programme und Manifeste zur Architektur des 20. Jahrhunderts* (Frankfurt: Ullstein, 1964), translated by Michael Bullock *Programs and Manifestoes on Twentieth-Century Architecture*, (Cambridge, MA: MIT Press, 2001), 81–82.

19 Ibid.

20 Hilberseimer first formulated his ideas about a modular city in 1924. They were most famously published in *The New City* (Chicago: Paul Theobald, 1944).

21 According to Gropius, the ratio between the amount of dwelling space and intensity of natural light was best in an 8–12-story building. Walter Gropius, *The New Architecture and the Bauhaus* (1934), 100–105.

22 Ernst May, "Fünf Jahre Wohnungsbautätigkeit in Frankfurt/M.," *Das Neue Frankfurt* 4 (1930), 2–5.

23 Anatole Kopp, *Town and revolution; Soviet architecture and city planning 1917–1935* (New York: Braziller, 1970), 135–138.

24 Selim Chan-Magometow, *Pioniere der sowjetischen Architektur* (Dresden: Verlag der Kunst, 1983), 398.

25 Christine Hannemann, *Die Platte* (Berlin: Schelzky und Jeep, 2000), 55.

26 Le Corbusier, *Urbanisme* (Paris: G. Crès, 1925).

27 Le Corbusier, *Vers une architecture* (Paris: G. Crès, 1924) translated by Hans Hildebrandt *Kommende Baukunst* (Stuttgart: DVA, 1926), 204.

28 Peter Hall, *Cities of Tomorrow* (Oxford: Blackwell, 1988), 204–206.

29 Vkhutemas = *Vysshie gosudarstvennye khudozhestvenno-tekhnicheskye masterskye*, National Superior Artistic-Technical Workshops.

30 Stefan Muthesius and Miles Glendinning, *Tower Block* (New Haven: Yale University Press, 1994), 39.

31 Ibid., 73–75.

32 Ibid., 53.

33 Ibid., 54.

34 Twelve 9–15-story slab buildings went up on the site of destroyed prewar housing. See Axel Schildt, *Die Grindelhochhäuser* (Hamburg: Christians, 1988).

35 See Alexander Davidson, *A Home of One's Own – Housing Policy in Sweden and New Zealand from the 1840s to the 1990s* (Stockholm: Almqvist and Wiksell International, 1994).

36 The Bijlmermeer development was projected for 100,000 inhabitants—almost 12 percent of the 870,000 inhabitants that the city counted in 1963. Apartments for approximately 85,000 inhabitants were eventually erected.

37 Annie Fourcaut, "Le cas français à l'épreuve du comparatisme," in *Le monde des grands ensembles*, ed. Frédéric Dufaux and Annie Fourcaut (Paris: Éditions Créaphis, 2004), 17.

38 Isabelle Amestoy, "Les grands ensembles en Russie, de l'adoption d'un modèle à la désaffection. Le cas de l'habitat khrouchtchévien," in *Le monde des grands ensembles*, ed. Frédéric Dufaux and Annie Fourcaut (Paris: Éditions Créaphis, 2004), 130.

39 Zhang Shouyi and Wang Tao, "Housing Development in the Socialist Planned Economy from 1949–1978," in *Modern Urban Housing in China: 1841–2000*, ed. Lü Junhua, Peter G. Rowe, and Zhang Jie (Munich: Prestel, 2001), 112 and 125.

40 Michael Franklin Ross, *Beyond Metabolism: the New Japanese Architecture* (New York: McGraw and Hill, 1978), 70–71.

41 Yassamine Tayab, "L'habitat collectif à Téhéran, produit de luxe ou logement social?" in *Le monde des grands ensembles*, ed. Frédéric Dufaux and Annie Fourcaut (Paris: Éditions Créaphis, 2004), 216.

42 Ibid., 217–218.

43 Ibid., 222.

44 Lin Kuo Ching and Amina Tyabji, "Home ownership policy in Singapore: An assessment," *Housing Studies* 6 (1991), 15–28. Originally provided for renters, the HDB shifted its policy toward homeownership and from 1971 allowed for reselling at market price. Bae-Gyoon Park, "Where Do Tigers Sleep at Night? The State's Role in Housing Policy in South Korea and Singapore," *Economic Geography* 74 n. 3 (July 1998), 283–284 and 274.

45 Peter Hall, *Cities of Tomorrow*, Second Edition (Oxford: Blackwell, 1998), 356.

46 Valérie Gelézeau, "Les *tanji* sud-coréens: des grands ensembles au coeur de la ville," in *Le monde des grands ensembles*, ed. Frédéric Dufaux and Annie Fourcaut (Paris: Éditions Créaphis, 2004), 199–201.

47 Korea's first modernist apartment blocks were built in Seoul in the late 1930s for employees of the Japanese colonial authorities. The Japanese also established the Korean Housing Authority in 1941 (*Choson chut'aek yongdan*), which after the country's independence became the driving force for the mass production of housing blocks. Ibid., 199–210.

48 Bae-Gyoon Park, "Where Do Tigers Sleep at Night? The State's Role in Housing Policy in South Korea and Singapore," *Economic Geography* 74 n. 3 (July 1998), 272–288, particularly 274–275.

49 Urbanización Veintitres de Enero was originally called Urbanización Dos de Diciembre. It consists of 38 superblocks for approximately 60,000 inhabitants.

50 Myriam Houssay-Holzschuch, "Paradoxes et perversions: le *township* sud-africain," in *Le monde des grands ensembles*, ed. Frédéric Dufaux and Annie Fourcaut (Paris: Éditions Créaphis, 2004), 242–253.

51 Charles Jencks, *The Language of Post-Modern Architecture* (New York: Rizzoli, 1977), 9.

52 The differentiation of housing estates in European countries—including the Netherlands, Britain, Hungary, Spain, and Slovenia—is stressed, for example, in Rob Rowlands, Sako Musterd, and Ronald van Kempen, eds., *Mass Housing in Europe: Multiple Faces of Development, Change, and Response* (Basingstoke: Palgrave McMillan, 2009).

2 Mass Housing in Chicago

1 Roberta Feldman, interview with the author, Chicago, April 10, 2007. Feldman is a professor of urban planning at the University of Illinois, Chicago.

2 *New York Times*, June 2, 1996, quoted by Arnold Hirsch, *Making the Second Ghetto*, second edition (Chicago: University of Chicago Press, 1998), vii.

3 For a detailed analysis of the cultural particularities that determined the way housing was built in the United States see Gwendolyn Wright, *Building the Dream—a Social History of Housing in America* (New York: Pantheon, 1981). For a history of public housing in the US and its underlying ideologies see Alex Schwartz, *Housing Policy in the United States* (New York: Routledge, 2006, second revised edition 2010), R. Allen Hays, *The Federal Government and Urban Housing: Ideology and Change in Public Policy* (Albany: State University of New York Press, 1985, second edition 1995), and John F. Bauman, Roger Biles, and Kristin Szylvian, eds., *From Tenements to the Taylor Homes: In Search of an Urban Housing Policy in Twentieth Century America* (University Park, PA: Pennsylvania State University Press, 2000).

4 Bradford Hunt, "Understanding Chicago's High-Rise Public Housing Disaster," in *Chicago Architecture,* ed. Charles Waldheim and Katerina Rüedi Ray (Chicago: University of Chicago Press, 2005), 302. See also Bradford Hunt, *Blueprints for Disaster: The Unraveling of Chicago Public Housing* (Chicago: University of Chicago Press, 2009).

5 The city of Chicago had approximately 3.4 million inhabitants in 1940 and 3.55 million in 1960. U. S. Bureau of the Census—Population Division, *Population of the 100 Largest Cities and Other Urban Places in the United States 1790–1990* (Washington DC: U. S. Bureau of the Census 1998), available online at http://www.census.gov/population/www/documentation/twps0027.html (accessed March 2008).

6 Arnold Hirsch, *Making the Second Ghetto-Race and Housing in Chicago 1940–1960* (Cambridge: Cambridge University Press, 1983), 135–170.

7   Bradford Hunt, "Understanding Chicago's High-Rise Public Housing Disaster," in *Chicago Architecture*, ed. Charles Waldheim and Katerina Rüedi Ray (Chicago: University of Chicago Press, 2005), 302.

8   Ibid.

9   Ibid., 304.

10 Nicholas Lehmann, *The Promised Land: The Great Black Migration and How It Changed America* (New York: Vintage, 1992), 92.

11 The development was located immediately north of the Illinois Institute of Technology campus, between 27th Street, 30th Street, and State Street.

12 Bradford Hunt, "Understanding Chicago's High-Rise Public Housing Disaster," in *Chicago Architecture,* ed. Charles Waldheim and Katerina Rüedi Ray (Chicago: University of Chicago Press, 2005), 305.

13 T. Y. Lin and S. D. Stotesbury, "Recent Technological Developments in Industrialized Production of Housing," *Proceedings of the National Academy of Sciences of the United States of America* 67 n. 2, (October 15, 1970), 861–876.

14 Report of the President's Committee on Urban Housing (Kaiser Committee), *A Decent Home* (U.S. Govt. Printing Office 0-313-937, 1969).

15 Bradford Hunt, "What Went Wrong with Public Housing in Chicago? A History of the Robert Taylor Homes," *Journal of the Illinois State Historical Society* 94 n. 1 (2001), 103.

16 Bradford Hunt, "Understanding Chicago's High-Rise Public Housing Disaster," in *Chicago Architecture,* ed. Charles Waldheim and Katerina Rüedi Ray (Chicago: University of Chicago Press, 2005), 302.

17 An emblematic account is given in Alex Kotlowitz, *There Are No Children Here* (New York: Doubleday, 1991), 19–22.

18 The Robert Taylor Homes were situated along the Dan Ryan Expressway on State Street between 39th and 54th Streets.

19 Gwendolyn Wright, "End of the Experiment," *Architecture* 91 n. 3 (March 20002), 29.

20 See, for example, Kenneth Jackson, *Crabgrass Frontier – The Suburbanization of the United States* (Oxford: Oxford University Press, 1985), 219–230, Peter Hall, *Cities of Tomorrow* (Oxford: Blackwell, 1988), 361–400, Arnold Hirsch, *Making the Second Ghetto-Race and Housing in Chicago 1940–1960* (Cambridge: Cambridge University Press, 1983).

21 Ibid., 272.

22 Ibid., 264.

23 "Chicago Clinging to Color Lines," *Sunday Sun-Times*, March 18, 2001.

24 Jacob Riis, *How the Other Half Lives* (New York: Scribner and Sons, 1890).

25 Max Page, *The Creative Destruction of Manhattan* (Chicago: University of Chicago Press, 1999), 78.

26 Edith Elmer Wood, *The Housing of the Unskilled Wage Earner* (New York: Macmillian, 1919). See also *The Tenement House Problem*, ed. Robert De Forest and Lawrence Veiller (New York: Macmillian, 1903), Lawrence Veiller, *Housing Reform* (New York: Charities Publication Committee/Russell Sage Foundation, 1920) (Veiller lived from 1872–1959), Catherine Bauer, "Low Buildings? Catherine Bauer Questions Mr. Yamasaki's Arguments," *Journal of Housing* 9 (1952), 227, Catherine Bauer Wurster, *Modern Housing* (Boston: Houghton Mifflin, 1934).

27 Peter Hall, *Cities of Tomorrow* (Oxford: Blackwell, 1988), 229.

28 Quoted by Henry Morton, "Housing in the Soviet Union," *Proceedings of the Academy of Political Science* 35 n. 3 (1984), 69. This opinion was also repeatedly uttered by author Gore Vidal.

29 Kenneth Jackson, *Crabgrass Frontier – The Suburbanization of the United States* (Oxford: Oxford University Press, 1985), 203–205.

30 Bradford Hunt, "Understanding Chicago's High-Rise Public Housing Disaster," in *Chicago Architecture,* ed. Charles Waldheim and Katerina Rüedi Ray (Chicago: University of Chicago Press, 2005), 304.

31 Arnold Hirsch, *Making the Second Ghetto-Race and Housing in Chicago 1940–1960* (Cambridge: Cambridge University Press, 1983), 269–272.

32   Peter Hall, *Cities of Tomorrow* (Oxford: Blackwell, 1988), 229.

33   Ibid.

34   Alex Kotlowitz, *There Are No Children Here* (New York: Doubleday, 1991), 28.

35   Gwendolyn Wright, "End of the Experiment," *Architecture* 91 n. 3 (March 2002), 29–32.

36   M. W. Newman, six-part series, *Daily News* April 10–April 16.

37   Alex Kotlowitz, *There Are No Children Here* (New York: Doubleday, 1991).

38   Oscar Newman, *Defensible Spaces: Crime Prevention and Urban Design* (New York: Macmillian, 1972), 59.

39   George Kelling and James Wilson, "Broken Windows," *Atlantic Monthly* (March 1982), 29–37.

40   Peter Blake, *Form Follows Fiasco: Why Modern Architecture Hasn't Worked* (Boston: Atlantic Monthly Press, 1977), and Tom Wolfe, *From Bauhaus to Our House* (New York: Farrar, Straus, Giroux, 1981) [first published in the June and July 1981 issues of *Harper's Magazine*].

41   Jane Jacobs, *Death and Life of Great American Cities* (New York: Vintage, 1961), Richard Sennet, *The Uses of Disorder. Personal Identity and City Life* (1970).

42   Roberta Feldman, interview with the author, Chicago, April 10, 2007.

43   See, for example, Martin Anderson, *The Federal Bulldozer—a Critical Analysis of Urban Renewal* (Cambridge, MA: MIT Press, 1964), and the unmasking of the allegedly incorruptible city official in Robert Caro, *The Power Broker—Robert Moses and the Fall of New York* (New York: Knopf, 1974).

44   See, for example, *Architects Journal* July 26, 1972, "St. Louis Blues," *Architectural Forum* 136 (May 1972), or "The Experiment that Failed," *Architecture Plus* (October 1973), and Charles Jencks, *The Language of Post-Modern Architecture* (New York: Rizzoli, 1977), 4.

45   Roberta Feldman, interview with the author, Chicago, April 10, 2007. Venkatesh also mentioned that a significant share of Robert Taylor Home tenants wanted to stay. Sudhir Venkatesh, *American Project—the Rise and Fall of an American Ghetto* (Cambridge, MA: Harvard University Press, 2000), 267–268.

46   The total number of applications was 56,000; each application corresponds to one family. Chicago Housing Authority, *Moving to Work—Annual Plan for Transformation, Year* 7 (2006) appendix 5, p. 137, available online at http://www.thecha.org/transformplan/plans.html (accessed July 2008).

47   For a history of public housing in New York City see Nicholas Dagen Bloom, *Public Housing That Worked: New York in the Twentieth Century* (Philadelphia: University of Pennsylvania Press, 2008).

48   Michael Gross, "Where the Boldface Bunk," *New York Times*, March 11, 2004. See also Michael Gross, *740 Park—The Story of the World's Richest Apartment Building* (New York: Broadway, 2005).

49   First Houses, designed by Fredrick Ackerman, is located at Avenue A and East 3rd Street in the Lower East Side. Tenants were carefully screened—those who the administrators felt were too poor, too rich, too lazy, or too dirty were rejected. Christopher Gray, "Streetscapes/Public Housing; In the Beginning, New York Created First Houses," *New York Times*, September 24, 1995. Harlem River Houses is situated around Adam Clayton Powell Boulevard and East 151st Street in northern Manhattan. Architect John Louis Wilson in 1928 was the first black graduate of Columbia University's architecture school. David Dunlap, "At 50, Harlem River Houses Is Still Special," *New York Times*, April 23, 1987.

50   Ibid., Christopher Gray, "Streetscapes/Public Housing; In the Beginning, New York Created First Houses," *New York Times*, September 24, 1995.

51   Max Page, *The Creative Destruction of Manhattan* (Chicago: University of Chicago Press, 1999), 104.

52   The controlled rent level stands in sharp contrast to skyrocketing market rents. Today, for working- and lower-middle-class families it is the only option for surviving in New York City. Tenants paid 424 dollars for a two-bedroom apartment in the above-mentioned First Houses in 1995, compared to several thousand dollars for a similar market-rent apartment in the Lower East Side neighborhood. Christopher Gray, "Streetscapes/Public Housing; In the Beginning, New York Created First Houses," *New York Times*, September 24, 1995, and Damaris Reyes, interview with the author, New York, October 9, 2007.

53   Roberta Feldman, interview with the author, Chicago, April 10, 2007.

54 See the official website of the Chicago Housing Authority http://thecha.org/housingdev/robert_taylor.html (accessed March 2007), and Susan J. Popkin et al., *A Decade of HOPE VI: Research Findings and Policy Challenges* (Washington, DC: The Urban Institute, 2004).

55 Chicago Housing Authority, *Moving to Work—Annual Plan for Transformation, Year 5* (2004), chapter 1, p. 8, available online at http://www.thecha.org/transformplan/plans.htm (accessed March 2008).

56 Stateway Gardens (once 1,600 units): 440 public housing units, 440 market rate, and 440 "affordable." Robert Taylor Homes (once 4,200 units): 850 public housing units, 870 market rate, and 890 "affordable." See Chicago Housing Authority, *Moving to Work—Annual Plan for Transformation, Year 5* (2004), chapter 1, p. 8, available online at http://www.thecha.org/transform plan/plans.html (accessed March 2008).

57 Susan J. Popkin et al., *A Decade of HOPE VI: Research Findings and Policy Challenges* (Washington, DC: The Urban Institute, 2004).

58 Bradford Hunt, interview with the author, Chicago, April 10, 2007.

59 This tension is the subject of Leo Marx's famous analysis of American nineteenth-century literature, *The Machine in the Garden—Technology and the Pastoral Idea in America* (New York: Oxford University Press, 1964).

60 See, for example, Gwendolyn Wright, "End of the Experiment," *Architecture* 91 n. 3 (March 2002), 29–32.

61 Katharine G. Bristol, "The Pruitt-Igoe Myth," *Journal of Architectural Education* 44 no. 3 (May 1991), 163–171.

62 Lawrence Vale, *Reclaiming Public Housing* (Cambridge, MA: Harvard University Press, 2002).

63 Sudhir Venkatesh, *American Project—the Rise and Fall of an American Ghetto* (Cambridge, MA: Harvard University Press, 2000). See, for example, p. xvi.

64 Eugene J., Meehan, "The Rise and Fall of Public Housing: Condemnation without Trial," in *A Decent Home and Environment: Housing Urban America,* ed. D. Phares (Cambridge, MA: Ballinger, 1977).

65 This idea is put forward, for example, by Kenneth Jackson, *Crabgrass Frontier – The Suburbanization of the United States* (Oxford: Oxford University Press, 1985), 229.

3 The Concrete Cordon Around Paris

1   Marc Zitzmann, "Kinder der Banlieue – Opfer der Moderne, Täter aus Wut," *Neue Zürcher Zeitung* November 14, 2005.

2   Annie Fourcaut, "Le cas français à l'épreuve du comparatisme," in *Le monde des grands ensembles*, ed. Frédéric Dufaux and Annie Fourcaut (Paris: Éditions Créaphis, 2004), 15.

3   Frédéric Dufaux, Annie Fourcaut, and Rémy Skoutelsky, *Faire l'histoire des grands ensembles. Bibliographie 1950–1980* (Lyon: ENS Editions, 2003).

4   Annie Fourcaut, "Trois discours, une politique?" *Urbanisme* 322 n. 1 (January–February 2002), 44.

5   Paul Chemetov, "D'Athènes à La Courneuve, à qui la faute?" *Revue Urbanisme* 322 n. 1 (January–February 2002), 51.

6   Hervé Vieillard-Baron, "Sur l'origine des grands ensembles," in *Le monde des grands ensembles,* ed. Frédéric Dufaux and Annie Fourcaut (Paris: Éditions Créaphis, 2004), 60–61.

7   See, for example, Gwendolyn Wright, *The Politics of Design in French Colonial Urbanism* (Chicago: University of Chicago Press, 1991).

8   Maurice Rotival, "Les grands ensembles," *L'Architecture d'aujourd'hui* 1 n. 6 (1935), 57 and 72.

9   Pierre Sudreau, interview with Bernard Champigneulle, *L'Architecture d'aujourd'hui 30* n. 85 (September 1959), v (first published in *Le Figaro litteraire* August 15, 1959).

10 Eugène Claudius-Petit, introduction to the theme issue "Reconstruction France 1950," *L'Architecture d'aujourd'hui* 20 n. 34 (October–November 1950), 7.

11 Pierre Sudreau, "Introduction," *Urbanisme* 28 n. 62–63 (1959), 3.

12 See, for example, Gwendolyn Wright, *The Politics of Design in French Colonial Urbanism* (Chicago: University of Chicago Press, 1991), or Mercedes Volait and Joseph Nasr, eds., *Urbanism: Imported or Exported? Native Aspirations and Foreign Plans* (London: Wiley, 2003).

13 Chantal Dunoyer, "Chronologie Janvier 1994 Ephéméride," *Le Monde* February 15, 1994.

14 Andreas Jaeggli, "Wohnungsbau – ein Problem der menschlichen Gesellschaft," *Bauen und Wohnen* 15 n. 8 (August 1960), 2–3.

15 Figures by the Institut national de la statistique et des études économiques (INSEE), quoted by Chantal Dunoyer, "Chronologie Janvier 1994 Ephéméride," *Le Monde* February 15, 1994.

16 Jean Lemoine, "Le crise du logement," *La Vie Urbaine* 57 (July–September 1950), M. Bertrand, "Le Confort des logements à Paris en 1954*," La Vie Urbaine* 3 (1964), 23–71.

17 See, for example, Bernard Philippe, "Trois quarts de siècle d'immigration nord-africaine dans la capitale," *Le Monde* March 3, 1991.

18 For example Office de Radiodiffusion Télévision Française (ORTF), "Centre d'hébergement nord africain à Marseille et Lille," report in the newscast *Les Actualités Françaises*, May 22, 1957, Office de Radiodiffusion Télévision Française (ORTF), "Ils sont trois millions de travailleurs étrangers en France," report in the newscast *Sept jours du monde*, June 12, 1964, both available online at http://www.ina.fr/archivespourtous/index (accessed March 2008).

19 Michael Kimmelman, "Ready or Not, France Opens Museum On Immigration," *New York Times*, October 17, 2007.

20 Ministry of Interior census, quoted by Rosemary Wakeman, *Public Space and Confrontation* unpublished manuscript, p. 48.

21 Ministère de l'Equipement et du Logement, *Etudes sur la résorption des bidonvilles,* Report No. 771142C3569, 1966. In the early 1960s, the inhabitants of the *bidonvilles* outside Paris were mostly but not exclusively immigrants. A national survey conducted in 1966 by Eugène Mannoni found 42 percent North Africans, 21 percent Portuguese, 6 percent Spaniards, and 20 percent French. "Du Maghreb à la Seine," *Le Monde*, April 19, 1960, both quoted by Yvan Gastaut, "Les bidonvilles, lieux d'exclusion et de marginalité en France durant les trente glorieuses," *Cahiers de la Méditerranée* 69 (2004).

22 Jean-Luc Einaudi and Maurice Rajsfus, *Les Silences de la police – 16 juillet 1942, 17 octobre 1961* (Paris: L'Esprit frappeur, 2001), 82.

23 Dominique Barjot, "Un âge d'or de la construction," *Urbanisme* 322 n. 1 (January–February 2002), 72–74.

24 Annie Fourcaut, "Trois discours, une politique?," *Urbanisme* 322 n. 1 (January–February 2002), 40.

25 Dominique Barjot, "Un âge d'or de la construction," *Urbanisme* 322 n. 1 (January–February 2002), 73.

26 The decree remained valid until 1967. During these ten years, 197 ZUPs were incorporated. Edouard d'Eudeville and Gwénael Lecocq, "Urbanisme," *Revue Urbanisme* 322 n. 1 (January–February 2002), 70.

27 Le Corbusier, *The Athens Charter*, ed. Josep Lluis Sert (New York: Grossman, 1973), part 2, section 1, 1, 20.

28 "Région parisienne: quelques grandes réalisations en cours," *L'Architecture d'aujourd'hui* 29 n. 80 (October–November 1958), 14–15 [issue edited by Renée Diamant-Berger].

29 Paul Chemetov, "D'Athènes à La Courneuve, à qui la faute?" *Urbanisme* 322 n. 1 (January–February 2002), 51.

30 Eugène Claudius-Petit, introduction to the theme issue "Reconstruction France 1950, *L'Architecture d'aujourd'hui* 20 n. 34 (October–November 1950), 7.

31 Pierre Sudreau, "Introduction," *Urbanisme* 28 n. 62–63 (1959), 3.

32 Gérard Dupont, "Le grand ensemble, facteur de progrès social et de progrès humain," *Urbanisme* 28 n. 62–63 (1959), 6–7.

33 Alexandre Persitz on the proposal by Pierre Dalloz, *L'Architecture d'aujourd'hui* n. 34 (February 1951), quoted by Edouard d'Eudeville, "L'Architecture d'aujourd'hui," *Revue Urbanisme* 322 n. 1 (January–February 2002), 69.

Notes **185**

34 "Les grands ensembles, naissance d'une civilisation. Edifier des cités, ce n'est pas seulement construire des logements," *La Croix* February 1, 1960.

35 See, for example, A[lexandre] P[ersitz], "Les grands ensembles et l'architecture," *L'Architecture d'aujourd'hui 30* n. 85 (September 1959), V. For Persitz, mass-produced houses should be subjected to an "architectural spirit" that has the potential to relieve a great number of society's ills.

36 "Les grands ensembles, pensés pour l'homme, au service d'une politique active et humanisée de l'habitat," *L'Architecture d'aujourd'hui* n. 46 (1953). Over the following years, the magazine reviewed about a hundred projects.

37 The term *sarcellite* ("sarcellitis") was first used on the radio station Europe 1. "La sarcellite," *L'Echo Régional* March 22, 1962, "Les varies raisons de la sarcellite," *L'Humanité*, November 5, 1965, "Des médecins nous parlent du nouveau mal du siècle, la 'sarcellite'. Faut-il condemner les cités termitières?" *Lectures pour tous*, May 1965. "Budget social record en Seine-et-Oise," *La vie française*, April 13, 1962.

38 "Les grands ensembles immobiliers sont des fabriques de blousons noirs," *L'Aurore*, July 2, 1962.

39 Christiane Rochefort (1917–1998), *Les petits enfants du siècle* (Paris: Grasset, 1961), translated as *Children of Heaven* (1962).

40 Alexandre Persitz, "Les grands ensembles et l'architecture," *L'Architecture d'aujourd'hui 30* n. 85 (September 1959), v.

41 Pierre Sudreau, "Un coup d'arrêt du ministre de la construction: fault-il que les grandes cités d'habitation aient la forideur des casernes ou ressemblent à des clapiers perfectionnés?" [interview with Bernard Champigneulle] *Le Figaro littéraire*, August 15, 1959, "Des médecins nous parlent du nouveau mal du siècle, la 'sarcellite'. Faut-il condemner les cités termitières?," *Lectures pour tous*, May 1965. For the other monikers see Hervé Vieillard-Baron, "Des images aux échelles de la mémoire," in *Les grands ensembles entre histoire et mémoire* [report of an academic conference in Paris on April 24, 2001], available online at http://i.ville.gouv.fr/divbib/doc/GrdsEnsembles.PDF (accessed December 2007), 16.

42 Caption to the reportage by Jacques Windenberger, "Sarcelles," *L'Architecture d'aujourd'hui* n. 95 (April 1961), 8. In 1958 journalist Louis Caro had already spoken of "un monde concentrationnaire" hidden under a "faux modernism": Louis Caro, "Les psychiatres et sociologues denoncent a folie des grands ensembles," *Science et Vie* n. 504 (September 1959), 30.

43 Geographer Jean Gravier in 1945 described tenements in Saint-Denis as "a sordid concentration camp for immigrants." Jean Gravier, *Paris et le Désert Français* (Paris: Le Portulan, 1947), 191. Thanks to Rosemary Wakeman.

44 Andreas Jaeggli, "Wohnungsbau – ein Problem der menschlichen Gesellschaft," *Bauen und Wohnen* 15 n. 8 (August 1960), 2–3.

45 Louis Caro, "Les psychiatres et sociologues denoncent a folie des grands ensembles," *Science et Vie* n. 504 (September 1959), 30–37. See also Anonymous, "Les grands ensembles: mal inevitable mais mal tout de meme," *L'Habitation* n. 72 (April 1959), 7–10, followed by short expert opinions in the same issue. In the years before, scientists published critical opinions: Paul-Henry Chombart de Lauwe and Paul Vieille, ed., "Logement et comportement des ménages dans trois cités nouvelles de l'agglomération parisienne," *Cahiers du centre scentifique et technique du bâtiment* 30 (1957), Guy Houist, *Groupes d'habitations, urbanisme et vie sociale* (Paris: Conseil économique et social, 1960), Robert Caillot, *Enquête sur les réactions des nouveaux occupants d'HLM* [copied report] (Paris: Centre scientifique et technique du bâtiment, 1959), Robert-Henri Hazemann, "Les implications psychologiques de l'habitation populaire," *Gazette de la santé publique* n. 26 (1959), 41–52.

46 See, for example, Françoise Choay, "Cités-jardins ou 'cages à lapins'," *France Observateur* (June 4, 1959), Françoise Choay "Nouvelle zone ou cités-jardins?" *L'Oeuil* (July 1959), Pierre Sudreau, "Un coup d'arrêt du minister de la construction: fault-il que les grandes cités d'habitation aient la forideur des casernes ou ressemblent à des clapiers perfectionnés?" [interview with Bernard Champigneulle] *Le Figaro littéraire*, August 15, 1959, "Les risques des cités poussés trop vite," *Le Figaro littéraire,* November 28, 1959, or the contributions in *Panorama Chrétien* (September 1959), *La France catholique* (October 1959), *Combat* (November 1959), and *Études* (December 1959).

47 Pierre Sudreau, personal conversation with Prefects and other leading state officials, in "Urbanisme et Architecture," October 1960, quoted by Annie Fourcaut, "Trois discours, une politique?" *Urbanisme* 322 n. 1 (January–February 2002), 42.

48 Pierre Sudreau, interview with Bernard Champigneulle *Le Figaro littéraire*, August 15, 1959, partially reprinted *L'Architecture d'aujourd'hui* 30 n. 85 (September 1959), v.

49 Eugène Beaudouin, "La composition des grands ensembles d'habitations en France de 1950 à 1957," *Urbanisme* n. 59 (1958).

50 Among the targets of criticism were the Cité des Courtilières in Pantin by Emile Aillaud, the university residences in Antony by Eugène Beaudouin, and the Mont-Mesly ensemble in Créteil by Charles-Gustave Stoskopf. Theme issue "Urbanisme des capitals." In the context of a "Proposition of the Committee of *L'Architecture d'aujourd'hui*" the editors censure the *grands ensembles* as "Les grandes réalisations: dispersion, médiocrité," *L'Architecture d'aujourd'hui* n. 88 (February/March 1960), 7.

51 "Pour un 'musée' des erreurs," *L'Architecture d'aujourd'hui* n. 95 (April 1961), 10–11 [collection of photos of *grands ensembles*].

52 Alexandre Persitz, "Les grands ensembles et l'architecture," *L'Architecture d'aujourd'hui* 30 n. 85 (September 1959), V.

53 Paul-Henry Chombart de Lauwe, quoted by Louis Caro, "Les psychiatres et sociologues denoncent a folie des grands ensembles," *Science et Vie* n. 504 (September 1959), 32.

54 Henri Lefebvre, "Les nouveaux ensembles urbains: Un cas concret: Lacq-Mourenx et les problèmes urbains de la nouvelle classe ouvrière," *Revue Française de Sociologie* 1 n. 2, (April–June 1960), 201

55 Louis Caro, "Les psychiatres et sociologues denoncent a folie des grands ensembles," *Science et Vie* n. 504 (September 1959), 31.

56 On the medical terminology of German modern reformers see Harald Bodenschatz, "Krebsgeschwür Hinterhof," *Bauwelt* 79 (March 1988), 506–513.

57 See, for example, Alexandre Persitz, "Les grands ensembles et l'architecture," *L'Architecture d'aujourd'hui* 30 n. 85 (September 1959), V.

58 Leonard Downie, "Paris: Under Construction" [1972], written for the *Washington Post*, available online at http://www.aliciapatterson.org/APF001971/Downie/Downie08/Downie08.html (accessed May 2008).

59 Gérard Dupont, "Le grand ensemble, facteur de progrès social et de progrès humain," *Urbanisme* 28 n. 62–63 (1959), 6 or Conference "Comment réussir la construction et l'aménagement des grands ensembles," reviewed in D. V. "Colloque sur les grands ensembles," *L'Architecture d'aujourd'hui* 31 n. 88 (February–March 1960), p ix.

60 Anonymous: "Les grands ensembles: mal inevitable mais mal tout de meme," *L'Habitation* n. 72 (April 1959), 10. See also Louis Caro, "Les psychiatres et sociologues denoncent a folie des grands ensembles," *Science et Vie* n. 504 (September 1959), 32.

61 The documentation program was run by DATAR (Délégation à l'Aménagement du Territoire et à l'Action Régionale). DATAR was a governmental institution designed to improve the living environment in France and coordinate local action. Olivier Guichard, who became Minister of Territorial Planning in 1973 and signed the 1973 law that officially ended the construction of satellite cities in France, was in charge of DATAR from 1963 to 1967. See Antoine Picon, "Anxious Landscapes: From the Ruin to Rust," *Grey Room* 1 n. 1 (Fall 2000), 64–83. In 2006, DATAR was replaced by the Délégation interministérielle à l'aménagement et à la compétitivité des territoires (DIACT).

62 See "Grille Dupont," *Urbanisme* 62–63 (1958), quoted by Edouard d'Eudeville and Gwénael Lecocq, "Urbanisme," *Urbanisme* 322 n. 1 (January–February 2002), 70.

63 Quoted in D. V. "Colloque sur les grands ensembles" [report on the conference "Comment réussir la construction et l'aménagement des grands ensembles" at the UNESCO in Paris, January 1960], *L'Architecture d'aujourd'hui* 31 n. 88 (February–March 1960), ix.

64 Pierre Sudreau, "Introduction," *Urbanisme* 28 n. 62–63 (1959), 3.

65 Pierre Sudreau, interview with Bernard Champigneulle [first published *in Le Figaro litteraire* August 15, 1959], *L'Architecture d'aujourd'hui 30* n. 85 (September 1959), vii.

66 Gérard Dupont, "Le grand ensemble, facteur de progrès social et de progrès humain" *Urbanisme* 28 n. 62–63 (1959), 6.

67 "Sarcelles, premier grand complexe d'habitation de la région parisienne. Louables efforts pour l'aménager à l'échelle humaine," *Le Figaro*, September 27, 1960, Gérard Dupont, "Le grand ensemble, facteur de progrès social et de progrès humain," *Urbanisme* 28 n. 62–63 (1959), 6–7.

68 André Bloc, "Paris et région parisienne," *L'Architecture d'aujourd'hui* n. 97 (August 1962), 6. See also pictures on pages 8–15.

69 "Proposition du comité de L'Architecture d'aujourd'hui," *L'Architecture d'aujourd'hui* n. 88 (February–March 1960), 3–11. The proposition was signed, among others, by André Bloc, George Candilis, Marcel Lods, Alexandre Persitz, Jean Prouvé, Pierre Vago, and Bernard Zehrfuss.

70 Marcel Lods and Jacques Beufe, "Projet pour une cité d'aujourd'hui," *L'Architecture d'aujourd'hui* 31 n. 88 (February–March 1960), 15–19.

71 Dominique Barjot, "Un âge d'or de la construction," *Urbanisme* 322 n. 1 (January–February 2002), 73.

72 The government passed a law on the formation of *zones d'aménagement concerté* (ZAC, "concerted development zone"). The two last ZUPs were launched in 1969. Edouard d'Eudeville and Gwénaèl Lecocq, "Urbanisme," *Urbanisme* 322 n. 1 (January–February 2002), 70–71.

73 Annie Fourcaut, "Trois discours, une politique?" *Urbanisme* 322 n. 1 (January–February 2002), 42–43.

74 Comité national du mémorial du camp de Drancy, *Drancy: Le camp d'internement pour la déportation des juifs* (Société Drancéene d'Histoire et d'Archéologie et le Service Culturel Municipal, n.d.), quoted by Robert Weddle, "Housing and Technological Reform in Interwar France: The Case of the Cité de la Muette," *Journal of Architectural Education* 54 n. 3 (February 2001), 168.

75 According to Bauman, the Holocaust was grounded not on a suspension of civilization in Germany, but rather on the loss of morality as a result of the process of civilization/modernization. Zygmunt Bauman, *Modernity and the Holocaust* (Ithaca, NY: Cornell University Press, 1989).

76 Robert Weddle, "Housing and Technological Reform in Interwar France: The Case of the Cité de la Muette," *Journal of Architectural Education* 54 n. 3 (February 2001), 167–75.

77 For some scholars this is evidence enough for interpreting the taylorized (after Frederic Taylor) settlement from the beginning as a colonial enterprise, designed by a powerful state for the oppression of workers rather than their liberation. Jean-Louis Cohen, "Frankreichs Vorstädte – Architekturexperimente zwischen Utopie und sozialen Unruhen," Public Lecture, Berlin Technical University, June 21, 2006.

78 Wells Bennet, "Products and Practice," *Architectural Forum* 64 n. 2 (February 1936), 21–23, Robert Weddle, "Housing and Technological Reform in Interwar France: The Case of the Cité de la Muette," *Journal of Architectural Education* 54 n. 3 (February 2001), 167–75.

79 Several other projects were modeled after the Cité de la Muette. Examples include the Grandes Terres by Lods in Marly and the Point du Jour development by Pouillon in Boulogne. The Grandes Terres comprise 1,500 apartments and were designed by Lods, Honneger, and Beufé. They are 16 identical rectangular 5-story bars. Paul Chemetov, "D'Athènes à La Courneuve, à qui la faute?," *Revue Urbanisme* 322 n. 1 (January–February 2002), 51.

80 Wells Bennet, "Products and Practice," [on Cité de la Muette] *Architectural Forum* 64 n. 2 (February 1936), 22.

81 Anonymous, "These Towers Have Scientific Shadows" *Architectural Record* 79 n. 5 (May 1936), 341.

82 Pierre Bordier, "La Cité de la Muette à Drancy," *Art et Décoration* 40 (January 1936), 4–7.

83 The latter number refers to the estimate by the organizers. Marc Zitzmann, "Kinder der Banlieue – Opfer der Moderne, Täter aus Wut," *Neue Zürcher Zeitung*, November 14, 2005.

84 Of course the prejudice is rarely admitted. Hiring companies officially explain their bias against housing project dwellers with the fact that workers from outside Paris are more likely to be late for work due to delayed trains. Cp. Christel Brigaudeau, "Les enterprises n'aiment pas les banlieusards," *Le Parisien* June 4, 2007. For the discrimination based on Muslim first names see the 2006 study by Jean François Amadieu and Sylvain Giry, who worked for the Institut National de la Statistique et des Etudes Economiques (INSEE): *Olivier, Gérard et Mohammed ont-ils les mêmes chances*

de faire carrière? Available online at http://cergors.univ-paris1.fr/docsatelecharger/Pr%E9sentation%
E9tudepr%E9nomsavril2006%5B2%5D.pdf (accessed February 2008).

85   Bruce Cumley, "Building Hope in the Banlieues," *Time* 166 n. 20, November 14, 2005.

86   François Tomas, "La place des grands ensembles dans l'histoire de l'habitat social français," in *Les Grands Ensembles – Une histoire qui continue*, ed. François Tomas, Jean-Noel Blanc, and Mario Bonilla (Saint-Etienne: Publications de l'Université de Saint-Etienne, 2000), 17.

87   Craig Smith, "What makes someone French?" *International Herald Tribune*, November 11, 2005.

88   Ibid.

4 Slabs versus Tenements in East and West Berlin

1   Anna Teut, "Huldigung an die städtebauliche Tradition," *Die Welt*, November 8, 1966, 13.

2   "Hoffnungsschimmer für die Städtebauer in halb Europa," *BZ* (Berlin), October 19, 1967.

3   *Der Tagesspiegel,* October 3, 1969, quoted by Alexander Wilde, *Das Märkische Viertel* (West Berlin: Nicolai, 1989), 127.

4   Gerd Wegner, "Reinickendorf: Erster Wohnblock in Farbe," *Die Welt*, September 27, 1966.

5   Anna Teut, "Huldigung an die städtebauliche Tradition," *Die Welt*, November 8, 1966: 13.

6   *Die Welt*, December 22, 1968, quoted by Alexander Wilde, *Das Märkische Viertel* (West Berlin: Nicolai, 1989), 127.

7   Hans Bernhard Reichow, *Organische Stadtbaukunst* (Braunschweig: Westermann, 1948). Reichow's approach was also codified in Johannes Göderitz, Roland Rainer, and Hubert Hoffmann, *Die gegliederte und aufgelockerte Stadt* (Tübingen: Wasmuth, 1957).

8   Josef Nipper, "Gute Zeiten, schlechte Zeiten – Das 20. Jahrhundert," in *Köln – der historisch-topographische Atlas*, ed. Dorothea Wiktorin et al. (Cologne: Emons, 2001).

9   See Jürgen Dobberke, "Märkisches Viertel, Star der Bauwochen," *Berliner Leben* n. 9 (1966), *Welt am Sonntag,* July 3, 1966, *Die Welt,* August 30, 1966, *Berliner Morgenpost,* August 30, 1966, and Alexander Wilde, *Das Märkische Viertel* (West Berlin: Nicolai, 1989), 126.

10   Günter Peters, *Gesamtberliner Stadtentwicklung* (Berlin: Hochschule der Künste, 1992), 22.

11   Hans Bernhard Reichow, *Organische Stadtbaukunst* (Braunschweig: Westermann, 1948), 3–55.

12   For an account of the bad reputation of Berlin's tenements see Harald Bodenschatz, *Platz frei für das Neue Berlin! Geschichte der Stadterneuerung in der "größten Mietskasernenstadt der Welt" seit 1871* (West Berlin: Transit, 1987).

13   "Slums verschoben," *Der Spiegel* 22 n. 37 (September 9, 1968), 134–138.

14   Ibid., 138.

15   "Es bröckelt," *Der Spiegel* n. 6 (1969), 38–42.

16   *Frankfurter Rundschau,* January 20, 1969, *Allgemeines Deutsches Sonntagsblatt,* June 22, 1969, *Stuttgarter Zeitung,* May 16, 1970, all quoted by Alexander Wilde, *Das Märkische Viertel* (West Berlin: Nicolai, 1989), 127.

17   Gerhard Ullmann, "Kritischer Zwischenbericht über das Märkische Viertel," *Süddeutsche Zeitung*, June 10, 1970.

18   Alexander Wilde, *Das Märkische Viertel* (West Berlin: Nicolai, 1989), 107.

19   Gwendolyn Wright, "End of the Experiment," *Architecture* 91 n. 3 (March 2002), 29–32.

20   Wolf-Jobst Siedler and Elisabeth Niggemeyer, *Die gemordete Stadt* (West Berlin: Herbig, 1964) (The Murdered City).

21   Alexander Mitscherlich, *Die Unwirtlichkeit unserer Städte* (Frankfurt/Main: Suhrkamp, 1965) (The Inhospitability of Our Cities). Mitscherlich was born in 1908 and died in 1982.

22   Ibid., 28.

23   West Berlin: For the First Urban Renewal Program of 1963, affecting approximately 10 percent of the city's population, see Senator für Bau- und Wohnungswesen, ed., *Stadterneuerung in Berlin* (West Berlin: Senator für Bau- und Wohnungswesen, 1964). East Berlin: For a list of the projected

demolition dates of the tenements in the Prenzlauer Berg district see Günter Peters, *Möglichkeiten und Probleme der langfristigen Planung von komplexen Modernisierungsmaßnahmen am Wohnungsbestand in Großstädten, dargestellt am Beispiel der Hauptstadt der DDR, Berlin*, Dissertation A (doctoral thesis), Hochschule für Ökonomie Bruno Leuschner, East Berlin, 1972: A57.

24 "Slums verschoben," *Der Spiegel* 22 n. 37, September 9, 1968, 137–138.

25 Ibid., 138.

26 Ibid., 137.

27 Hellmut Maurer, "Menschenfeindliche Gettos statt sinnvoller Ordnung," *Frankfurter Rundschau*, January 20, 1969.

28 Ibid.

29 Alexander Mitscherlich, *Die Unwirtlichkeit unserer Städte* (Frankfurt/Main: Suhrkamp, 1965), 12.

30 Wolf-Jobst Siedler and Elisabeth Niggemeyer, *Die gemordete Stadt* (West Berlin: Herbig, 1964), 33.

31 Harald Bodenschatz, *Platz frei für das neue Berlin!* (West Berlin: Transit, 1987), 233.

32 "Es bröckelt," *Der Spiegel* n. 6 (1969), 38–42.

33 Ibid.

34 Ulrike Meinhof, "Vorläufiges Strategie-Papier Märkisches Viertel," reprinted in *"Jetzt reden wir": Betroffene des Märkischen Viertels. Wohnste sozial, haste die Qual*, ed. Johannes Beck, Heiner Boehnke and Gerhard Vinnai (Hamburg, 1975), 95.

35 Ibid., 130.

36 Johannes Hieber, "Berlin war eine Reise wert," *Süddeutsche Zeitung,* Regionalanzeiger Nord, October 9, 1973, Alexander Wilde, *Das Märkische Viertel (West Berlin:* Nikolai, 1989), 112.

37 Ibid., 114–115. See also Harald Bodenschatz, *Platz frei für das neue Berlin!* (West Berlin: Transit, 1987), 246.

38 Christoph Haller, *Leerstand im Plattenbau, Ausmaß, Ursachen, Gegenstrategien* (Berlin: Leue 2002).

39 Christine Hannemann, *Die Platte* (Berlin: Schelzky und Jeep, 2000).

40 Klaus Schroeder, *Der SED-Staat* (Munich: Landeszentrale für politische Bildungsarbeit, 1998), 283.

41 See, for example, Hermann Henselmann "Der Einfluss der sozialistischen Lebensweise auf den Städtebau und die Architektur in der DDR," *Deutsche Architektur* n. 5 (1966), 264–265 or Fred Staufenbiel "Kultursoziologie und Städtebau," *Deutsche Architektur* n. 6 (1966), 326–327.

42 "Architekturanalyse im Bezirk Leipzig," presented to the *Abteilung Bauwesen* (Department of Construction) at the Central Committee, led by Gerhard Trölitzsch, in November 1975. Berlin Federal Archive DY 30/18088.

43 Bruno Flierl, *Industriegesellschaftstheorie im Städtebau* (East Berlin: Akademie-Verlag, 1973), 120.

44 Ibid.

45 Bruno Flierl, *Zur Wahrnehmung der Stadtgestalt. Beispieluntersuchung im Stadtzentrum von Berlin* (East Berlin: Bauakademie der DDR, 1979).

46 Olaf Weber and Gerd Zimmermann, "Orientierungen in der Stadt," *Form und Zweck* no. 4 (1980), 21.

47 *Grundsätze für die sozialistische Entwicklung von Städtebau und Architektur in der DDR*, minutes of the Politbüro meeting on May 18, 1982, final copy, Berlin Federal Archive DY 30/J IV 2/2 1947: 238.

48 Institut für Städtebau (Bauakademie) and Bezirksplankommission, "Wohnungsbau in Berlin 1991–2000 Vorschlag einer strategischen Grundlinie," unpublished proposal dated August 25, 1989, Berlin Federal Archive DH 2 F2/198.

49 Ibid., 2.

50 Christiane F., *Wir Kinder vom Bahnhof Zoo,* transcribed after tape recordings by Kai Hermann and Horst Rieck [journalists with the news magazine *Stern*], first edition (Hamburg: Gruner und Jahr, 1978), 48th edition in 2006.

51 "Durchführungsbestimmung zur Verordnung über die Planung, Vorbereitung und Durchführung von Folgeinvestitionen—Abriß von Gebäuden und baulichen Anlagen," *Gesetzblatt der DDR I*, n. 34 (October 19, 1979), 325–326.

52 Jan Bauditz, "Aufbruch gegen den Abriß—Die Bürgerinitiative Spandauer Vorstadt," in *Die Spandauer Vorstadt*, ed. Gesellschaft Hackesche Höfe (Berlin: Argon, 1995), 42–56.

53 Harald Bodenschatz, *Platz frei für das Neue Berlin! Geschichte der Stadterneuerung in der "größten Mietskasernenstadt der Welt" seit 1871* (West Berlin: Transit, 1987), 207.

54 The negative image of the backyard as a "cancer" is summarized in Harald Bodenschatz, "Krebsgeschwür Hinterhof," *Bauwelt* 79 (March 1988), 506–513. A very late example of the trope of the "deceptive stucco ornament" can be found in the East German magazine *Architektur der DDR*, Dorothea Krause, Uwe Klasen, and Wolfgang Penzel, "Rekonstruktion im Stil der Jahrhundertwende. Husemannstraße in Berlin," *Architektur der DDR* n. 10 (1987), 14–17.

55 Census data, published by the Statistisches Landesamt Berlin, available online at http://www.statistik-berlin.de/framesets/berl.htm (accessed June 2008).

56 Günter Peters, *Gesamtberliner Stadtentwicklung* (Berlin: Hochschule der Künste, 1992): 22.

57 David Clay Large, *Berlin* (New York: Basic Books, 2000), 466.

58 pi (abbreviation), "'Züge von modernem Sklavenhandel'," *Berliner Zeitung,* November 2, 1996, Josefine Janert, "Ethnologien untersuchen die Gettos in Berlin und die Regeln, die sie schufen," *Der Tagesspiegel,* February 21, 2000.

59 Descriptions from the early 1970s, both commending and critical, mentioned a proletarian milieu, but remained silent about non-German residents. See, for example, Eberhard Schulz, "Die Hölle ist es nicht – Plädoyer für das Märkische Viertel," *Frankfurter Allgemeine Zeitung*, November 10, 1973.

60 Census data from 2004 for "Berlin" (p. 191), for the neighborhood "Märkisches Viertel" (p. 191), and for the neighborhood "Mariannenplatz" (p. 188), both published by Senatsverwaltung für Stadtentwicklung, available online at http://www.stadtentwicklung.berlin.de/planen/basisdaten_stadtentwicklung/monitoring/de/2006/index.shtml (accessed August 2008). The numbers of course do not include nationalized foreigners or German nationals with foreign parents.

61 Census data from 2004 for the neighborhood "Lipschitzallee," ibid.: 191.

62 Census data from 2005, Statistisches Landesamt Berlin, available online at http://www.statistik-berlin.de/framesets/such.htm (accessed June 2008).

63 Hellmut Maurer, "Menschenfeindliche Gettos statt sinnvoller Ordnung," *Frankfurter Rundschau*, January 20, 1969.

64 For example in Cologne-Chorweiler 37.7 percent (Cologne average: 17.2 percent), in Munich-Neuperlach more than 27.1 percent (Munich average: 23 percent), and in Hamburg-Mümmelmannsberg 22.7 percent (Hamburg average: 14.9 percent). For Munich, the number is an estimate, since the census district border does not align with that of the tower block development. Census data from 2007, available online at http://www.stadt-koeln.de/zahlen/bevoelkerung/artikel/04620/index.html. Census data from 2008, Landeshauptstadt München, *Statistisches Jahrbuch 2008* (Munich: Statistisches Amt München, 2008), 191, census data from 2005, Statistisches Amt für Hamburg und Schleswig Holstein, "Stadtteilprofil Mümmelmannsberg," available online at http://fhh1.hamburg.de/fhh/behoerden/behoerde_fuer_inneres/statistisches_landesamt/profile/muemmelmannsberg.htm (accessed July 2008).

65 "Vergessene Trabanten," *Mieter-Magazin* (Berlin) (September 2004), 2.

66 Alexander Wilde, *Das Märkische Viertel* (West Berlin: Nicolai, 1989), 159.

67 Institut für Markt und Medienforschung, *Märkisches Viertel* (West Berlin, 1986)

68 Census data from 2005, Senatsverwaltung für Stadtentwicklung, available online at http://www.stadtentwicklung.berlin.de/planen/basisdaten_stadtentwicklung/monitoring/de/2006/index.shtml, p. 214, (accessed August 2008).

69 Census data, Senatsverwaltung für Stadtentwicklung, available online at http://www.stadtentwicklung.berlin.de/planen/basisdaten_stadtentwicklung/monitoring/de/2006/index.shtml (accessed August 2008).

70 Institut für Markt und Medienforschung, *Märkisches Viertel* (West Berlin, 1986).

71 "Ein Stadtteil überwand seinen schlechten Ruf," *Der Tagesspiegel* August 3, 1980, Thomas Schardt, "Hochhausstadt besser als ihr Ruf," January 31, 1986, Gabriele Gethke, "Früher verschrien, heute begehrt: Wohnungen im MV," *Der Nord-Berliner*, July 6, 1979.

72 By 1979, the number of Märkisches Viertel tenants moving out of their homes had gone down to the West Berlin average of 4 percent per year. Gabriele Gethke, "Früher verschrien, heute begehrt:

Wohnungen im MV," *Der Nord-Berliner*, July 6, 1979. Similarly, observers detected a "growing attachment to one's home district." Alexander Wilde, *Das Märkische Viertel (West Berlin:* Nicolai, 1989), 140. See also "Ein Stadtteil überwand seinen schlechten Ruf," *Der Tagesspiegel* August 3, 1980.

73 Gerlind Staemmler, *Rekonstruktion innerstädtischer Wohngebiete in der DDR* (West Berlin: IWOS-Bericht zur Stadtforschung, 1981), 300–303.

74 See Christian Böhm, "Hochhaus mit drei Etagen," *Der Tagesspiegel* August 10, 2004, "Ahrensfelder Terrassen sind vollendet," *Die Welt* July 12, 2005.

5 Brasília, the Slab Block Capital

1   2001 census data, quoted by Eduard Rodrìguez i Villaescusa, "Brasília querida y mantenida," in *Brasília 1956–2006*, ed. Eduard Rodrìguez i Villaescusa and Cibele Vieira Figueira (Lleida: Editorial Milenio, 2006), 180.

2   Juscelino Kubitschek, "JK escreve: Brasília 16 anos depois," *Manchete*, May 1, 1976: 34.

3   For a study of the superquadra's spatial syntax see Frederico de Holanda, *O espaço do exeção* (Brasília: Editora Universidade de Brasília, 2002).

4   Maria Elisa Costa, "The *Superquadra* in Numbers and Context," in *Lúcio Costa – Brasília's Superquadra,* ed. Farès El-Dahdah (Munich and New York: Prestel, 2005), 27.

5   Ibid.

6   Briane Panitz Bicca et al., "Caracterización preliminar de Brasília: Plano Piloto," *Summarios* (Buenos Aires) 9 n. 97–98 (January–February 1986), 11.

7   Lawrence Vale, *Architecture, Power and National Identity* (New Haven: Yale University Press, 1992), 120.

8   Sylvia Ficher et al. "The Residential Building Slab in the *Superquadra*," in *Lúcio Costa – Brasília's Superquadra,* ed. Farès El-Dahdah (Munich: Prestel Verlag, 2005), 53. See also Frederico de Holanda, "A morfología interna da capital," in *Brasília, ideologia e realidade: Espaço urbano em questão*, ed. Aldo Paviani (São Paulo: Projeto, 1985).

9   Norma Evenson, *Two Brazilian Capitals* (New Haven, CT: Yale University Press, 1973), 187.

10 Ana Paula Koury, Nabil Bonduki, and Sálua Kairuz Manoel, "Análise Tipológica da Produção de Habitação Econômica no Brasil (1930–1964)," *Proceedings of the 5th Docomomo Seminar in São Carlos, Brazil* (October 2003), 5.

11 Sylvia Ficher et al., "The Residential Building Slab in the *Superquadra*," in *Lúcio Costa – Brasília's Superquadra,* ed. Farès El-Dahdah (Munich: Prestel Verlag, 2005), 53.

12 Ibid.

13 Ibid., 61.

14 Tanja Thung, *Brasília SQS 103 – Fallstudie über den öffentlichen Raum in einer Superquadra* (Diploma thesis, Institut für Städtebau, University of Stuttgart, 2003), 119.

15 Novacap journal, 1958, quoted by James Holston, *The Modernist City: an Anthropological Critique of Brasília* (Chicago: University of Chicago Press, 1989), 20.

16 For a Marxist critique of Brasília as a deceptive project see, for example, the article of the Cuban author Roberto Segre, "Brasília," *Cuadernos Arquitectura Latinoamericana* (Mexico City) 1, n.1 (June 1976), 26–33.

17 See, for example, Safira Bezerra Ammann, "Excluídos sim. Invasores não," in *Urbanização e metropolização: a gestão dos conflitos em Brasília*, ed. Aldo Paviani (Brasília: Editora Universidade de Brasília, Codeplan, 1987).

18 Given the complexity of parameters to gauge lifestyle and inequality, this number can only be an estimate. Alexander Fils, "Brasília 2000," in *Brasília – Archtektur der Moderne in Brasilien* ed. Alexander Fils, Beate Eckstein, and Martina Merklinger (Berlin: Ifa-Galerie, 2000), 50.

19 Nabil Bonduki, *Origens da habitação social no Brasil.* (São Paulo: Estação Liberdade, 1998), 12–13.

20 Marta Ferreira Santos Farah, *Estado, previdência social e habitação* (master's thesis in sociology, Department of Social Science, University of São Paulo, 1983), 25.

21 Sigrid de Lima, "Brazil Builds a New City," *American Journal of Economics and Sociology* 6 n. 3 (April 1947), 335–344. For a plan, see *L'architecture d'aujourd'hui* 13–14 (September 1947), 100.

22 Nabil Bonduki, *Origens da habitação social no Brasil.* (São Paulo: Estação Liberdade, 1998), 12–13.

23 René Galesi and Candido Malta Campos, "Edifício Japurá: Pioneiro na aplicação do conceito de 'unité d'habitation' de Le Corbusier no Brasil," *Arquitextos* 31 (December 2002).

24 Nabil Bonduki, *Origens da habitação social no Brasil.* (São Paulo: Estação Liberdade, 1998), 12–14.

25 Alberto Gawryszewski, *Agonia de morar: Urbanização e habitação na cidade do Rio de Janeiro (1945–50)* (Ph.D. dissertation, Department of History, Faculdade de Filosofia, Letras e Ciências Humanas, Universidade de São Paulo, 1996), 156.

26 Ibid.

27 Sylvia Ficher et al., "Brasília: la historia de un planeamiento," in *Brasília 1956–2006*, ed. Eduard Rodrìguez i Villaescusa and Cibele Vieira Figueira (Lleida: Editorial Milenio, 2006), 82–83.

28 Lúcio Costa, "Saudação aos críticos de arte" [1959], quoted in ibid., 84.

29 Articles and interviews by Juscelino Kubitschek: "Brasília – Interview de Juscelino Kubitschek," *L'architecture d'aujourd'hui* 31 n. 90 (June–July 1961), 2–3 and "Introduction," in *Brasília* by Willy Stäubli (Stuttgart: Koch, 1965). Articles and interviews by Oscar Niemeyer: "Brasília," *Architectural Design* 30 n. 12 (1960), 524–525, "Brasília," in *Brasília* by Willy Stäubli (Stuttgart: Koch, 1965), "Mes experiences de Brasília," *L'architecture d'aujourd'hui* 31 n. 90 (June–July 1960), 8–9, "Minha experiencia de Brasília", *Módulo* n.3 (June 1960), 11–27, "Unternehmen Brasília," interview with Henry E. Moeller, *Bauwelt* 53 n. 21 (1962), 583–588. See also the article by the Brazilian consul in Zurich: José-Osvaldo de Meira Penna, "Urbanisme Politique," *L'architecture d'aujourd'hui* 31 n. 90 (June–July 1961), 4–7.

30 Sigfried Giedion, "Stadtform und die Gründung von Brasília," *Bauen und Wohnen* 15 n. 7 (July 1960), 292.

31 David Snyder, "Alternate Perspectives on Brasília," *Economic Geography* 40 n. 1 (January 1964), 35.

32 Willy Stäubli, *Brasília* (Stuttgart: Koch, 1965), 10.

33 Lucien Hervé, "Brasília," *L'architecture d'aujourd'hui* 33 n. 101 (April–May 1962), 2.

34 Henry Moeller, "Wohnen in Brasília," *Bauwelt* 53 n. 21 (1962), 593.

35 Octávio Costa, "Brasília ano 10 – a *superquadra* da esperança," *Manchete* April 25, 1970: 85.

36 Frank Arnau, *Brasília – Phantasie und Wirklichkeit* (Munich: Prestel, 1960), 9.

37 See article 10 and 17 of "Relatorio do Plan Piloto de Brasília," quoted by Eduard Rodrìguez i Villaescusa, "Brasília querida y mantenida," in *Brasília 1956–2006*, ed. Eduard Rodrìguez i Villaescusa and Cibele Vieira Figueira (Lleida: Editorial Milenio, 2006), 183.

38 Quoted and used as the title of an article by Colin Buchanan, "The Moon's Backside," *RIBA Journal* 74 n. 4 (April 1967), 159–160.

39 James Holston, *The Modernist City: an Anthropological Critique of Brasília* (Chicago: University of Chicago Press, 1989), 24–25.

40 Simone de Beauvoir, *La force des choses* [autobiography] (Paris, 1963), 535.

41 See, for example, Oscar Niemeyer, "Fizemos Brasília contra todas as incompreensões," *Manchete*, April 29, 1978: 76–78.

42 See, for example, Klaus Zuck, "Ein Student sieht Brasília," *Bauwelt* 53 n. 21 (1962), 594–595, Marta Valentin, "Brasília," *Bauwelt* 51 n. 37 (1960), 1097–1098, or Frank Arnau, *Brasília – Phantasie und Wirklichkeit* (Munich: Prestel, 1960).

43 William Holford, "Problemas e perspectivas de Brasília," *Módulo* 3 n. 17 (April 1960), 2. See also David Crease, "Progress in Brasília," *Architectural Review* 133 (1962), 262.

44 Klaus Zuck, "Ein Student sieht Brasília," *Bauwelt* 53 n. 21 (1962), 594.

45 David Snyder, "Alternate Perspectives on Brasília," *Economic Geography* 40 n. 1 (January1964), 44.

46 Henry Moeller, "Wohnen in Brasília," *Bauwelt* 53 n. 21 (1962), 590.

47 Frank Arnau, *Brasília – Phantasie und Wirklichkeit* (Munich: Prestel, 1960), 36, Marta Valentin, "Brasília," *Bauwelt* 51 n. 37 (1960), 1098.

48 Photo reportage by Colin Buchanan, "The Moon's Backside," *RIBA Journal* 74 n. 4 (April 1967), 159–160.

49   Simone de Beauvoir, *La force des choses* [autobiography] (Paris, 1963), 576–578.

50   Richard Williams, "Modernist Civic Space and the Case of Brasília," *Journal of Urban History* 32 n. 1 (November 2005), 128.

51   Lord Nathan and Lawrence Dudley Stamp, "Brasília: The Federal Capital of Brazil" [Discussion at the Royal Geographical Society], *Geographical Journal* 128 n. 1 (March 1962), 18.

52   Carlos Moreira Teixeira, "La vraie nature de Brasília," *L'architecture d'aujourd'hui* 79 n. 359 (July–August 2005), 100–105, photographs by Emmanuel Pinard.

53   See quotes in Ruth Verde Zein, "Brasília, modernidade radical à deriva," in *O lugar da crítica – Ensaios oportunos de arquitetura* (Porto Alegre: Centro Universitário Ritter dos Reis, 2001), 179.

54   The term was coined by Leo Marx in his analysis of the tensions between modernization and pastoral life in nineteenth-century American literature. Leo Marx, *The Machine in the Garden—Technology and the Pastoral Idea in America* (New York: Oxford University Press, 1964).

55   For a history of Brazilian architecture that takes into account the *favela* as an inspiration for development see Richard Williams, *Brazil: Modern Architectures in History* (London: Reaktion, 2009).

56   Gustavo Lins Ribeiro, "Arqueologia de uma cidade: Brasília e suas cidades satélites," *Espaço e debates* (São Paulo) 2 n. 5 (March–June 1982), 116.

57   David Epstein, *Brasília, Plan and Reality: A Study of Planned and Spontaneous Urban Development* (Berkeley: University of California Press, 1973), 10.

58   Gustavo Lins Ribeiro, "Arqueologia de uma cidade: Brasília e suas cidades satélites," *Espaço e debates* (São Paulo) 2 n. 5 (March–June 1982), 120–122.

59   Ibid.

60   Tanja Thung, *Brasília SQS 103 – Fallstudie über den öffentlichen Raum in einer Superquadra* (diploma thesis, Institut für Städtebau, University of Stuttgart, 2003), 23.

61   Philippe Panerai, "Brasília 2006, una ciudad de 2,5 millones de habitantes," in *Brasília 1956–2006*, ed. Eduard Rodrìguez i Villaescusa and Cibele Vieira Figueira (Lleida: Editorial Milenio, 2006), 107.

62   Eduard Rodrìguez i Villaescusa, "Brasília querida y mantenida," in *Brasília 1956–2006*, ed. Eduard Rodrìguez i Villaescusa and Cibele Vieira Figueira (Lleida: Editorial Milenio, 2006), 198.

63   David Snyder, "Alternate Perspectives on Brasília," *Economic Geography* 40 n. 1 (January 1964), 45.

64   Ibid., 42.

65   Philippe Panerai, "Brasília 2006, una ciudad de 2,5 millones de habitantes," in *Brasília 1956–2006*, ed. Eduard Rodrìguez i Villaescusa and Cibele Vieira Figueira (Lleida: Editorial Milenio, 2006), 118.

66   Eduard Rodrìguez i Villaescusa, "Brasília querida y mantenida," in *Brasília 1956–2006*, ed. Eduard Rodrìguez i Villaescusa and Cibele Vieira Figueira (Lleida: Editorial Milenio, 2006), 198.

67   Philippe Panerai, "Brasília 2006, una ciudad de 2,5 millones de habitantes," in *Brasília 1956–2006*, ed. Eduard Rodrìguez i Villaescusa and Cibele Vieira Figueira (Lleida: Editorial Milenio, 2006), 115.

68   Aldo Paviani, "Questões a respeito do planejamento urbano em Brasília," in, *Brasília –a metrópole em crise. Ensaios sobre Urbanização,* ed. Aldo Paviani (Brasília: Editora Universidade de Brasília, 1989), 99–105. For a similar approach see architectural historian Richard Williams's account of Águas Claras, Richard Williams, "Brasília after Brasília," *Progress in Planning* 67 (2007), 301–366.

69   Gustavo Lins Ribeiro, "Arqueologia de uma cidade: Brasília e suas cidades satellites," *Espaço e debates* (São Paulo) 2 n. 5 (March–June 1982), 124.

70   Census data from 1997, SEDUH, Anuário Estatistico do D. F., 2000, quoted by Tanja Thung, *Brasília SQS 103 – Fallstudie über den öffentlichen Raum in einer Superquadra* (diploma thesis, Institut für Städtebau, University of Stuttgart, 2003), 110.

71   Tanja Thung, *Brasília SQS 103 – Fallstudie über den öffentlichen Raum in einer Superquadra,* (diploma thesis, Institut für Städtebau, University of Stuttgart, 2003), 110–111.

72   Ibid.

73   Ibid.

74   Leonel Rocha, "Cerco às *superquadras*: Corrente na porta," *Veja* 29 n. 1504, July 16, 1997.

75   Clifford Pearson, "Brazil May Be Poised for an Architectural Comeback," *Architectural Record* 188 n. 3 (March 2000), 49–50.

76   Ibid., 50.

77 Jean-Louis Cohen, "The Future of the Modern," *Architecture* 98 n. 12 (December 2000), 61.

78 Richard Williams, "Modernist Civic Space and the Case of Brasília," *Journal of Urban History* 32 n. 1 (November 2005), 121–122.

79 Matheus Gorovitz, "*Unidade de Vizinhança*: Brasília's 'Neighborhood Unit'," in *Lúcio Costa: Brasília's Superquadra,* ed. Farès El-Dahdah (Munich: Prestel, 2005), 41–47.

80 For example Carlos Moreira Teixeira, "La vraie nature de Brasília," *L'architecture d'aujourd'hui* 359 (July–August 2005), 100–105, Carmen Stephan, "'Diesmal bauen wir die Hauptstadt von Brasilien'," *Du – die Zeitschrift für Kultur* (Zurich) 742 (December 2003), 75–77.

81 See photographs by Todd Eberle in David Morton, "Through the Viewfinder: Brasília's Modernism Emptied," *Architectural Record* 186 n. 9 (September 1998), 82–87.

82 Leonel Rocha, "Cerco às *superquadras*: Corrente na porta," *Veja* 29 n. 1504, July 16, 1997.

6 Mumbai—Mass Housing for the Upper Crust

1 In 1995, the local government changed the colonial name Bombay officially into its Marathi version, Mumbai. In contemporary Mumbai, both names are used interchangeably and often in the same sentence. To avoid confusion, in this book the city will consistently be called Mumbai.

2 Chandrashekhar Prabhu, "Housing for All?" *Economic Digest* (Mumbai) 32 n. 5 (May 2003), 19.

3 Bradford Hunt, "Understanding Chicago's High-Rise Public Housing Disaster," in *Chicago Architecture*, ed. Charles Waldheim and Katerina Rüedi Ray (Chicago: University of Chicago Press, 2005), 302.

4 In 1957, the number of slum dwellers was estimated at approximately 415,000 in the Mumbai area, or approximately 10 percent of the area's 4.1 million inhabitants. At the turn of the millennium estimates ranged around 55 percent of the 10 million inhabitants within Mumbai's city borders. Next to these approximately 5.5 million there are another 2 million who live in dilapidated formal buildings, and another 1 million sidewalk dwellers. P. K. Das, "Slums: The Continuing Struggle for Housing," in *Bombay and Mumbai – The City in Transition,* ed. Sujata Patel and Jim Masselos (New Delhi: Oxford University Press, 2003), 210. For an analysis of the layered community structures in Mumbai's informal settlements see Robert Neuwirth, *Shadow Cities: A Billion Squatters, a New Urban World* (London: Routledge, 2005), 101–142. For a rather pessimistic account of the slum as the new global paradigm of urbanization see Mike Davis, *Planet of Slums* (London: Verso, 2006).

5 P. K. Das, "Slums: The Continuing Struggle for Housing," in *Bombay and Mumbai – The City in Transition,* ed. Sujata Patel and Jim Masselos (New Delhi: Oxford University Press, 2003), 212.

6 Harini Narayanan, "In Search for Shelter: The Politics of the Implementation of the Urban Land (Ceiling and Regulation) Act 1976 in Greater Mumbai," in *Bombay and Mumbai – The City in Transition,* ed. Sujata Patel and Jim Masselos (New Delhi: Oxford University Press, 2003), 183–184.

7 2001 numbers, quoted from the official city website http://portal.mcgm.gov.in (accessed December 2007).

8 Norma Evenson, *The Indian Metropolis. A View Toward the West* (New Haven: Yale University Press, 1989), 206.

9 P. S. A. Sundaram, *Bombay: Can it House its Millions?* (New Delhi: Clarion Books, 1989), 32–37.

10 Norma Evenson, *The Indian Metropolis. A View Toward the West* (New Haven: Yale University Press, 1989), 239.

11 Ibid., 252.

12 M. B. Achwal, "Low-Cost Housing," *Architectural Review* 150 n. 898 (December 1971), 367.

13 Vidyadhar Phatak, interview with the author, Mumbai, June 11, 2008.

14 Swapna Banerjee-Guha, "Who are the Beneficiaries? Evaluation of a Public Housing Project for the Poor in New Bombay," *Ekistics* 58 n. 347 (March–April 1991), 63.

15 Chandrashekhar Prabhu, "Rent Control," *Economic Digest* (Mumbai) 34 n. 3 (March 2005), 23–25 Sulakshana Mahajan, interview with the author, Mumbai, June 5, 2008.

16 Neelima Risbud, *The Case of Mumbai. Case Study commissioned in preparation for the UN Global Report on Human Settlements 2003 – The Challenge of Slums* (New Delhi, 2003), 12, available online at http://www.ucl.ac.uk/dpu-projects/Global_Report/cities/mumbai.htm (accessed August 2007).

17 Government of India, National Buildings Organisation, *A Collection of Designs of Houses for Low Income Groups* (New Delhi: National Buildings Organisation, and UN Regional Housing Centre ECAFE, 1973). The collection of plans was started in 1965, eight years (!) before the book was eventually published.

18 Jaysukh Mehta, "Typification in Housing," *Journal of the Indian Institute of Architects* 38 n. 1 (January–March 1972), 22–24.

19 P. S. A. Sundaram, *Bombay: Can it House its Millions?* (New Delhi: Clarion Books, 1989), 68. See also Chandrashekhar Prabhu, "Rent Control," *Economic Digest* (Mumbai) 34 n. 3 (March 2005), 23.

20 Chandrashekhar Prabhu, "Future of Tenants in Mumbai," *Economic Digest* (Mumbai) 35 n. 3 (March 2006), 17–18.

21 Sahakar Nagar I is situated west of the Tilak Nagar suburban railroad station on the southern side of the railroad line.

22 Pankaj Joshi, interview with the author, Mumbai, June 10, 2008. Sahyadri Nagar is situated two blocks north of Mahatma Gandhi Road (Charkop Road) and east of Dr. Babasaheb Ambedkar Road.

23 The colony is situated between Nadkarni Marg and Wadala Railway Station.

24 The Mudran Press Colony lies north of Jai Prakash Road (Versova Road) and west of Lokhandiwala Complex Road.

25 Chandrashekhar Prabhu, "A Summing-Up," *Economic Digest* (Mumbai) 38 n. 6 (June 2007), 19–21.

26 The Slum Redevelopment Authority was formed in March 1995 by a right-wing coalition between Shiv Sena (the Marathi nationalist party) and the BJP (the conservative Indian People's Union) that had replaced Mumbai's moderate left-leaning Congress Party government in that year. The new program was based on the preceding Slum Redevelopment Scheme (SRD), which was launched in 1991 by the Congress Party government and also attempted to involve private actors.

27 Most of the author's interviewed Mumbai architects and housing activists thought of self-redevelopment as the only viable solution in a market economy, including Anirudh Paul, June 10, 2008, Chandrashekhar Prabhu, June 7, 2008, Shirish Patel, June 2, 2008.

28 The area is located south of Wasi Naka Road, north of Bharat Petroleum Road, east of Ghatkopar-Mahul Road, and west of a hilly shrub.

29 Chandrashekhar Prabhu, interview with the author, Mumbai, June 7, 2008

30 Ibid.

31 Sudhir Diwan and Vakhariya Kamnaiya, "Big Money and Political Power Have Made Bombay's Back Bay Scheme India's Biggest Urban Fraud," *Design* (New Delhi) 24 (January–March 1980), 25–36.

32 Ibid.

33 Norma Evenson, *The Indian Metropolis. A View Toward the West* (New Haven: Yale University Press, 1989), 244.

34 Ibid.

35 Ibid., 213.

36 Sharada Dwivedi and Rahul Mehrotra, *Bombay, the Cities Within* (Mumbai: India Book House, 1995), 291.

37 Uttam Jain, "Editorially," *Journal of the Indian Institute of Architects* 42 (October–December 1976), 15.

38 Sharada Dwivedi and Rahul Mehrotra, *Bombay, the Cities Within* (Mumbai: India Book House, 1995), 293.

39 "A Capital of Quality," *Design* (New Delhi) 28 (January–March 1984), 21, quoted by Norma Evenson, *The Indian Metropolis. A View Toward the West* (New Haven: Yale University Press, 1989), 244.

40 Arun Ranade, "What Has Gone Wrong at Back Bay?" *Journal of the Indian Institute of Architects* 42 (October–December 1976), 14–18.

41 Norma Evenson, *The Indian Metropolis. A View Toward the West* (New Haven: Yale University Press, 1989), 213.

42 Rakesh Chandra, "Minimum Housing Standards for Low-income Group Housing," *Journal of the Indian Institute of Architects* 42 n. 4 (October–December 1976), 19–21. The author is an architect teaching at the University of Roorkee.

43 "An Experiment in System Building," *Architectural Review* 150 n. 898 (December 1971), 374–375 and S. K. Dutta, "New Technic [sic] of Low-Income Group Housing," *Journal of the Indian Institute of Architects* 38 n. 2 (April–June 1972), 21–23.

44 M. B. Achwal, "Low-Cost Housing," *Architectural Review* 150 n. 898 (December 1971), 367–369.

45 Shirish Patel, interview with the author, Mumbai, June 2, 2008.

46 Ibid. Patel's office did the structural engineering for both buildings.

47 Among John F. C. Turner's most important publications is "The Squatter Settlement: Architecture that Works," *Architectural Design* 38 (1968), 355–360. For similar approaches from India see Shri Manohar, "Developing a Radically New Approach to Urban Housing," *Journal of the Indian Institute of Architects* 36 n. 4–6 (April–June 1970), 16 or M. B. Achwal, "Low-Cost Housing," *Architectural Review* 150 n. 898 (December 1971), 367.

48 Vidyadhar Phatak, interview with the author, Mumbai, June 11, 2008.

49 One of the many sites is the area between Mahatma Gandhi Road (Charkop Road) in Charkop and the Gorai Khadi Creek in Kandivali (West). Sites and Services projects are situated, for example, along Dr. Babasaheb Abedkar Road and its prolongation to the north, RDP Road No. 6 (Gorai Link Road).

50 This estimation was confirmed by many of the author's Mumbai interview partners, including Shirish Patel, June 2, 2008, Vidyadhar Phatak, June 11, 2008, Sulakshana Mahajan, June 5, 2008, Swapna Banerjee-Guha, June 9, 2008.

51 Since the 1970s, historic preservation is also gaining ground in India, but mostly focuses on buildings that are considered "artistically valuable." Norma Evenson, *The Indian Metropolis. A View Toward the West* (New Haven: Yale University Press, 1989), 248.

52 This estimation was confirmed many of the author's Mumbai interview partners, including Hafeez Contractor, June 3, 2008, and Shirish Patel, June 2, 2008.

53 "Bombay's Multi-Story Growth Without a Plan," *Indian Architect* 17 n. 6 (June 1975), 85–87. See also Vijay Kumar, "High Rise Mass Housing," *Journal of the Indian Institute of Architects* 36 n. 4–6 (April–June 1970), 14.

54 Abu Nadeem, "How Form Follows Fiasco: An American Writer Unwittingly Mirrors the Ongoing Fiasco in India," *Design* (New Delhi) 26 n. 1 (January–March 1982), 39–42

55 M. B. Achwal, "Low-Cost Housing," *Architectural Review* 150 n. 898 (December 1971), 368.

56 Shahnaz Anklesaria, "Lost in the Concrete Jungle," *Design* (New Delhi) 28 n. 3 (July–September 1984), 31–35.

57 M. B. Achwal, "Low-Cost Housing," *Architectural Review* 158 (December 1971), 367.

7 Prefab Moscow

1 This was stated by the director of the Central Research and Design Institute for Dwelling, quoted by Robert McCutcheon, "Technology and the State in the Provision of Low-Income Accommodation: The Case of Industrialized House-Building, 1955–77," *Social Studies of Science* 22 n. 2 (May 1992), 360.

2 "Deshevle skinut'sia na rekonstruktsiyu chem platit' po schetchiku," *Rossiiskaya Gazeta,* March 4, 2004, quoted by Thomas Lahusen, "Decay or Endurance? The Ruins of Socialism," *Slavic Review* 65 n. 4 (Winter 2006), 736–746.

3 The dual nature of the slab building as both home and symbol for the socialist system was very thoughtfully analyzed in the East German context by Christine Hannemann, *Die Platte* (Berlin: Schelzky und Jeep: 2000). For a history of housing in the Soviet Union in general and in Moscow in particular see the great work by Timothy Colton, *Moscow: Governing the Socialist Metropolis* (Cambridge, MA: Harvard University Press, 1995). See also R. Antony French, *Plans, Pragmatism,*

and *People—the Legacy of Soviet Planning for Today's Cities* (Pittsburgh: University of Pittsburgh Press, 1995), and Henry Morton, "Who Gets What, When and How? Housing in the Soviet Union," *Soviet Studies* 32 n. 2 (April 1980), 235–259.

4   Between 1926 and 1959, the population of the USSR rose from 148.7 to 209 million, reaching 241.7 in 1970 and 293.1 million in 1991. E. M. Andreev et al., *Naselenie Sovyetskogo Soyuza, 1922–1991* (Moscow: Nauka, 1993). At the same time, the urban population had risen from 17 percent of the total population in 1926 to 47.9 percent in 1959 and 56.3 percent in 1970—in 1989 it was 65.8 percent. R. Antony French, *Plans, Pragmatism, and People—the Legacy of Soviet Planning for Today's Cities* (Pittsburgh: University of Pittsburgh Press, 1995), 52.

5   It had been 6.4 square meters in 1913. By 1970 it rose again to 11.2 square meters. These figures refer to the entire Soviet Union. *Narodnoye Khozyaystvo SSSR 1956* (Moscow: Gosudarstvennoye Statisticheskoye Izdatel'stvo, 1956), 163 and *Narodnoye Khozyaystvo SSSR v 1970g* (Moscow: Statistika), 7, 68, and 546, both quoted after R. Antony French, *Plans, Pragmatism, and People—the Legacy of Soviet Planning for Today's Cities* (Pittsburgh: University of Pittsburgh Press, 1995), 58. Statistics from Soviet sources deserve a general caveat. It is one of the ironies of real existing socialism that despite the socialist bureaucrats' obsession with hard numbers, reliable data remains scarce. For most of the Soviet period and even afterward, censorship made detailed censuses unavailable to researchers. In politically sensitive contexts, such as the state-provoked famine of 1931–32 that led to millions of deaths, it is almost certain that the census data has been falsified. The post-Stalinist censuses are likely to be more reliable. See Paul R. Josephson, *New Atlantis Revisited. Akademgorodok, the Siberian City of Science* (Princeton: Princeton University Press, 1997), 6 and 52.

6   Selim Chan-Magometow, *Pioniere der sowjetischen Architektur* (Dresden: Verlag der Kunst, 1983), 398.

7   The Architectural Planning Directorate evolved from the Architectural Affairs Directorate; the renaming went with an extension of responsibilities. Timothy Colton, *Moscow: Governing the Socialist Metropolis* (Cambridge, MA: Harvard University Press, 1995), 326 and 371.

8   Nikita Khrushchev, *Khrushchev Remembers: The Last Testament* (Boston: Little, Brown, and Co., 1974), 102.

9   At the same time, industrial production continued to be predominant over housing. Thomas Lahusen, "Decay or Endurance? The Ruins of Socialism," *Slavic Review* 65 n. 4 (Winter, 2006), 743

10 R. Antony French, *Plans, Pragmatism, and People—the Legacy of Soviet Planning for Today's Cities* (Pittsburgh: University of Pittsburgh Press, 1995), 75. Half a year later, the Central Committee officially announced the industrialization of the construction industry. Postanovlenie TsK KPSS i Soveta Ministrov SSSR, "O merakh po dal'neishey ey industrializatsii, uluchsheniyu kachestva i snizheniyu stoymosti stroitel'stva" (August 23, 1955), in *Resheniya partii i pravitel'stva po khozyaystvennym voprosam 1917–1967 g.*, ed. E. Tyagay (Moscow: Izdatel'stvo politicheskoy literatury, 1968) (Resolution of the Central Committee of the KPSU and the Council of Ministers of the USSR "On the measures for a future industrialization, improvement of the quality and decrease of cost of construction"). The resolution was specified and extended two years later, on July 31, 1957. See also *Postanovleniya partii i pravitel'stva ob arkhitekture i stroitel'stve. Krotkiy istorikobibliograficheskiy spravotchnik* (Moscow: 1974) (Resolutions of the Party and the Government on Architecture and Construction. A short historical-bibliographical handbook).

11 Postanovlenie TsK KPSS i Soveta Ministrov SSSR, "Ob unstranenii islishestv v proektirovanii i stroitel'stve" (November 4, 1955), in *Institut Marksizma-Leninisma pri TsK KPSS, Kommunisticheskaya partiya sovetskogo soyuza v rezolyutsiyakh s"ezdov konferentsii i plenumov TsK* (Moscow: Izdatel'stvo politicheskoy literatury, 1985) (Resolution of the Central Committee of the KPSU and the Council of Ministers of the USSR "on the elimination of excess in planning and construction").

12 R. Antony French, *Plans, Pragmatism, and People—the Legacy of Soviet Planning for Today's Cities* (Pittsburgh: University of Pittsburgh Press, 1995), 75.

13 Timothy Colton, *Moscow: Governing the Socialist Metropolis* (Cambridge, MA: Harvard University Press, 1995), 371.

14 E. Gigovskaya, "Inzhenyer Lagutenko, portret mastera," *Arkhitektura i stroitel'stvo Moskvy* n. 5, October 4, 2002 (The Engineer Lagutenko, a Portrait of the Master), available online at

http://www.stroi.ru/periodical/detail.asp?d=2498&dc=2498&dr=72337 (accessed December 2007).

15 Timothy Colton, *Moscow: Governing the Socialist Metropolis* (Cambridge, MA: Harvard University Press, 1995), 371.

16 R. Antony French, *Plans, Pragmatism, and People—the Legacy of Soviet Planning for Today's Cities* (Pittsburgh: University of Pittsburgh Press, 1995), 76.

17 Timothy Colton, *Moscow: Governing the Socialist Metropolis* (Cambridge, MA: Harvard University Press, 1995), 373.

18 Ibid., 376.

19 Katerina Gerasimova, "Privacy in the Soviet Communal Apartment," *Socialist Spaces: Sites of Everyday Life in the Eastern Bloc,* David Crowley and Susan E. Reid (Oxford, 2002), 210.

20 Ministerium für Bauwesen der DDR and Gosgrazhdanstroi, ed., *Neue Wohnkomplexe in der DDR und der UdSSR* (East Berlin: Verlag für Bauwesen and Moscow: Strojizdat, 1987), 41.

21 Ibid.

22 Timothy Colton, *Moscow: Governing the Socialist Metropolis* (Cambridge, MA: Harvard University Press, 1995), 491.

23 See, for example, Isabelle Amestoy, "Les grands ensembles en Russie, de l'adoption d'un modèle à la désaffection. Le cas de l'habitat khrouchtchévien," in *Le monde des grands ensembles,* ed. Frédéric Dufaux and Annie Fourcaut (Paris: Éditions Créaphis, 2004), 137.

24 Z. A. Yankova and I. Yu. Rodzinskaya, *Problemy bol'shogo goroda* (Problems of Big Cities) (Moscow: Nauka, 1982), 63–64.

25 *Moskva v tsifrakh* (Moscow in Numbers) (Moscow: Finansy i statistika, 1985), 144, quoted after Timothy Colton, *Moscow: Governing the Socialist Metropolis* (Cambridge, MA: Harvard University Press, 1995), 488.

26 Günter Peters, *Gesamtberliner Stadtentwicklung von 1949–1990* (Berlin: Hochschule der Künste, 1992), 22.

27 This sentiment is still noticeable to date. Nicolai Ouroussoff, "Russian Icons," *New York Times* May 15, 2005. See also Barbara Engel, "'Blaue Städte' in Sibirien," *Der Architekt* 4/2001: 50.

28 N. Bobrovnikov, "Razvitie zhilishchnogo stroitel'stva v tekushchei pyatiletke," *Voprosi ekonomiki* (Moscow) n. 5 (1972), 24, quoted by Henry Morton, "Who Gets What, When and How? Housing in the Soviet Union," *Soviet Studies* 32 n. 2, (April 1980), 236.

29 V. Promyslov, (chairman of the city soviet) "Za obraztsovyi kommunisticheskii," *Sovety deputatov trudyashchikhsya* n. 12 (1975), 24, quoted by Henry Morton, "Who Gets What, When and How? Housing in the Soviet Union," *Soviet Studies* 32 n. 2, (April 1980), 236.

30 Starting with the five-year plan 1956–60, close to 300 million square meters of residential space were completed in the Soviet Union per five-year plan, a number that remained approximately the same until 1990. In the preceding five-year plans the number was only half to one-third: approximately 150 million square meters in 1951–55 and approximately 100 million square meters 1946–50. In all preceding five-year plans, the number oscillated around 50 million square meters. Isabelle Amestoy, "Les grands ensembles en Russie, de l'adoption d'un modèle à la désaffection. Le cas de l'habitat khrouchtchévien," in *Le monde des grands ensembles*, ed. Frédéric Dufaux and Annie Fourcaut (Paris: Éditions Créaphis, 2004), 131.

31 Henry Morton, "Housing in the Soviet Union," *Proceedings of the Academy of Political Science* 35 n. 3 (1984), 70.

32 R. Antony French, *Plans, Pragmatism, and People—the Legacy of Soviet Planning for Today's Cities* (Pittsburgh: University of Pittsburgh Press, 1995), 135–136.

33 Ibid., 136. See also Timothy Colton, *Moscow: Governing the Socialist Metropolis* (Cambridge, MA: Harvard University Press, 1995), 403.

34 Timothy Colton, *Moscow: Governing the Socialist Metropolis* (Cambridge, MA: Harvard University Press, 1995), 407.

35 Ibid.. 502–503.

36 Ibid., 415–416.

37 Ibid., 506–507.

38 Research based on *zayavki* has to be taken with a pinch of salt, since most likely the ads convoluted people's desires with a more or less pragmatic estimation of what kind of exchanges might be successful. Examples of such research include G. L. Vasilyev, "Sotsial'naya otsenka gorodskoy territorii," *Goroda i sistemy rasseleniya 6: Dostizheniya i perspektivy* 43, 59–66, N. B. Barbash, "Otsenka naseleniyem uchastkov gorodskoy sredy (na osnove dannykh o zayavkakh na obmen zhil'ya)," *Isvestiya AN SSSR; Seriya Geograficheskaya* n. 5 (1984), 81–91, and G. L. Vasilyev and O. L. Privalova, "Sotsial'no-geograficheskaya otsenka vnutrigorodskikh razlichiy," *Vestnik MGU* n. 4 (1982), 9–15, transl. "A Socio-Geographic Evaluation of Differences within a City," *Soviet Geography* 25/7 (1984), 488–496.

39 Ibid.

40 Ibid. The preference for the western inner districts is confirmed by Yuri G. Veshninskiy, "Sotsial'no-esteticheskiye predpochteniya moskvichey (otsenka gorodskoy sredy razlichnykh chastey territorii Moskvy)," in *Sotsial'nyye problemy arkhitekturno-gradostroitel'nogo razvitiya Moskvy*, ed. M. V. Borshchevskiy (Moscow: TSNIIP Gradostritel'stva, 1988), 98. There were also contradictions—in Moscow and Leningrad, for example, a large number of tenants who wanted to move to the center stood against a similarly large group who desired an apartment on the periphery. Natasha B. Babash, *Metodika izucheniya territorial'noy differentsiatsii gorodskoy sredy* (Moscow: IG AN SSSR, 1986), 141.

41 Robert Rudolph, "Segregation Tendencies in Large Russian Cities: The Development of Elitist Housing in St. Petersburg," in *Die Städte Russlands im Wandel*, ed. Isolde Brade (Leipzig: Institut für Länderkunde, 2002), 209, and R. Antony French, *Plans, Pragmatism, and People—the Legacy of Soviet Planning for Today's Cities* (Pittsburgh: University of Pittsburgh Press, 1995), 135.

42 Robert Rudolph, "Die Moskauer Region zwischen Planung und Profit," in *Die Städte Russlands im Wandel*, ed. Isolde Brade (Leipzig: Institut für Länderkunde, 2002), 240. See also L. Kalyanina, "Seson pokopuk: Samaya deshyovaya i samaya dorogaya nedvizhimost v Moskvye pochti vsya raskuplyena" (Sale season: The cheapest and most expensive pieces of real estate in Moscow are almost sold out), *Expert*, December 6, 1999: 44–51.

43 Timothy Colton, *Moscow: Governing the Socialist Metropolis* (Cambridge, MA: Harvard University Press, 1995), 407–408.

44 In a 1986 survey, 80 percent of respondents who lived in the outer parts of Moscow desired to live closer to a metro station. Natasha B. Babash, *Metodika izucheniya territorial'noy differentsiatsii gorodskoy sredy* (Moscow: IG AN SSSR, 1986), 140. In a 1978 survey undertaken in Leningrad, 40 percent of those who wanted to move to a different neighborhood mentioned "quality of environment" as a reason, which of course might include the quality of an apartment. "Proximity to work" was mentioned by 13 percent. "Aesthetic perceptions" were only mentioned by 4.7 percent and "proximity to the center" only by 5.4 percent. *Gorod: Problemy Sotsial'nogo Razvitiya* (The City: Problems of Social Development), ed. A. V. Dimitryev and M. N. Mezhevich (Leningrad: Nauka, 1982), 114.

45 Henry Morton, "Who Gets What, When and How? Housing in the Soviet Union," *Soviet Studies* 32 n. 2, (April 1980), 245.

46 Isabelle Amestoy, "Les grands ensembles en Russie, de l'adoption d'un modèle à la désaffection. Le cas de l'habitat khrouchtchévien," in *Le monde des grands ensembles,* ed. Frédéric Dufaux and Annie Fourcaut (Paris: Éditions Créaphis, 2004), 138. It has to be pointed out that the study, carried out in 1999, was very limited in its scope and comprised only 257 individuals.

47 V. Ruzhzhe, "Sotsial'noye kachestovo zhiloy sredy," *Sotsiologicheskiye issledovaniya* n. 1 (1974), 38.

48 G. L. Vasil'yev, D. A. Sidorov, and S. E. Khanin, "Vyyavleniye potrebitel'skikh predpochteniy v sfere rasseleniya," *Vestnik MGU Seriya 5 Geografiya* n. 2 (1988), 44.

49 See also Ol'ga Evgenevna Trushchenko, *Prestizh tsentra – gorodskaya sotsial'naya segregatsiya v Moskve* (Moscow: Izdatel'stvo Sotsio-Logos 1995) (The prestige of the center—urban social segregation in Moscow).

50 Robert Rudolph, "Segregation Tendencies in Large Russian Cities: The Development of Elitist Housing in St. Petersburg," in *Die Städte Russlands im Wandel*, ed. Isolde Brade (Leipzig: Institut für Länderkunde, 2002), 206. Russian real estate dealers use all kinds of legal and illegal methods to remove *kommunalka* inhabitants from central apartments; they mostly end up in the high-rise

buildings on the periphery where they are far from the center but at least enjoy individual sanitary facilities.

51 For a study of the *propiska* system see Mervyn Matthews, *The Passport Society: Controlling Movement in Russia and the USSR* (Boulder, CO: Westview Press, 1993)

52 In the ranking of most desirable cities, Moscow held the top position, followed, with a big difference, by Leningrad. Siberian and Central Asian cities were ranked lowest. G. L. Vasil'ev, D. A. Sidorov, and S. Ye. Khanin, *Vyyavleniye potrebitel'skikh predpochteniy v grafichesikiy analiz* (Moscow: Statistika, 1988).

53 Hillary Pilkington, *Migration, Displacement, and Identity in Post-Socialist Russia* (London: Routledge, 1998), 40–42. See also Tova Höjdestrand, "The Soviet-Russian Production of Homelessness – Propiska, Housing, Privatization," available online at http://www.anthrobase.com/Txt/H/Hoejdestrand_T_01.htm (accessed March 2007). The author teaches at the Department of Anthropology, Stockholm University.

54 Raymond J. Struyk, "Housing Privatization in the Former Soviet Bloc to 1995," in *Cities after Socialism*, ed. Gregory Andrusz, Michael Harloe, and Ivan Szeleny (Oxford: Blackwell, 1996), 196.

55 R. Antony French, *Plans, Pragmatism, and People—the Legacy of Soviet Planning for Today's Cities* (Pittsburgh: University of Pittsburgh Press, 1995), 150.

56 Michael Gordon, "Yeltsin Attacks Soviet-Era Housing Benefits," *New York Times,* July 13, 1997

57 Robert Rudolph, "Segregation Tendencies in Large Russian Cities: The Development of Elitist Housing in St. Petersburg," in *Die Städte Russlands im Wandel*, ed. Isolde Brade (Leipzig: Institut für Länderkunde, 2002), 204. See also Raymond J. Struyk, "Housing Privatization in the Former Soviet Bloc to 1995," in *Cities after Socialism*, ed. Gregory Andrusz, Michael Harloe, and Ivan Szeleny (Oxford: Blackwell, 1996).

58 The figure is from 1997. Robert Rudolph, "Segregation Tendencies in Large Russian Cities: The Development of Elitist Housing in St. Petersburg," in *Die Städte Russlands im Wandel*, ed. Isolde Brade (Leipzig: Institut für Länderkunde, 2002), 205.

59 Aleksander Rakhlin [member of European Net of Housing Research], *Social Housing in Russia* (2002), available online at http://www.hic-net.org/articles.asp?PID=226 (accessed March 2008).

60 Raymond J. Struyk, "Housing Privatization in the Former Soviet Bloc to 1995," in *Cities after Socialism*, ed. Gregory Andrusz, Michael Harloe, and Ivan Szeleny (Oxford: Blackwell, 1996): 196–198.

61 Ibid.

62 World Bank Data, available online at http://siteresources.worldbank.org/INTRUSSIAN FEDERATION/Resources/macromay2006.pdf (accessed June 2007).

63 Based on a calculation of the national food basket in 2005, 15.8 percent of the Russian population lived below the poverty line. Based on national averages, the statistics do not reflect the immense gap in living expenses between urban and rural areas. Ibid.

64 Robert Rudolph, "Die Moskauer Region zwischen Planung und Profit," in *Die Städte Russlands im Wandel*, ed. Isolde Brade (Leipzig: Institut für Länderkunde, 2002), 237.

65 2006 data, "Deshevle skinut'sia na rekonstruktsiiu chem platit' po schetchiku," *Rossiyskaia Gazeta* March 4, 2004, quoted in Thomas Lahusen, "Decay or Endurance? The Ruins of Socialism," *Slavic Review* 65 n. 4 (Winter, 2006), 736–746.

66 R. Antony French, *Plans, Pragmatism, and People—the Legacy of Soviet Planning for Today's Cities* (Pittsburgh: University of Pittsburgh Press, 1995), 78.

67 Ibid.

68 Michael Gordon, "Yeltsin Attacks Soviet-Era Housing Benefits," *New York Times,* July 13, 1997.

69 Anna Svetlichnaya, "Panel'nye pyatetazhki stanovyatsya redkost'yu," *Kommersant* December 12, 2005 (Five-Story Panel Buildings Are Becoming Rare), online version http://www.irn.ru/articles/5611.html (accessed March 2007).

70 Ibid.

71 Ibid. See also Resin, "Vse 'Khrushchëvki-piatetazhki' budut sneseny k 2010 godu," *Nezavisimaya gazeta*, November 10, 2005. These buildings are situated in different neighborhoods, for example in the Khoroshevo-Mnëvniki rayon.

72 Ibid.

73 The buildings are situated on n. 24 and 30, Ulitsa Mezhdunarodnaya, and on 12/1 and 18/1 Ulitsa Khodynskaya; panels are taken from the P-32 series. The model was to be completed by 2006. Anna Svetlichnaya, "Panel'nye pyatetazhki stanovyatsya redkost'yu," *Kommersant* December 12, 2005 (Five-Story Panel Buildings Are Becoming Rare), available online at http://www.irn.ru/articles/5611.html (accessed March 2007).

74 Alye Parusa is located at Aviatsionnaya Ulitsa 77–79, Vorob'ëvy Gory on Mosfil'movskaya Ulitsa 4–6.

75 For example the so-called Tsarskoye Selo (Tsar's Village), a development of 14-story slab buildings with comparatively high standards at 43–45 Profsoyuznaya and 60–62 Novocherëmushkinskaya ulitsa. It was built for approximately 10,000 residents. Timothy Colton, *Moscow: Governing the Socialist Metropolis* (Cambridge, MA: Harvard University Press, 1995), 510.

76 http://www.moscowresidencies.com (accessed January 2007). For the average monthly wages as calculated in 2006 see World Bank Data, available online at http://siteresources.worldbank.org/INTRUSSIANFEDERATION/Resources/macromay2006.pdf (accessed June 2007).

77 Sonja Zekri, "Wir sind reich! Wir sind da!" *Süddeutsche Zeitung*, September 11, 2007: 15.

78 Ibid.

79 Isabelle Amestoy, "Les grands ensembles en Russie, de l'adoption d'un modèle à la désaffection. Le cas de l'habitat khrouchtchévien," in *Le monde des grands ensembles*, ed. Frédéric Dufaux and Annie Fourcaut (Paris: Éditions Créaphis, 2004), 140.

80 Ibid.

81 Ibid.

8 High-Rise Shanghai

1 Figures by the UN Population Division, *World Urbanization Prospects, 1999 Revision*, available online at http://www.un.org/esa/population/publications/wup1999/wup99ch6.pdf p. 95 (accessed July 2008). The figures in the literature differ significantly.

2 Zhang Jie and Wang Tao, "Housing Development in the Socialist Planned Economy from 1949 to 1978," in *Modern Urban Housing in China 1840–2000*, ed. Lü Junhua, Peter Rowe, and Zhang Jie (Munich: Prestel, 2001), 151 and 174. See also Xue Qiuli and Ernie Scoffham, "China's Housing in Transition: a Case Study of Shanghai," *Housing Science* 20 n. 4 (1996), 232.

3 *Narodnoye Khozyaystvo SSSR 1956* (Moscow: Gosudarstvennoye Statisticheskoye Izdatel'stvo, 1956), 163 quoted by R. Antony French, *Plans, Pragmatism, and People—the Legacy of Soviet Planning for Today's Cities* (Pittsburgh: University of Pittsburgh Press, 1995), 58.

4 Li Zhengyu, conversation with the author, Shanghai, August 24, 2007.

5 Zhang Shouyi and Tan Ying, "An Important Period of the Early Development of Housing in Modern Cities," in *Modern Urban Housing in China: 1841–2000*, ed. Lü Junhua, Peter Rowe, and Zhang Jie (Munich: Prestel, 2001), 80.

6 Peter Rowe and Seng Kuang, *Architectural Encounters with Essence and Form in Modern China* (Cambridge, MA: MIT Press, 2002), 98.

7 Zhang Shouyi and Wang Tao, "Housing Development in the Socialist Planned Economy from 1949–1978" in *Modern Urban Housing in China: 1841–2000*, ed. Lü Junhua, Peter Rowe, and Zhang Jie (Munich: Prestel, 2001), 130.

8 Cheng [Zheng] Shounan and Chang [Zhang] Min, "Designs for Experimental Works of Great Panel Construction Dwellings in Shanghai 1964," *Jianzhu Xuebao* (Architectural Journal) 8 (1964), 1–3.

9 Li Zhengyu, interview with the author, Shanghai, August 24, 2007. Zhang Shouyi and Wang Tao, "Housing Development in the Socialist Planned Economy from 1949–1978," *Modern Urban Housing in China: 1841–2000*, ed. Lü Junhua, Peter Rowe, and Zhang Jie (Munich: Prestel, 2001), 183.

10   Shanghai Municipal Institute of Civil Building-Design, "The Prefabricated Housing in Shanghai with Non-Steam-Pressed, Large Sized Silicate Blocks," *Jianzhu Xuebao* (Architectural Journal) 3 (1960), 2–5.

11   Zhang Shouyi and Wang Tao, "Housing Development in the Socialist Planned Economy from 1949–1978," in *Modern Urban Housing in China: 1841–2000*, ed. Lü Junhua, Peter Rowe, and Zhang Jie (Munich: Prestel, 2001), 125.

12   Ibid., 132 and 182

13   Li Zhengyu, *Cheng Shi, Zhu Zhai, Cheng Shi* (City, Housing, City) (Nanjing: Dong Nan Da Xue, 2004), 249. Li is the vice dean of the College for Architecture and Urban Planning at Tongji University, Shanghai.

14   Wang Dingzeng, "The Planning and Design of the Cáoyáng Xīncūn Residential Area in Shanghai," *Jianzhu Xuebao* (Architectural Journal) 2 (1956), 1–15. See also Li Zhengyu, *Cheng Shi, Zhu Zhai, Cheng Shi* (City, Housing, City) (Nanjing: Dong Nan Da Xue, 2004), 325–326.

15   Ibid., 249.

16   *Shanghai Kexue Jushu Wenxian Chubanshi 1951–1996 – Housing in Shanghai 1951–1996* (in English and Chinese) (Shanghai: Publisher for Documents of Science and Technology, 1998), 82.

17   The development is bordered by the Shanghai–Nanjing railroad, the New Gonghe Road Overpass, West Tianmu Road, and Datong Road.

18   Ho Wingchung, "The (Un-)Making of the Shanghai Socialist 'Model Community'," *Journal of Asian and African Studies* 39 n. 5 (2004), 379–405.

19   Li Zhengyu, *Cheng Shi, Zhu Zhai, Cheng Shi* (City, Housing, City) (Nanjing: Dong Nan Da Xue, 2004), 151.

20   Ho Wingchung, "The (Un-)Making of the Shanghai Socialist 'Model Community'," *Journal of Asian and African Studies* 39 n. 5 (2004), 379–405.

21   Zhang Shouyi and Wang Tao, "Housing Development in the Socialist Planned Economy from 1949–1978," in *Modern Urban Housing in China: 1841–2000*, ed. Lü Junhua, Peter Rowe, and Zhang Jie (Munich: Prestel, 2001), 175.

22   *Shanghai Kexue Jushu Wenxian Chubanshi 1951–1996 – Housing in Shanghai 1951–1996* (in English and Chinese) (Shanghai: Publisher for Documents of Science and Technology, 1998), 169–171. See also Robert Kaltenbrunner, *"Minhang, Shanghai: Die Satellitenstadt als intermediäre Planung* (Berlin: Fachgebiet Geschichte und Theorie der Landschaftsentwicklung, Technische Universität, 1993) [Ph.D. thesis].

23   Li Zhengyu, interview with the author, Shanghai, August 24, 2007. See also Zhang Shouyi and Wang Tao, "Housing Development in the Socialist Planned Economy from 1949–1978," in *Modern Urban Housing in China: 1841–2000*, ed. Lü Junhua, Peter Rowe, and Zhang Jie (Munich: Prestel, 2001), 180.

24   Li Zhengyu, *Cheng Shi, Zhu Zhai, Cheng Shi* (City, Housing, City) (Nanjing: Dong Nan Da Xue, 2004), 51–52. See also picture on p. 52, 2.49.

25   Zhang Shouyi and Wang Tao, "Housing Development in the Socialist Planned Economy from 1949–1978," in *Modern Urban Housing in China: 1841–2000*, ed. Lü Junhua, Peter Rowe, and Zhang Jie (Munich: Prestel, 2001), 1184.

26   Zheng Naigui, "On High-Rise Buildings," *Jianzhu Xuebao* (Architectural Journal) 3 (1981), 40–42 (in Chinese with English summary).

27   Jonathan Spence, *The Search for Modern China* (New York: Norton, 1990), 767–773.

28   Ibid., 851.

29   Li Zhengyu, conversation with the author, Shanghai, August 24, 2007.

30   Lü Junhua and Shao Lei, "Housing Development from 1978 to 2000 after China Adopted Reform and Opening-Up Policies," in *Modern Urban Housing in China: 1841–2000*, ed. Lü Junhua, Peter Rowe, and Zhang Jie (Munich: Prestel, 2001), 242.

31   Xue Qiuli and Ernie Scoffham, "China's Housing in Transition: a Case Study of Shanghai," *Housing Science* 20 n. 4 (1996), 232.

32 Lü Junhua and Shao Lei, "Housing Development from 1978 to 2000 after China Adopted Reform and Opening-Up Policies," in *Modern Urban Housing in China: 1841–2000*, ed. Lü Junhua, Peter Rowe, and Zhang Jie (Munich: Prestel, 2001), 243.

33 Li Zhengyu, *Cheng Shi, Zhu Zhai, Cheng Shi* (City, Housing, City) (Nanjing: Dong Nan Da Xue, 2004), 263.

34 In 1991 there were approximately 3,000 realty developers; two years later, already more than 30,000. Approximately two-thirds were Chinese-foreign joint ventures. *China Reform and Development Report 1992–1993* (Chinese Economic Publishing House, 1994), quoted by Lü Junhua and Shao Lei, "Housing Development from 1978 to 2000 after China Adopted Reform and Opening-Up Policies," in *Modern Urban Housing in China: 1841–2000*, ed. Lü Junhua, Peter Rowe, and Zhang Jie (Munich: Prestel, 2001), 251.

35 Xueguang Zhou, Nancy Brandon Tuma, and Phyllis Moen, "Stratification Dynamics under State Socialism: The Case of Urban China, 1949–1993," *Social Forces* 74 n. 3 (March 1996), 764.

36 Xue Qiuli and Ernie Scoffham, "China's Housing in Transition: a Case Study of Shanghai," *Housing Science* 20 n. 4 (1996), 238.

37 Jonathan Spence, *The Search for Modern China* (New York: Norton, 1990), 810.

38 Wu Waiping and Emily Rosenbaum, "Migration and Housing: Comparing China with the United States," in *Urban China in Transition*, ed. John Logan (London, New York: Routledge, 2008), 251.

39 Zhigang Li and Fulong Wu, "Tenure-Based Residential Segregation in Post-Reform Chinese Cities: A Case Study of Shanghai," *Transactions of the Institute of British Geographers* 33 n. 3 (July 2008), 404–419.

40 In a state-owned apartment, the rent averaged 0.13 yuan per square meter in 1988—the same as in 1949. Xue Qiuli and Ernie Scoffham, "China's Housing in Transition: a Case Study of Shanghai," *Housing Science* 20 n. 4 (1996), 236.

41 Ibid.

42 Lü Junhua and Shao Lei, "Housing Development from 1978 to 2000 after China Adopted Reform and Opening-Up Policies," in *Modern Urban Housing in China: 1841–2000*, ed. Lü Junhua, Peter Rowe, and Zhang Jie (Munich: Prestel, 2001), 225–226.

43 Starting with the "Suggestions on Promoting All-Round Reform of the Housing System in Urban Areas" in 1991, the state set most of the institutional goals in 1994. Ibid., 255.

44 For example, in 1996 rents in 35 Chinese large and medium-size cities on the average accounted for only 3.64 percent of a household income. Ibid., 258.

45 Zhang Lixin, interview with the author, Shanghai, August 29, 2007.

46 Xue Qiuli and Ernie Scoffham, "China's Housing in Transition: a Case Study of Shanghai," *Housing Science* 20 n. 4 (1996), 240–242, Li Zhengyu, interview with the author, Shanghai, August 24, 2007.

47 Ibid.

48 Ibid., confirmed by Zhang Lixin, interview with the author, Shanghai, August 29, 2007.

49 Lü Junhua and Shao Lei, "Housing Development from 1978 to 2000 after China Adopted Reform and Opening-Up Policies," in *Modern Urban Housing in China: 1841–2000*, ed. Lü Junhua, Peter Rowe, and Zhang Jie (Munich: Prestel, 2001), 267.

50 Ibid., 254.

51 Huang Yiru, interview with the author, Shanghai, August 29, 2007.

52 Gu Zhongtao, "Yandang High-Rise Residential Building, Shanghai," *Jianzhu Xuebao* (Architectural Journal) 3 (1986), 52–53.

53 For a detailed description see Yao Jinling und Wang Yongmei, "Some High-Standard Apartment Buildings for Chinese expatriates" (in Chinese), *Jianzhu Xuebao* (Architectural Journal) 1 (1985), 25–27. The Àijiàn Development is situated at 590 South Wanping Road, on the corner of Línglíng Road.

54 Zhang Lixin, interview with the author, Shanghai, August 29, 2007.

55 Lü Junhua and Shao Lei, "Housing Development from 1978 to 2000 after China Adopted Reform and Opening-Up Policies," in *Modern Urban Housing in China: 1841–2000*, ed. Lü Junhua, Peter Rowe, and Zhang Jie (Munich: Prestel, 2001), 228.

56 The Qūyáng development is situated in the Hóngkǒu District, bordered by Miyun Road, East Tiyuhui Road, West Dailian Road, and Yuanlin Road. Li Zhengyu, *Cheng Shi, Zhu Zhai, Cheng Shi* (City, Housing, City) (Nanjing: Dong Nan Da Xue, 2004), 64 and 326.

57 *Shanghai Kexue Jushu Wenxian Chubanshi 1951–1996 – Housing in Shanghai 1951–1996* (in English and Chinese) (Shanghai: Publisher for Documents of Science and Technology, 1998), 26.

58 Li Zhengyu, interview with the author, Shanghai, August 24, 2007. Ye Ang, interview with the author, Shanghai, August 24, 2007.

59 Arthur Lubow, "The China Syndrome," *New York Times* May 21, 2006.

60 The compound is situated at 531–541 North Henan Road.

61 Zheng Shiling, interview with the author, Shanghai, August 28, 2007.

62 Ibid.

63 For protection as a historic monument, there are four categories. The highest forbids any change, the lowest allows for demolition (!), but the building has to be reconstructed in a similar way. Criteria for attaining the status of protection are not precisely defined; they might include such diverse factors as age, architectural uniqueness, or general artistic value. Zheng Shiling, interview with the author, Shanghai, August 28, 2007.

64 For the categories of historic preservation see Shanghai Municipal Urban Planning Administration, *Shang Hai Cheng Shi Gui Hua Guan Li Shi Jian* (Urban Planning Administration Practices in Shanghai) (Shanghai: Chinese Architectural Industry, 2007), 237. Table 5–56 on page 168 shows the degrees of protection in Shanghai's Old Town. For the vast majority of the "preservation areas" demolition is still allowed as long as the replacement building has the same proportions as the original.

65 Zheng Shiling, interview with the author, Shanghai, August 28, 2007.

66 Ibid.

67 Ibid., Huang Yiru, interview with the author, Shanghai, August 29, 2007.

68 Ibid.

69 Ibid.

70 For example Jim Yardley, "Little Building Defies Beijing's Olympic Ambitions," *New York Times*, August 9, 2007.

71 Yanlord Gardens is situated west of Pucheng Road between Dongchang Road and Shangcheng Road.

72 Shinmao Riviera Gardens is located two blocks south of Yanlord Gardens, west of Pudong Road between Zhangyang Road and Weifang Road.

73 Li Zhengyu, *Cheng Shi, Zhu Zhai, Cheng Shi* (City, Housing, City) (Nanjing: Dong Nan Da Xue, 2004), 195. See also photograph of model on p. 195, 1.151.

74 Ibid. Brilliant City is situated on Zhongtan Road, between the Zhongtan Road railroad station and the Wúsōng River.

75 Ibid., 76.

76 Shanghai Municipal Urban Planning Administration, *Shang Hai Cheng Shi Gui Hua Guan Li Shi Jian* (Urban Planning Administration Practices in Shanghai) (Shanghai: Chinese Architectural Industry, 2007), 253.

77 Huang Yiru, interview with the author, Shanghai, August 29, 2007.

78 Ibid., 259–260.

79 Everest Town is situated in the Pǔdòng district, south of Gaoqing Road between Pusan Road and South Yanggao Road. In August 2007, the shells of most buildings were finished.

80 Huang Yiru, interview with the author, Shanghai, August 29, 2007.

Index

Buildings and Projects